Esperanza,

May the Lord bless you and encourage you

as you read this book in you time of need.

May it help to give you resolve when you

face your daily and extreme trials. May

you give God the glory for He alone is

worthy!

Blessings,

I pray that you will
grow in grace as you
read this and that it will
encourage you!

HOPE AMID HOPELESSNESS

Our Abba Father Provides a Straight Path Through Mental Illness

JIM HANSEN

WESTBOW
PRESS®

A DIVISION OF THOMAS NELSON
& ZONDERVAN

WestBow Press books may be ordered through booksellers or by contacting:

WestBow Press
A Division of Thomas Nelson & Zondervan
1663 Liberty Drive
Bloomington, IN 47403
www.westbowpress.com
1 (866) 928-1240

ISBN: 978-1-9736-5266-3 (sc)
ISBN: 978-1-9736-5267-0 (e)

Print information available on the last page.

WestBow Press rev. date: 02/13/2019

CONTENTS

DEDICATION

This book is dedicated to my wife, Laura, whose difficult journey inspired its writing. More importantly, I have dedicated it to my Abba Father and His Son, the Lord Jesus Christ, and His Holy Spirit, for their Glory. God and Jesus were my principle source of sustenance during this difficult time.

ACKNOWLEDGEMENT

I would not have made it through this time without the sustaining love of God and Jesus, nor could I have endured without the aid of my Christian brothers and sisters. Thank you to Steve and Paula Crane, Gib and Tina Coleman, Tom and Leann Lebarre, Bob and Donna Oehrig, Dale and Sharon Stephens, Tom Swanson, and Steve and Louise Wentworth. I also would like to thank all those pastors I dealt with in my work, in particular Jim Anderson, Troy Dobbs, Stephen Goold, Mike Haseltine, and Tom Parrish.

This book would have never been written if it were not for the encouragement and help from Dan MacKinnon who first suggested that I write this book, my Pastor Troy Dobbs whose sermon lead me to start writing, Bret Waldman who helped me walk through the process, and the Holy Spirit who helped me know what to write.

FOREWORD

For most of my life I have been intrigued by relationships and how they work, particularly between 1) God and individuals, and 2) between a husband and wife. While I have read many books on relationships and learned much from personal experience, I have also gained much from watching other people work through their own relationships with God and their spouse. One such couple I have learned from was Jim and Laura Hansen.

I met Jim and Laura 14 years ago at church. My wife and I had several opportunities to go on triple dates with them. Their love and appreciation for God and one another was very evident. They enjoyed spending time with God and spending time with each other. When Laura started to struggle with mental illness, their devotion to God and one another seemed to grow in new ways.

I had the privilege to talk with them individually as well as together, during this time. I saw Jim's faith grow as Laura's illness worsened. The love, patience, hope, and strength he drew from God was passed on to Laura. This was of great help to Laura especially when the illness seemed to lessen its grip. During these times Laura's love for God and people was demonstrated by her volunteer work with the Salvation Army.

Their love for God and each other grew even though the mental illness kept returning. I saw first-hand what keeping the vow "for better or worse" looked like. As you read this book you will see how having a growing relationship with God will enable you to love and hope even when things appear impossible. Thank you, Jim and Laura, for the many lessons you have taught me.

Steve Crane
Care Pastor
Grace Church Roseville

PRELUDE

Why I Wrote This Book

Writing a book about depression and thinking someone will want to read it may seem difficult to understand, if not impossible. I, however, know the outcome of my wife Laura's depression, having lived with its pathologies for so long – it's why I believe this book is important.

Over time I have come to understand that anyone who has a heart for God can benefit by exposure to the stories, ideas, concepts, and scriptures I share in the pages ahead. In fact, I know that the understanding and insight a person will gain by reading this book and thinking about it could be liberating, perhaps life-saving, though in ways not understandable until the last page.

"I'm not a writer," I said to Dan McKinnon, a friend of mine who first suggested this book many years ago. Dan believed that others could greatly benefit from a candid telling of my story. I dismissed Dan's suggestion at the time.

Several years later another friend of mine suggested a book about my experiences. "But I'm not a writer," I said once again. This time, however, I went home and produced a book outline as if I were going to write it. The book outline then sat dormant, tucked away in a file, for several years.

One Sunday morning, Pastor Troy Dobbs, Senior Pastor at Grace Church in Eden Prairie, Minnesota, preached on Matthew 25. Specifically, he spoke about God's end time judgment and the separation of the sheep from the goats.

"When the Son of Man comes in His glory, and all the angels with Him, then He will sit on His glorious throne. Before Him will be gathered all the nations, and He will separate people one from another as a shepherd separates the sheep from the goats." (Matt. 25:31-32) [1]

Pastor Troy's words connected with my longing to see God use my experiences to teach others. The Holy Spirit showed me that His Church needed something from me. The Spirit then clarified it for me, and I understood exactly what I had to offer the Church. That afternoon I went home, turned on my computer, and started to write this book.

"Who should and will read this book?" I knew immediately that had such a book been available to me, it would have helped immensely as I dealt with Laura, her illness and the challenges associated. I also knew it would have helped the church, my friends, and colleagues. Primary caretakers, like myself, who are helping a loved one deal with mental illness will benefit from my story.

My faith and experiences taught me that Christians would want to look to the Bible for guidance and comfort. In short, my story could help others - especially Christians - who faced the challenges of living with and ministering to a family member suffering from mental illness.

I will not tell anybody how to deal with their own situation in these pages. Frankly, there is no such construct as "Seven Steps to Perfect Mental Health." What I will show you is what God taught me during my journey, and I believe it will help you in yours.

Incorporating Scripture is vitally important as a Christian confronts the challenges of mental illness. This book features multiple passages from Scripture, many of which God used to teach me about my situation.

"All Scripture is inspired by God and profitable for teaching, for reproof, for correction, for training in righteousness; so that the man of God may be adequate, equipped for every good work." (2 Timothy 3:16-17) (NASB)[2]

As I struggled with Laura's mental illness, I searched for books to help me. There are scores of books written by secularists, but they lack an essential consideration – the Christian perspective. As a Christian it is critical to understand mental illness in the context of God's perspective – revealed in Scripture.

---

[1] All scriptures in this book are from The Holy Bible, English Standard Version. ESV® Permanent Text Edition® (2016). Copyright © 2001 by Crossway Bibles, a publishing ministry of Good News Publishers. Unless otherwise noted.

[2] Scripture quotations taken from the New American Standard Bible® (NASB), Copyright © 1960, 1962, 1963, 1968, 1971, 1972, 1973, 1975, 1977, 1995 by The Lockman Foundation Used by permission. www.Lockman.org" All others will be marked as (NASB)

During my search, I only found one book written from a Christian perspective that had anything to help me. That book had only two chapters that might help the loved ones of someone suffering from mental illness.

We are all too familiar with how an individual may say something to help another person, but the words are received as cutting criticism. We know that no matter how well-intentioned, helpful words can be hurtful. Sadly, Christian platitudes often sound like judgmental attitudes. I hope to provide insight into this all-too-common problem and how to turn Christian brotherhood into providing help when needed.

I have learned that Christians and society as a whole have very little understanding of depression and mental illness. During my time trying to help Laura, most people with whom I spoke didn't want to talk about it. Moreover, Believers *and* society often attach a stigma to mental illness.

Christians have told me they believe mental illness does not exist, and saw Laura's challenges as spiritual deficits. They often questioned my efforts in trying to help Laura and keep myself healthy as a failure of faith.

Mental illness, then, is difficult for everyone to grasp and to provide useful help to those suffering from it. Many Christians I have met refer to mental health as a mental *health* issue fearing labeling it an illness.

Let me appeal to facts. Facts helped me to better understand the pervasiveness of mental illness. I have listed some below. I have spared you from an extensive fact list only because there are so many, and it would overwhelm you. An Internet search on the term "facts about mental illness" at Google.com showed more than five million hits, while "mental health statistics" showed almost seventeen million. I am only providing you with a few.

According to the National Institute of Mental Health, in 2015, 17.9% of all Americans 18 years and older suffered from mental illness and 9.8 million or 4% suffered from a serious mental illness.

In 2002 the economic cost of mental illness was $317.6 billion. Mental illness is a significant cause for suicide, which is the 10th leading cause of death.

The evidence of the destructive and pervasive nature of mental illness is persuasive. Mental illness is real.

According to the Center for Disease Control, 78% of adults with mental health symptoms and 89% of adults without mental health symptoms agreed that treatment can help persons with mental illness lead normal lives. Fifty-seven percent of *all* adults believed that people are caring and sympathetic to persons with mental illness. On the other hand, only 25% of adults *with* mental health symptoms believed that people are caring and sympathetic to persons with mental illness.

Let's explore this more deeply. I will use the story of Laura and Jim Hansen to show you how mental illness affects individuals. I believe you will find yourself and/or someone you know in this book and as a result, will be better able to minister to them and care for yourself.

"Now may the God of hope fill you with all joy and peace in believing, so that you will abound in hope by the power of the Holy Spirit." (Romans 15:13) (NASB)

CHAPTER 1

The Diagnosis

My Abba Father Is in Control

On August 19, 2002, my wife Laura and I woke up as usual at 6:00 AM on our own. As we got out of bed, we both expected it to be a normal day with no surprises. Laura headed to the shower, and I headed to the kitchen to make Laura's coffee. She thought I made coffee better than she did, but maybe it was the act of love behind the coffee that made her think it was better. After starting the coffee, I headed into the bathroom to shave and brush my teeth. Laura was now finished with her shower so I jumped in and took mine. We both proceeded to get ready for work. This particular day Laura would go to the doctor for her annual check-up before going to the bank where she was an operations officer, and I headed off to work at a state political party. That normal morning, however, neither of us had an inkling about the tragedy and trials we would face during the next several years.

That day ended up *anything* but normal.

Laura went to the doctor that morning for her annual physical. The doctor did a routine exam, including blood work. Something he saw as he examined Laura indicated that he needed to include a blood alcohol test in the blood work

The afternoon of the blood test, the doctor called Laura. He reported that the test result showed a blood alcohol level of .063. "Mrs. Hansen, I want you to find help to control your alcohol use," he instructed. As a result, Laura set up an appointment with a psychologist.

That night after work I came home and made dinner as usual. During dinner Laura told me about her blood test results and subsequent appointment with the psychologist as if were no big deal. To me it was a big deal in part because Laura was raised in a home with two alcoholic parents. I was stunned. I had no idea that Laura was struggling with alcohol. To some extent I was afraid. All sorts of questions came into my mind. Why was she drinking? When was she drinking? How bad is it? Is this a consistent activity? How long has it been going on? How could she do this to me? How can I fix the problem? I had no way of knowing how that news would affect our future – but it changed our lives forever. Neither did I know that God would use Laura's illness to prepare me for the days that lay ahead, as I worked to help Laura, maintain my own health, and contend with other people.

I looked back to when Laura and I first met. At the time I owned a shoe store in the Alderwood Mall in Lynnwood, Washington. Sometime in late April or early May I needed to hire a salesperson. Two of my friends, sisters Sharon and Rhonda, worked at Casual Corners in the mall and knew that I was looking for someone. Rhonda had a roommate who she thought would be good. It was Laura.

The next day Laura came in for an interview. After interviewing her, I was unsure if she was the right fit. I saw that she was introverted – not a strong trait for a good salesperson. So I went to Casual Corners to talk to Sharon to get her thoughts; she knew Laura well. Sharon told me that Laura would do fine once I trained her, and that Laura had some great qualities. She knew Laura as dedicated, a hard worker, trainable, intelligent and committed to her tasks.

The next day I called Laura and offered her the job.

I was actually surprised that I had never met her before the interview as it turned out we both went to the same church and had several friends in common. After she started working for me, I started to run into her outside of work whenever I hung out with Sharon and her husband Russ, Rhonda, and her other roommate, Tamara. As I saw her more often, I became attracted to her and asked her out. (As her employer, perhaps dating Laura was not a good idea, but I did it anyway.)

There were several traits I wanted in a potential spouse. The first and most important issue for me was that the woman I married needed to have a personal relationship with Jesus. Having been a Christian for about 18 years at the time, I knew for certain that I wanted a Christian spouse, someone who loved Jesus as I did. My wife, I had also decided, needed to desire to be in fellowship with other believers and to have children. I wanted a woman who would love me, and that included tolerating if not liking baseball because I really like baseball. It made no difference to me if my spouse liked to cook because cooking is one of my hobbies. I wanted a wife who loved to travel, as I did. As I watched her and began to know her better, I saw that Laura met most of my criteria except I was not sure she loved me – yet – and I was not sure about her feelings toward baseball. So, I asked her to go with me to a baseball game between the Minnesota Twins, my team, and the Seattle Mariners, the hometown team.

Laura had no idea what to wear to a baseball game. She asked Rhonda who said, "Wear something casual. You are going to a baseball game. I am sure Jim will be dressed casual." It was a night game and I was at work where I got tied up with a customer. I had no time to go home and change – I cannot stand missing the first pitch. I showed up at Laura's wearing a suit and tie. Laura was mortified. I saw that she had dressed in jeans and a tee shirt and there I stood, in a suit and tie. I wondered how this would sit with her. I explained my attire and apologized and thankfully, Laura understood and we headed to the game. I removed my tie, suit jacket, and vest before we got to the game. We survived the first date, the Twins won, and we kept on dating.

A few weeks later, on the Fourth of July, one of my vendors invited me to join them at their home on Lake Chelan. So, I took the weekend off and went to the lake. I left Laura to work the weekend at the store. Typically, sales are slow on the Fourth of July weekend and this weekend was no exception. When I returned to the city that evening, I saw Laura. "How was the weekend?" I asked. "It was particularly slow today. In fact, the only sale we had was the pair of sandals I bought," she said. "I bought the sandals because I didn't want you to feel bad because we had no sales."

As we continued to date, I learned that Laura's sole ambition was to be a mom. She had chosen not to go to college because she felt it would be a waste of money – she wanted to be a mom. As we got together with our friends, I watched Laura interacting with their children and I saw that she would be a great mom. She showed tenderness and great care for the children and wanted to make sure they were having fun. She engaged them in conversation, entertained and played with them. The longer we were together the more I realized that Laura would be a great mom to the children that she and I wanted in the future.

That abnormal day in 2002, my Abba Father began a new and intense work in me to train and discipline me in ways I could not anticipate – and if I had my choice, I would have avoided. God began the difficult and sometimes painful process to instill in me three critical realities: He is in control, He has a plan, and He is faithful.

Before I tell you more of our story - how Laura's alcoholism and depression disrupted our lives - I want to share several concepts that I learned and still cling to that helped me manage my life. More importantly, these principles made it possible for me to grow closer to God and taught me how to deal with other well-meaning people.

My Abba Father Is in Control

Coming to accept and internalize the fact that God is in control in all aspects of life, and having the conviction to act on this fact, is one of the toughest lessons I needed to learn. I also had to learn that it is an ongoing lifetime challenge because it is natural for me to want to control my own life.

As I witnessed my beloved Laura suffering from mental illness, I wanted to know why. I went to God for answers. All manner of questions surfaced. Did Laura's sin cause her to be afflicted with such a difficult disease? Did I do something that caused or worsened it? Why does God, who is love, let a Believer or a good person suffer? Why didn't God heal Laura the way I wanted Him to heal her? I struggled constantly with questions like these, but found only partial answers.

As long as I have breath, I know I will continue to search for definitive answers. Maybe someday while I am still here on earth, God will answer the "why" questions. One lesson, however, became perfectly clear to me – I needed to wait on the Lord, stay patient, and trust that God is in control.

As a human, I tend to think God needs me to agree with Him before He decides what to do in my life. Of course, that is not true. God's control over His creation – over me – does not require my consent. For my own good I had to choose to embrace and internalize the fact that God is in control of *my* life. I could have chosen otherwise.

I could have decided that Satan is in control of all things that happened on earth, other sinful people were in control, I was in control, or nobody was in control. Instead, I chose to trust that a loving, personal, holy, truthful, faithful, righteous, and just God was in control. I realized I had head-knowledge about God and needed heart-knowledge. I had to internalize the truth that He cares for me beyond what I can understand, and that He is absolutely just. Eventually, I chose to trust that He is in control.

Choosing to accept the fact that God is in control is vitally important. The challenge, however, is making the decisions to act on that trust.

The Bible repeatedly demonstrates that God is in control, not Satan, self, or others. The book of Job is perhaps the best narrative about God's sovereignty and human suffering. It shows us how God and Satan contended for the soul of a righteous man. When I struggle with questions about who is in control, I carefully study Job.

Job has become one of my favorite books of the Bible because it shows how God dealt with Job and his friends. It reflects how well-meaning friends can misunderstand the events in a person's life, and contribute to their pain and suffering. Most importantly Job helps me understand and more deeply trust in God and accept what is happening to me.

Just before Jesus ascended into heaven, He explained to His disciples how God controlled the future: "He said to them, 'It is not for you to know times or seasons that the Father has fixed by His own authority.'" (Acts 1:7) This statement was also meant to teach the fact that God is always in control. I should not worry about the future.

The Bible, from cover to cover, and especially in Job taught me that God *does* allow bad things to happen to people. I see the evidence of this all around me. My question, then, was does it somehow please Him to watch people suffer? The answer to that is a resounding no, because God is love and there is no evil in Him. However, to be able to answer *why* He allows it to happen even though such a conclusion seems counterintuitive, the fact is I cannot answer the question because I do not know. I do know that whatever He does or allows to happen in our lives will work for our good because He loves us – He is in control.

I found many Scriptures that helped me internalize the fact that God is in control. One in particular that stands out to me is Paul writing in Romans 8:26-28 "the Spirit helps us in our weakness. For we do not know what to pray for as we ought, but the Spirit Himself intercedes for us with groanings too deep for words. And He who searches hearts knows what is the mind of the Spirit, because the Spirit intercedes for the saints according to the will of God. And we know that for those who love God all things work together for good, for those who are called according to His purpose." Not only does this show me that God is in control of my life, but the Holy Spirit is actively working on my behalf.

When Laura and I first began to deal with her mental illness, I realized I had not yet fully accepted the fact that God was in control. As He began teaching me about His control in the context of Laura's struggles, I quickly saw that it is not an easy belief to accept or act upon, but over time, it began to take hold.

It was natural for me to struggle with the fact that God is in control of everything and especially Laura and my individual lives. To begin to better understand this, I read and study the Bible and learn from Him. I ponder His holiness, perfection, and purity, and understand that His absolute holiness cannot tolerate sin. I understand that Adam's fall ushered sin into the world and as a consequence, made human illness possible. These truths helped me to understand the truth about God's control of our lives.

Whenever I ask, "Why do bad things happen to good people?", I must consider the better question: "Why don't more bad things happen to sinful men?" As I ask the question from that point of view, I will better understand a profound truth – it is only by God's grace that you and I do not experience more bad outcomes. The ultimate reality is that as sinners, we deserve suffering and death, but God has given us eternal life through Jesus Christ, and He has added profound meaning and value to our days on earth. "I came that they may have life, and have *it* abundantly." (John 10:10b) (NASB)

God's forgiveness comes from His unfathomable love that sets a pattern for you and me as we deal with other people.

My Abba Father's Plan

When I chose to internalize the fact that God is in control, I also needed to accept that He has a plan for my life. His plan is comprehensive, but it starts with forgiveness of my sins. He delivered me from the consequences of my sin when He sent His Son, Christ Jesus, to the cross –

"But He was pierced through for our transgressions,

He was crushed for our iniquities;

The chastening for our well-being *fell* upon Him,

And by His scourging we are healed." (Isaiah 53:5) (NASB)

I received forgiveness of my sins as Jesus paid for my eternal penalties that result from my guilt. This wonderful forgiveness happened when I accepted God's free gift of salvation – this is God's plan for all who believe on the name of Jesus. It is cause for us all to offer praise to God.

"Now to Him who is able to keep you from stumbling, and to make you stand in the presence of His glory blameless with great joy, to the only God our Savior, through Jesus Christ our Lord, *be* glory, majesty, dominion and authority, before all time and now and forever. Amen." (Jude 24-25) (NASB)

My eternity is secure as a result of the sacrifice in death of Christ Jesus for my sins and the reality of His resurrection. This is a universal truth about God's plan – His plan gives eternal life to all who will believe in and trust His Son.

Knowing that God's plan includes giving eternal life to me as a believer in Jesus Christ makes it possible for me to accept the fact that He is control of every aspect of my life.

> "Trust in the Lord with all your heart
> And do not lean on your own understanding.
> In all your ways acknowledge Him,
> And He will make your paths straight." (Proverbs 3:5-6)
> (NASB)

I learned the only way to get over my need to have all my "why" questions answered rested upon these two truths: trust that God is in control and quit trusting in my own understanding. God's control and reign is absolute – Satan does not control the world. Satan has no authority over those who trust Jesus Christ. Because of this I am committed to live my life with Proverbs 3:5-6 as guiding verses.

Five Control Options

There are five options we humans can consider concerning this control issue: 1) someone else is in control, 2) I'm in control, 3) nobody is in control, 4) Satan is in control, or 5) God is in control.

First, I don't know any human who I would trust being in control of everything. Secondly, knowing myself as I do, I sure don't want to be in control – and you wouldn't like it if I were. Thirdly, although sometimes it looks like no one is in control, evidence suggests that as feeble and flawed as they are, the nation's rulers maintain some semblance of control over human interaction. Fourth, I certainly do not want Satan to be in control: when speaking to the Pharisees, the religious rulers of the day, Jesus said Satan is a liar and there is no truth in him:

"You are of your father the devil, and your will is to do your father's desires. He was a murderer from the beginning, and does not stand in the truth, because there is no truth in him. When he lies, he speaks out of his own character, for he is a liar and the father of lies." (John 8:44)

So, that leaves God in control – or more factually, control starts with God.

As events began to unfold regarding Laura's illness, God impressed numerous lessons on me about His character and nature. God's attributes strengthened my ability to trust Him with the events in my life. These attributes of God became more precious and important to me over time.

God is love.
God is faithful.
God is just.
God is righteous.
God is holy.

Knowing and internalizing these attributes of God helped me to surrender control of my life to Him, at least more frequently than before Laura's troubles started. Giving control of one's life to God does not happen overnight – it is incremental. I failed many times and still do. After all, God gave us a free will, and if you are like me, we too often prefer our will to His. Our sinful nature fights against the reality that God is in control and we can trust Him. Each day I work to trust Him more.

Accepting the fact that God is in control allows me to trust in the reality that He has a plan for my life. Knowing He will always keep His word seals the deal for me.

My Abba Father Is Faithful

What does it mean that I accept as true the fact that God is faithful? It means He is never going to desert me. He is never going to renege on His promises. He is always going to be with me. He is dependable. As I accept the fact that God is dependable – faithful – it helps me to also accept that He is in control and has a plan.

God's faithfulness remains particularly important to me as I go through trials. Even when I asked, "Why me?" I knew that God remained faithful.

Scripture is replete with references to God's faithfulness. "But You, O Lord, are a God merciful and gracious, slow to anger and abounding in steadfast love and faithfulness." (Psalms 86:15) Here I see that God is abundantly faithful, not just a little faithful. His faithfulness is unlimited, abundantly faithful above and beyond what I could expect or imagine.

There are several other passages I looked at to help me understand that God's faithfulness is forever. Deuteronomy 7:9 is just one of them.

Many Scriptural promises that I find are hard to comprehend, and some seem especially painful while I am going through trials. Sometimes I would rather not hear His clear voice speaking to me from those verses. Yet, He has remained faithful to His Word and to me as I go through them all.

God is faithful even when I am unfaithful. As Paul wrote to the Romans:

> "What if some were unfaithful? Does their faithlessness
> nullify the faithfulness of God? By no means! Let God be
> true though everyone were a liar, as it is written,
> 'That You may be justified in Your words,
> and prevail when You are judged.'" (Romans 3:3-4)

God will always be faithful even when I am not. When I do not pray, He is faithful. When I do not read His Word, He is faithful. When I do not fellowship with other believers, He is faithful. When I sin, He is faithful. When I do not believe in His faithfulness, He is faithful. All praise to God for His faithfulness that does not depend on me!

His faithfulness helps me to flee from temptations. 1 Corinthians 10:13

The stark truth is that there are many times when I am tempted to rebel against God's plan for me while I am going through trials. Knowing beyond the shadow of a doubt that He remains faithful at all times gives me the courage to find a way out.

2 Thessalonians 3:3 remains a powerful reminder to me of God's faithfulness as He is active in my life.

His faithfulness helps me to be certain of His truth so that I can have assurance in all things. "Let us hold fast the confession of our hope without wavering, for He who promised is faithful," (Hebrews 10:23) (NASB)

God's faithfulness is a powerful and profound truth that changes how I live and function each day, but especially during the many years of trials that were yet to come. No matter my circumstances, my trials, my joys, and my successes, He is faithful! This is why I can wholeheartedly accept the truth about trials.

> "Count it all joy, my brothers, when you meet trials of various kinds, for you know that the testing of your faith produces steadfastness. And let steadfastness have its full effect, that you may be perfect and complete, lacking in nothing." (James 1:2-4)

I cannot imagine life as I know it today without knowing as a certainty that God is faithful, though I have certainly failed to be faithful to Him. No matter your current relationship to God, you can be confident in this: He is faithful and wants you to rely on Him. He will never leave nor forsake you. Join with me to leave our lives in God's hands, knowing that He is faithful.

Okay, before I leave this subject, a confession is in order. I have not accomplished perfect trust in God. I am human, like you. I at least try to trust His faithfulness most of the time; maybe not most of the time, but perhaps half the time; sometimes not even half the time. For certain, however, some of the time. Here, however, is a powerful and profound truth: When I fail to be faithful and leave my life in His hands, He remains faithful to me and sends His Spirit to draw me back to Him.

My Abba Father Is Just

As I consider that God is in control, I also want to be sure He will always do what is best for me. As I accept the reality that God will only do what is best for me, that He is a just God, my trust in Him grows. I can know for certain that because He is just, I deserve His wrath instead of His mercy. I also know that Jesus took upon Himself my just reward as He died on the cross and I will not be punished.

The truth is that I am a sinner and deserve a guilty verdict from God's justice – I deserve His anger. Praise be to God that Christ's death satisfied

His demand for a penalty as He administers justice for my sin, so I have no condemnation or sentence of death upon me.

God's justice is spoken of throughout the Bible.

"The Rock, His work is perfect,
for all His ways are justice.
A God of faithfulness and without iniquity,
just and upright is he."
(Deuteronomy 32:4)

You may ask as I did, "If God is just then how come evil people sometimes prosper and have great wealth, while good people sometimes struggle and live in poverty?" Too often, humans look at a person's material possessions and their accomplishments to judge whether God has blessed them.

God has taught me that evidence of His justice viewed through the prism of earthly goods or pleasures is a false standard. The reality is that God's justice is not always revealed during our lifetime and we must die before receiving His final judgment.

Jesus gave us insight into God's justice with the story about the rich man and Lazarus (Luke 16:19ff). Jesus showed that the rich man, who had enjoyed immense earthly rewards, ended up in hell, suffering eternal torment. Lazarus, who lived in earthly poverty, ended up in heaven. The rich man cried out for relief, but his possessions and position meant nothing – God had judged him guilty. God's justice also rained on the poor man who had received forgiveness of his sin through Jesus Christ. God's riches in Christ Jesus made the difference, not earthly goods or accomplishments.

God's justice is administered on the day of each person's final judgment. As I came to understand and internalize the eternal nature of God's justice, it helped me to yield control of my life to Him and to accept life's events.

My Abba Father Is Righteous

Of the many attributes of God, that He is righteous also helped me know and trust in the fact He is in control.

What does it mean that God is righteous? To me it means that God is always right. He never makes a mistake. Since He never makes a mistake, it is folly for me to ask Him to change His mind or bend His will to mine. His decisions are right.

When I experience a trial, I can be confident that God is in control, and whatever is happening to me is right. I may not think it is right at the time – foresight is often a challenge. Hindsight, though, usually informs me why the situation I experienced was valuable for me. I confess too often my trials are the result of my errors, a lesson God continues to teach me.

Scripture is filled with references about God's righteousness. Two of my favorites are in the Psalms.

> "Your righteousness is righteous forever,
> and Your law is true."
> (Psalms 119:142)

> "The Lord is righteous in all His ways
> and kind in all His works."
> (Psalms 145:17)

In John 17:25 we read Jesus' prayer to God, referring to Him as righteous: "O righteous Father, even though the world does not know You, I know You, and these know that You have sent me."

My Abba Father Is Holy

What does it mean to say that God is holy? What is holy? God is perfect, transcendent, and spiritually pure. God has no flaws in His nature, person or character. God's holiness evokes adoration and reverence in me, and puts me in awe of Him.

Many times, the Scriptures tell us to fear God. Fearing God is the outcome of recognizing His holiness, being in awe of Him. His holiness demands perfection. Because I love God, I fear Him like young children fear their earthly parent. It is not that the child is afraid of punishment but rather the child is afraid of making their parent unhappy with their behavior. Hebrews 10:13 says: "It is a fearful thing to fall into the hands of the living God." It is right for me to fear God because He would be justified to punish me for my sin.

When I view God, His holiness, combined with His other attributes, I am continually reminded that He is in control and I can trust Him to always do the right thing for me. God's holiness comforts me and demands that I am best off when I obey Him.

I considered the picture Isaiah drew of God's holiness.

> In the year of King Uzziah's death I saw the Lord sitting on a throne, lofty and exalted, with the train of His robe filling the temple. Seraphim stood above Him, each having six wings: with two he covered his face, and with two he covered his feet, and with two he flew. And one called out to another and said,
>
> "Holy, Holy, Holy, is the Lord of hosts,
> The whole earth is full of His glory."
>
> And the foundations of the thresholds trembled at the voice of him who called out, while the temple was filling with smoke. Then I said,
>
> "Woe is me, for I am ruined!
> Because I am a man of unclean lips,
> And I live among a people of unclean lips;
> For my eyes have seen the King, the Lord of hosts."
>
> Then one of the seraphim flew to me with a burning coal in his hand, which he had taken from the altar with tongs. He touched my mouth *with it* and said, "Behold, this has touched your lips; and your iniquity is taken away and your sin is forgiven."
>
> Then I heard the voice of the Lord, saying, "Whom shall I send, and who will go for Us?" Then I said, "Here am I. Send me!" (Isaiah 6:1-8) (NASB)

Isaiah's awesome fear of God inspires me. Imagine standing in the presence of holiness! I know that I, like Isaiah, would confess I am a man of unclean lips, body, soul, and spirit. Yet with Isaiah, because of the fact that God is in control, I can also say, "Here I am. Send me," as a way of acknowledging my trust in His will for my life. I am far from being holy apart from the salvation God gave to me through Jesus Christ.

As Laura attempted to make her way through the morass of life created by her mental illness, and as I contended with her and those around us, I saw more clearly the misunderstanding most people have about mental illness. I saw that Christians, just as non-Christians, struggled to know how to deal with the trials Laura and I faced. During our interactions with well-meaning people, God increasingly revealed His holiness to me. I saw that people are imperfect and often undependable, but in contrast, I found that God was always perfect and wholly dependable. As people would unintentionally say hurtful things to us, God would reveal more of His holy truth to me.

Even though I still do not have the answer to the big "why" question, I do know that God did not cause Laura's illness; His Holiness would prevent Him from doing anything that is wrong. God's holiness gives me confidence that He always has my best in mind.

One day while I was talking with a group of fellow Christians, one of them made a profound statement that I believe demonstrates God's holiness. He said he had been praying, asking God, "What do I do if someone says something judgmental? I heard a voice saying 'Just respond that I am glad that *you* are not God."

Moses experienced several direct and personal conversations with God. As Moses approached the burning bush, he heard God say:

"Then He said, 'Do not come near; take your sandals off your feet, for the place on which you are standing is holy ground.' And He said, 'I am the God of your father, the God of Abraham, the God of Isaac, and the God of Jacob.' And Moses hid his face, for he was afraid to look at God." (Exodus 3:5-6)

From Moses' encounter with God at the burning bush, I learned that not only is God holy, but because of His holiness I am to fear Him. Taken out of context, considering God's love, faithfulness, justice, and plan for my life, it may sound odd to actually be afraid of Him. Yet there is a righteous fear of the Lord that is profoundly important, because my recognition of God's holiness is essential to activate all His other attributes in me.

Because of God's complete holiness, we can never have a relationship with Him except through the shed blood of Jesus Christ. Jesus put the fear of God into context for Laura and me: "And do not fear those who kill the body but cannot kill the soul. Rather fear Him who can destroy both soul and body in hell." (Matthew 10:28)

A proper fear of God is necessary if I want to gain wisdom and knowledge. "The fear of the Lord is the beginning of knowledge; fools despise wisdom and instruction." (Prov. 1:7), and "The fear of the LORD is the beginning of wisdom, and the knowledge of the Holy One is insight." (Prov. 9:10) Plainly said, unless I fear God I can never gain true knowledge, wisdom, or insight into my life's problems and challenges.

God's holiness reveals His glorious deeds. Knowing this helped me understand that the events occurring during my trials were God's miracles revealed to me because of His holiness. "Who is like You, O LORD, among the gods? Who is like You, majestic in holiness, awesome in glorious deeds, doing wonders?" (Exodus 15:11)

This is a foundational fact of faith: If I want God to perform miracles in my life as I go through trials, then I must acknowledge and accept His holiness.

God's holiness shows both His ability and desire to care for lowly and humble people.

"For thus says the One who is high and lifted up, who inhabits eternity, whose name is Holy: "I dwell in the high and holy place, and also with him who is of a contrite and lowly spirit, to revive the spirit of the lowly, and to revive the heart of the contrite." (Isaiah 57:15)

There were many times during my trials resulting from Laura's depression when I thought I had hit bottom. Laura, too, often found herself lowly in spirit. It gave us, and especially me, great comfort during these times to know that because God is holy, He cared for Laura and me.

Because God is holy, I learned I could depend upon Him to be my Rock, my light, and my hope. See 1 Samuel 2:2.

God's Word, revealing His holiness, gave me comfort during my journey with Laura because I knew I could depend upon Him.

God's holiness is the foundation of why He is to be worshipped. See Revelation 4:8.

Accepting and working to understand God's holiness brings my heart and mind into the right position so that I can hear what He wants me to hear and learn what He wants me to learn. If I fail to hold Him in absolute high esteem, the position that flows from His holiness and my neediness, I will not be able to trust Him as I go through trials.

As a result of God's holiness, I learned to try to conform more to the image of Christ. I will never be able to achieve God's holiness, but because I love Jesus and want to have a better relationship with Him, I can learn from Him how to live.

> "For I am the LORD your God. Consecrate yourselves therefore, and be holy, for I am holy." (Leviticus 11:44)

My Abba Father Is Personal

One of the most difficult truths to accept is that the God of the universe wants to have a relationship with me. Frankly, I cannot comprehend this, at least from a human perspective.

Controlling the universe seems like an exhausting and all-encompassing job. What makes me worthy of His desire to be personal with me?

For certain, I am imperfect and He is perfect. Why would the Perfect One want to bother with me?

Yet knowing that God wants to relate to me on a personal level – one-on-one – is hugely comforting to me. Like you, there are many people whom I would like to call personal friends. A personal relationship with God seems extraordinary because it is – only God could do this.

How is God personal with me? God speaks to me through His Word, the Bible. He speaks to me in His creation. He speaks to me through other believers as they encourage and counsel me through their love. He also speaks to me when I worship Him. He also speaks to me via the Holy Spirit whom He has sent to live within me.

I have experienced times when I have had an overwhelming sense that I needed to do something. When I act on that sense, I am amazed at the outcomes I observe. As I ponder this, I believe these are the times when God spoke to me through His Holy Spirit. For instance, I have long had an overwhelming sense that I should write this book.

I speak directly with My Abba Father through prayer. My prayers acknowledge Who He is. Often they are prayers of repentance and seeking forgiveness, essential for a good relationship with God. Sometimes my prayers intercede for others. And I pray for my own needs, which I found to be profoundly important during the years of dealing with Laura's illness – and these continue today.

Prayer is an essential factor in maintaining a personal relationship with

God. He's always ready for it and especially during my trials, I found how desperately I needed prayer. Yet, there were – and are – many times when I really don't know what to pray or what to say. I'm thankful that the Holy Spirit helps me.

> "Likewise the Spirit helps us in our weakness. For we do not know what to pray for as we ought, but the Spirit Himself intercedes for us with groanings too deep for words. And He who searches hearts knows what is the mind of the Spirit, because the Spirit intercedes for the saints according to the will of God." (Romans 8:26-27)

Sometimes I make prayer a chore, rather than a conversation. That is why Jesus taught me how to pray. He gave me The Lord's Prayer as an example.

> ""Pray, then, in this way:
> 'Our Father who is in heaven,
> Hallowed be Your name.
> 'Your kingdom come.
> Your will be done,
> On earth as it is in heaven.
> 'Give us this day our daily bread.
> 'And forgive us our debts, as we also have forgiven our debtors.
> 'And do not lead us into temptation, but deliver us from evil.'"
> (Matthew 6: 9- 13) (NASB)

The Lord's prayer is akin to an outline or a guide to effective prayer. It starts by acknowledging Who God is. That is, it starts with worship. Then it moves to seeking His will. Next, meeting my personal daily needs. A time to confess sins and receive forgiveness and offer repentance illustrates how important it is for us to acknowledge our sin and guilt. Lastly, it asks God for His personal protection for us from the evils of the world.

In my own prayer life, I have adopted the pattern Jesus provided in this prayer. I don't always get it right, and too often skip to the part about my needs – but God forgives me. So I start my prayer with worship of God. I move on to admitting my sin and finally I pray for others and myself. I try to make the first part the longest and most important because without God I am nothing.

Coming to grips with the fact that God is in control and that He wants to have a personal relationship with me are foundational truths that undergird everything I do and who I am. This is the starting line as God teaches me how important this personal relationship is to Him, a process that He used to teach me the fact that He is a jealous God.

CHAPTER 2

Start of Treatment

My Abba Fathers Draws Us Back to the Fellowship of Believers

On Friday of the week Laura's doctor recommended she seek help for alcohol abuse, she met with her psychologist for the first time. After talking together about Laura's life, the psychologist issued a diagnosis – Laura suffered from Major Depression Disorder. Soon after, Laura began talk therapy with her psychologist.

The diagnosis of clinical depression confused me. I knew Laura had always been introverted, but I didn't see any other signs of depression, at least at the time. She didn't appear sad and she didn't look any different to me. Ever since Laura and I had met, I think I could have counted on one hand the times I saw her cry or have a belly laugh. Instead, she would stifle her emotions, shoving them deep inside. At that time, I didn't recognize any of this as a sign of depression.

Instead, I felt confident we could work together to fix this. Fixing situations is one of my gifts, so I felt sure I could fix her depression, if she was willing to let me help.

I had found the fact she abused alcohol, however, to be especially disturbing and surprising. Laura and I would often enjoy a glass of wine or two with dinner, but as far as I knew, that was the limit of our alcohol consumption. It never occurred to me that when Laura went to bed earlier than me each night, she would drink from a bottle of brandy she had hidden under our bed. Both her parents were alcoholics – we had talked about this many times. Alcoholism had caused disruption in her family, and we had agreed it would not do so in ours. Yet, here it was, right in front of me. Laura abused alcohol. *I have to fix this,* I thought to myself. *We can overcome this.*

Together, Laura and I decided that we needed to reconnect to the local church. We had woefully neglected fellowshipping with Believers for several years. Our decision to return to church came as God convinced me that failing to do so added to our dilemma. Fellowshipping with other believers, God showed us, worked to strengthen us and provide needed support.

Both of us had read about the value of Christian fellowship in a church, but now, in the context of Laura's diagnosis, God's admonition became more real to us.

> Therefore, brethren, since we have confidence to enter the holy place by the blood of Jesus, by a new and living way which He inaugurated for us through the veil, that is, His flesh, and since *we have* a great priest over the house of God, let us draw near with a sincere heart in full assurance of faith, having our hearts sprinkled *clean* from an evil conscience and our bodies washed with pure water. Let us hold fast the confession of our hope without wavering, for He who promised is faithful; and let us consider how to stimulate one another to love and good deeds, not forsaking our own assembling together, as is the habit of some, but encouraging *one another*; and all the more as you see the day drawing near. (Hebrews 10:19-25) (NASB)

Over time, God continued to instruct me about the value of meeting together with other Christians in a church body. This need for Christian fellowship continued to grow, and became especially important to me as I was increasingly challenged by our situation.

Talk Therapy Begins

Laura began weekly talk therapy with her psychologist. She also continued to struggle with over-consumption of alcohol. During this time, I continued to struggle with the idea that Laura hid her drinking from me, creating increased communication challenges between us. Laura's secret alcohol abuse meant keeping me in the dark about how she acted out as a result of her root problem.

Each week Laura and her psychologist attempted to dig deeper into the causes of her depression. She never shared the gist of these discussions with me. I remained unaware of the extent or nature of the issues that troubled her. You might find it odd that a spouse would not share these details with her husband – I know I found it strange. At the same time, I am unsure that anyone suffering from mental illness would want to share intimate details with a loved one, at least not at the beginning of therapy.

During the first two months of Laura's therapy, God taught me that He was jealous for a closer relationship with me and about my need for forgiveness and my need to forgive others. He impressed on me my need for Christian fellowship. God continued to reinforce my dependence on Him and how He remained in control of what was going on in my life.

Laura's blood test showed us that her abuse of alcohol had become a physical and psychological issue. The psychologist's diagnosis of underlying causes of her alcohol abuse indicated clinical depression. These facts did not mitigate my own struggles about Laura's alcohol consumption. I did not understand why she drank. I struggled with whether alcoholism is a disease that caused her to drink habitually and to excess, or if it was her choice. Maybe, I thought to myself, it is a combination of a disease and a choice.

I found it difficult to believe that a disease caused her to abuse alcohol or made it harder for her to control herself. Instead, I concluded that she had made a decision to drink, that her excessive drinking related to a cause over which she could or should exercise control. Thinking that she had made the decision to drink and that she gave into this urge angered me. God saw that I needed to learn about forgiveness.

God taught me that I needed to forgive Laura concerning a broad range of issues. My forgiveness of Laura, God showed me, is rooted in His forgiveness of me. I had to come to understand that God forgave Laura, too. I needed to forgive Laura for keeping her drinking a secret for several years during our marriage – and that my forgiveness needed to extend to her excessive drinking.

God also taught me to forgive myself for failing to be the spiritual leader He would have me to be. I needed to forgive myself for my failure to love her as I ought to have loved her. I needed to forgive myself for my lack of understanding of Laura's excessive drinking and her depression.

Forgiveness

My Abba Father taught me a lot about forgiveness. Forgiveness starts with God. I learned that my ability to forgive others depends on understanding God's forgiveness of me. I remain unsure whether I could ever forgive others without first knowing that God had forgiven me.

To understand forgiveness also means understanding the nature of sin and that God sees all sins as equal. Sin separates us from God. Small sins, as men see them, like the bigger ones, meant that without the forgiveness given by Jesus Christ, I could not have a personal relationship with God. James wrote:

> If you really fulfill the royal law according to the Scripture, "You shall love your neighbor as yourself," you are doing well. But if you show partiality, you are committing sin and are convicted by the law as transgressors. For whoever keeps the whole law but fails in one point has become accountable for all of it. (James 2:8-10)

When I ponder God's forgiveness it produces awe in me and reveals His love to me. I cannot imagine how He could be forgiving because of how unworthy I am to be forgiven. Not only does He forgive me, but He also designed the plan that provided His forgiveness. He sacrificed His Son Jesus so that He could forgive me. How incredible is that? Certainly, enough to teach me that I need to forgive others as He forgives me.

> Bless the LORD, O my soul,
> and forget not all His benefits,
> who forgives all your iniquity,
> who heals all your diseases,

who redeems your life from the pit,
who crowns you with steadfast love and mercy,
who satisfies you with good
so that your youth is renewed like the eagle's. (Psalms 103:2-5)

In Lamentation Jeremiah discuses the abject sorrow that Jesus Christ would experience on the Cross as He took upon Himself the sins of the whole world.

"Is it nothing to you, all you who pass by?
Look and see
if there is any sorrow like my sorrow,
which was brought upon me,
which the Lord inflicted
on the day of His fierce anger." (Lamentations 1:12)

Ponder what Jesus said and did on the cross.

And about the ninth hour Jesus cried out with a loud voice, saying, "Eli, Eli, lema sabachthani?" that is, "My God, my God, why have You forsaken me?" And some of the bystanders, hearing it, said, "This man is calling Elijah." And one of them at once ran and took a sponge, filled it with sour wine, and put it on a reed and gave it to Him to drink. But the others said, "Wait, let us see whether Elijah will come to save Him." And Jesus cried out again with a loud voice and yielded up His spirit. (Matthew 27:46-50)

As soon as Jesus gave up His spirit, for the only time in eternity, He experienced the sense of brutality and hopelessness of separation from God the Father. At that moment, because of God's holiness, He could not be connected to Jesus, His Son. All of the past, present, and future sins of everyone, which Jesus had willingly taken upon Himself, were repugnant to God.

Jesus, in this incredible act of forgiveness, gave up His spirit. Man had failed to execute Him. Instead, Jesus gave up His life of His own free will for mankind.

There are times when I feel separated from God and during these times, I am miserable. The fact that in the past, before I had a personal relationship with Him, I had also experienced separation from Him, is different in this – once I knew and experienced fellowship with God, I became more acutely aware of separation from Him. Now that I am a believer in Jesus Christ, my separation from God is the result of unrepented sin and stubbornness, or stems from my lack of attention to my relationship with Him. This pales in comparison to what Jesus went through when He, the Son of God, for the first time in all eternity was separated from God the Father. Jesus' words on the cross testified to His unimaginable despair. Jesus experienced separation from God and died for me. What a forgiving God I serve!

Nearly every day, Laura and I dealt with complications from her depression and drinking. My misunderstanding of her disease made our relationship and ability to cope more difficult. These were the times when God reminded me of Jesus' sacrifice, and that made it easier to forgive her and myself.

The reality and power of God's forgiveness ebbed and flowed in my life. At times, I still struggled to forgive. But even in my fecklessness toward God, I could build my hope on the fact that God never forgot me, nor does He tire of teaching me how to forgive.

My Abba Father Is Jealous

Even though I found it hard to accept, I am convinced that God did not cause the trials Laura and I went through. He did allow Laura and me to go through her mental illness. He did this in part because He was jealous for us. Both of us had trusted Christ for salvation, but we had strayed from Him. God is jealous for our love and worship and wanted a relationship with us. I believe He allows events and conditions into our lives to draw us back to Him. These events and conditions can include great blessings and at other times, difficult trials (See Job, for instance). In our case, God used the trials surrounding Laura's mental illness to draw us to Him.

We had taken our eyes off Jesus and focused on other things, especially our overwhelming desire to have children. As we came to see that it was not in God's plan for us to have children, we both became bitter toward God. I dealt with bitterness by focusing on success in my job and in politics.

Laura, however, held it in, trying to stuff it down in her heart. This led to great depression. I knew at the time that not being able to have children bothered her deeply, but I don't think I comprehended how deeply. Besides, once we realized the issue of being childless had been settled, in my way of thinking we were able to move on to other issues that could continue to strengthen our relationship.

I not only did not comprehend the depth of despair being childless had caused her; at the time, I didn't understand the notion that she also had physiological and neurological issues with which to deal. Laura learned from her psychiatrist that he believed that Laura suffered from the lack of some or all the following chemicals that affect the transmission of information in the brain: acetylcholine, serotonin, norepinephrine, dopamine, glutamate, and gamma-aminobutyric acid. Her psychiatrist believed that there was something wrong with her chemical balance in her brain by observing CT scans of her brain. I do not believe that he took actual blood tests. When these essential natural body chemicals are lacking, it increases an individual's susceptibility to react and respond to outside situations. When the brain chemicals are not present in the correct amounts, this causes the synapses in the brain to either misfire or not fire at all. This leads to a person having an improper view of things. It breaks down certain responses and changes the thinking process. This can open the door to sin and as it takes a stronger hold it may cause major depression.

God is aware of our body's functions and temptations. He said, "You shall not bow down to them or serve them, for I the LORD your God am a jealous God, visiting the iniquity of the fathers on the children to the third and the fourth generation of those who hate me." (Exodus 20:5).

Laura and I came to understand that as individuals and as a couple dealing with our intense challenges, we needed to establish a stronger personal relationship with God.

God used a variety of events during this time to remind us that He is jealous of our affections as He drew us back to Himself. God is jealous for us! His is a righteous jealousy based on His nature and character.

Learning about God's jealous love for me and His willingness to discipline me to regain my devotion helped deliver me from my bitterness toward Him. I saw that God cared so much about me that He invested His attention in helping me find a better relationship with Him. It helped me to see that God pursued me even though I failed to pursue Him.

My experience was like that of the prodigal son we read of in the

Gospels. I wanted my way, so I went out and did my own thing. I had planned to fix Laura, but found it was not working. When I realized how destitute I had become and I approached God, He was like the father of the prodigal son – He rejoiced upon my return.

> But when he came to his senses, he said, 'How many of my father's hired men have more than enough bread, but I am dying here with hunger! I will get up and go to my father, and will say to him, "Father, I have sinned against heaven, and in your sight; I am no longer worthy to be called your son; make me as one of your hired men."' So he got up and came to his father. But while he was still a long way off, his father saw him and felt compassion *for him,* and ran and embraced him and kissed him. And the son said to him, 'Father, I have sinned against heaven and in your sight; I am no longer worthy to be called your son.' But the father said to his slaves, 'Quickly bring out the best robe and put it on him, and put a ring on his hand and sandals on his feet; and bring the fattened calf, kill it, and let us eat and celebrate; for this son of mine was dead and has come to life again; he was lost and has been found.' And they began to celebrate. (Luke 15:17-24) (NASB)

God the Father welcomed me home.

God saw that I was straying too far away from Him, and in His jealousy for me, He rescued me and drove me back to Himself. He did the same with Laura.

God showed us the value and necessity of meeting together with other Christians. We found a church that preached the Gospel and emphasized building personal relationships with believers, and became active in the church. We started to get back to His Word and into fellowship with Him. This act of reuniting with God and His people – the Church – helped build our spiritual strength and gave us encouragement. I saw that when I had abandoned going to church, I had also lost one of the primary vessels God uses to provide us with His help – His people.

God tells us that His name is Jealous.

Take care, lest you make a covenant with the inhabitants of the land to which you go, lest it become a snare in your midst. You shall tear down their altars and break their pillars and cut down their Asherim (for you shall worship no other god, **for the Lord, whose name is Jealous, is a jealous God**), lest you make a covenant with the inhabitants of the land, and when they whore after their gods and sacrifice to their gods and you are invited, you eat of his sacrifice, and you take of their daughters for your sons, and their daughters whore after their gods and make your sons whore after their gods. [Emphasis added] (Exodus 34:12-16)

As God led us to fellowship in a local church, He also challenged us to pursue Him in serious Bible study. As each of us studied the Bible, I saw hope for Laura and for our relationship. Since then, even with the complications that we eventually faced, I have made it a priority to pursue God. In all this, He continues to teach me that He loves me so much that He will even allow difficult or painful experiences in my life to draw me back to Him.

Effect, But Not Cause

As Laura and I made our pivot toward God, His Word, and His local church, He clarified to me that He did not cause Laura's illness, but He did allow it. God used two profound Scripture passages to teach me about cause and condition.

Then Satan answered the Lord and said "Does Job fear God for no reason? Have You not put a hedge around him and his house and all that he has, on every side? You have blessed the work of his hands, and his possessions have increased in the land. But stretch out Your hand and touch all that he has, and he will curse You to Your face." And the Lord said to Satan," Behold, all that he has is in Your hand. Only against him do not stretch out Your hand." So Satan went out from the presence of the Lord. (Job 1:9-12)

This is the second passage. Notice how it interacts with the first one.

> As He passed by, He saw a man blind from birth. And his
> disciples asked Him, "Rabbi, who sinned, this man or his
> parents, that he was born blind?" Jesus answered, "It was
> not that this man sinned, or his parents, but that the works
> of God might be displayed in him." (John 9:1-3)

These two passages taught me key lessons about Laura's illness and my situation. First, I learned that God did not give Laura mental illness – it would violate His own nature to inflict disease upon anyone. Secondly, diseases do not necessarily result from one's own sin, although disease is the result of original sin and death entering the world though Adam. This is not to say that sinful behavior will not result in disease, because common sense and observation make it clear they are often closely related. Jesus made it plain, however, that the man's blindness did not come from anyone's sin – rather, Jesus put the emphasis on how He healed the blind man to show God's might. This also brought glory to God.

Eventually I wanted to answer the question of whether God allowed Laura's disease to become a trial for us so that we might return to Him. I have come to believe the answer to that question is "Yes."

Since then, my life experience combined with my understanding of Scripture, taught me a second reason God allowed Laura to become ill – so that His glory might be seen in our response to that illness.

I Need Other Believers

In God's plan the Church has a specific role. To be clear, I am writing here about the local church, but in a broader sense, I include the Church made up of all believers.

God uses the Church to meet the needs of members of the body of believers – fellow believers. Scriptures is full of commands for the Church. These commands are there to remind us how important Christian fellowship is to our lives.

When or if we desert our responsibility to remain in fellowship with other believers, it is to our own peril. Among the many lessons God taught me, this one – about an active engagement with the body of believers – ranks among the most important.

Although Christians can come together in any number of ways, the fact is that Christian fellowship is most available in a local church. Laura and I heeded God's leading on this and began to regularly attend and participate in a local church.

The Scriptures are filled with what I call the "one another" commands – as in "love one another" and "serve one another." As I started to study the "one another" commands, I became more aware of how much I needed other believers in my life. These "one another" commands are vital to Christian life – to the abundant life about which Jesus taught.

The "one another" commands emphasize how the body of Christ is made up of individual parts, and when one part of the body of Christ is in crisis, all the body is affected. Each member of the Church is there to help lift up others and to be lifted up by others so we live in unity with each other, but we do this all for God's glory. Each member of the Church is there to show each other how to demonstrate God's love through action.

I have provided a list of many of these "one another" commands from the New Testament for your personal study. Each one has value for our daily lives. I try to practice these commands in my interaction with fellow believers, but I found that during trials, I desperately needed other believers to practice these with me.

- Mark 9:50 – be at peace with one another.
- John 13:34, 1 Peter 1:22, 1 Peter 4:8, 1 John 3:11, 1 John 3:23, John 15:12, John 15:17, 1 John 4:7, 1 John 4:11and 2 John 5 – love one another.
- Romans 12:10 – love one another and outdo one another in showing honor.
- Romans 12:16, Romans 15:5 – live in harmony with one another.
- Romans 14:13 – do not pass judgment on one another.
- Romans 15:7 – welcome one another.
- Romans 15:14 – instruct one another.
- Romans 16:16, 1 Corinthians 16:20 and 2 Corinthians 13:12 – greet one another with a holy kiss.
- 1 Corinthians 6:7 – do not have lawsuits against one another.
- 1 Corinthians 11:33 – wait on one another.
- 1 Corinthians 12:25 – care for one another.

- 2 Corinthians 13:11 – comfort one another and agree with one another.
- Galatians 5:13 and 1 Peter 4:10 – serve one another.
- Galatians 5:15 – do not consume one another.
- Galatians 5:26 – do not provoke or envy one another.
- Galatians 6:2 – bear one another's burdens.
- Colossians 3:13 – bearing with one another.
- Ephesians 4:32 – be kind to one another and forgive one another.
- Ephesians 5:19 – address one another with songs hymns and spiritual songs.
- Ephesians 5:21 – submit to one another.
- Colossians 3:16 – teach and admonish one another.
- 1 Thessalonians 4:13 – encourage one another.
- 1 Thessalonians 5:11 – encourage one another and build one another up.
- 1 Thessalonians 5:15 – seek to do good to one another.
- Hebrews 3:13 – exhort one another.
- Hebrews 10:24 – stir up one another to love and good works.
- Hebrews 10:25 – meet with one another and encourage one another.
- James 4:11 – do not speak evil of one another.
- James 5:9 – do not grumble against one another.
- James 5:16 – confess your sins to one another and pray for one another.
- 1 Peter 4:9 – show hospitality to one another.
- 1 Peter 5:5 – clothe yourself with humility to one another.
- 1 John 1:7 – fellowship with one another.

I do not fully understand why God chose to use human interaction to enrich our lives, and I have yet to fully comprehend why my journey back to Him started at this place of fellowship. I expect that getting my arms around the value of fellowship will be a lifelong quest.

During the tough days Laura and I faced together, I found great solace and comfort in the friendship and love of other believers through a local church. It helped me gain an understanding of and accept Job's view of the severe trial he experienced, a view that I have adopted for my own.

Then his wife said to him, "Do you still hold fast your integrity? Curse God and die!" But he said to her, "You speak as one of the foolish women speaks. Shall we indeed accept good from God and not accept adversity?" In all this Job did not sin with his lips. (Job 2:9-10) (NASB)

CHAPTER 3

Suicide Attempt

My Abba Father Is There for Laura and Me

About two months after Laura began therapy, I called home to check in. I had been attending a regular weekly staff meeting that concluded after 10 PM. Even though she was used to the demands of my job, I felt better letting her know I was on my way home. After learning that she abused alcohol, calling ahead was one of the ways I tried to ensure that she was not drinking. So, I wanted Laura to know that she could expect me in about 20 minutes.

The phone rang a couple of times, and then I heard a man's voice say, "Hansen residence."

"Who is this?" I asked, having never before experienced such a thing. It shocked me.

"I am a police officer. Are you related to Laura Hansen?" he asked.

"I am her husband. What has happened?" I asked, my heart beginning to race.

The officer explained that Laura had called 9-1-1 after attempting suicide. EMT and police had responded. She had taken a bottle of prescription drugs. *Why would she do this?* The thought shot through my mind like a piercing knife wound.

"She seems pretty stable and should be okay," the officer said. "She is on her way in an ambulance to Fairview on the West Bank." *Okay? What does he know?* I asked myself. *He's not a doctor!*

Along with the overdose of her prescription pills, Laura had also been drinking wine. The combination of wine with the pills caused her to throw up and probably saved her life. Later on, I found a red wine stain on the floor, mixed with vomit. Eventually I cleaned up that spot, which stood out as an emblem of my failure and frustration to fix Laura, and left me saddened.

Laura's suicide attempt came as a great surprise to me. Although I knew of her alcohol issues, I did not know she was suicidal. If Laura had been successful, I would have been completely in the dark.

I drove straight to the hospital. The word suicide reverberated in my mind, which began to race. *What if she doesn't make it?* I felt perplexed, confused, and asked why. It seemed illogical. *How could life have gotten this bad? Life is not perfect, but it can't be bad enough for Laura to take her life!* Then I went into my problem-solver mode. *We have to fix this problem,* I reasoned. At that point, my first reaction did not include God fixing it. As I drove toward the hospital, I prayed that God would protect Laura. *But why would she do this?* I repeatedly asked myself, but found no answers.

As I continued toward the hospital that night, terrible thoughts reverberated in my mind. I had no idea if Laura would live through the night. What would I do? I prayed for Laura about her condition. I began to ask God, Why *are You allowing Laura to go through this ordeal?* Then I thought again about how we could fix this, because people get over it, and surely, we can do this.

Upon arriving at the emergency room, the doctor told me Laura would be okay, at least physically. She had survived the suicide attempt. When they let me see her, she looked pale and sad, attached to a heart monitor with a blood pressure cuff regularly measuring her vital signs. I saw evidence of how effective the medications had been, as she seemed almost non-responsive. My heart sank, having to see her that way. They had given her charcoal to negate the effects of the drugs and alcohol, but told me to be patient.

I held her hand and tried to comfort her. "Everything will be okay," I said softly. "We can deal with this."

Soon I learned that hospitals treat suicidal patients carefully. The physician explained that they placed people who attempt suicide on a 72-hour hold and restricted access to her. I felt fear, anguish, and helplessness. The physician made it plain that I had no control over Laura's fate, at least for those 72 hours.

The physician went on to explain the legal aspects and the hospital's responsibilities. For one thing, they needed to ensure that there would be no second attempt, nor could they take the chance that Laura, in her depressed state, might try to hurt someone else.

At this point, I think I began to understand how serious this was, and though I didn't let anyone else see it, I felt my emotions welling up inside. *How can this be? Why? Oh God, what will we do?*

As I drove home that night, I found myself weeping. People who know me know that I am expressive and verbal, and I like to laugh. They know that I am not afraid to cry and sometimes let my emotions out by crying. In my car, alone with God, I could let the tears flow in between my questions. I slept poorly that night, and for many nights to follow. I could not turn my mind off, but in retrospect, I can see how this drove me to God.

A political party employed me at the time in a high stress job. After all, it was campaign season. Campaigns are time demanding and crammed with details and tasks that require immediate attention. I am grateful that God had provided the job, a job I loved to do, but more so in that He surrounded me with fellow Christians who encouraged and helped me. Still, the campaign season added to my physical stress and by itself, was enough to exhaust me. Trouble sleeping and my concern for Laura only compounded my dilemma.

While Laura was on 72-hour hold, I could only see her for two hours a day. During those visits, I saw other evidence of how seriously the hospital took her condition. Just like entering a jail, I had to go through two locked doors, hearing one close behind me before the second one would open. I knew this was not to keep me out, but to keep her in – to protect her.

After evaluation, however, the hospital admitted her to its psychiatric ward, where she stayed for more than 20 days in a locked ward. She shared a room with another patient, which I thought would make it harder for her to recover. I did notice, however, that each day she seemed better.

At this point I had mixed feelings. I felt like I was being unfairly separated from my wife, and felt it may not be the best for her. On the other hand, I felt relief because at least I knew she was safe.

During her stay in the psychiatric ward, her doctors started Laura on medication to treat her depression. That first day dragged on for hours as the physicians evaluated the potential for negative side effects caused by the psychotropic medication.

My mind and spirit fought about what it meant that Laura needed such powerful medicine to help her cope. I felt okay with the medication, but expected it would be for a short period of time. I prayed that God would intervene and heal her so she would be able to get off these drugs.

During her stay in the psychiatric ward, Laura began Cognitive Behavior Therapy (CBT), often in group settings. I cannot speak as an expert about the dynamics involved in CBT, but it strikes me that our small group Bible studies and home groups provide powerful, positive feedback and guidance for people under stress. In fact, in some cases, members of the Body of Christ might show by example how a person can cope with deep depression. Medical professionals have no problem putting a person into group therapy, but many Christians avoid or never even attempt to meet together to share burdens and pray for each other.

With her suicide attempt, Laura's illness suddenly became more serious to both of us. We felt the immense increase in intensity and focus of our trials, but I remained confident that God was there for us. His gracious kindness and love for us started to become a foundation for navigating our own struggles.

After Laura attempted suicide, I began to wonder if God was really in control, even though only a few weeks earlier while I had been reading Job, Scripture had convinced me that God was in control. The reality was that I am bullheaded. I reverted to doubting whether God is in control. What is marvelous, however, was that God looked past my unbelief. My Abba Father showed me something that His Son Jesus said: "Are not two sparrows sold for a penny? And not one of them will fall to the ground apart from Your Father." (Matthew 10:29)

In this verse, Jesus showed me that God is in control of what happens to one of His smallest creatures. I recalled how the book of Genesis told me that God created humans in His own image. Therefore, I saw in this verse that as God cares for the sparrow, to a greater extent He will care for me. As I pondered this powerful truth, it became immensely comforting to know that God watched over me and provided for my needs.

Once Laura left the hospital, she seemed much better. Her doctors left her with many instructions, including taking medications and limiting her weekly works hours to no more than 40. Laura worried that she would lose her job if she didn't go back to her more rigorous work schedule. She quit taking her medications, complaining about how they made her feel, although she did continue taking sleep medications.

I started to struggle with Laura's continued defiance of her doctors' orders. It appeared to me she had made a willful decision to ignore their good advice. She did not seem to care how her actions were affecting others, particularly me. Her actions and attitudes frustrated me. I did not understand that as she continued to struggle, I needed to be more understanding and forgiving. I needed to be more like my Abba Father.

As I struggled with the need to continuously forgive Laura, God pointed me to a familiar passage in the Bible. "If we confess our sins, He is faithful and just to forgive us our sins and to cleanse us from all unrighteousness." (I John 1:9) In this passage God reminded me that He is faithful and just, and because of how He treats me, I needed to be more like Him. It was an awesome sensation to realize how much I deserved judgment, but how much more He forgave me. I have quoted this verse countless times to remind myself of God's justice and forgiveness.

My Abba Father's Love and Concern

No one can adequately explain how gracious God is to us, but I do know the basis of my confidence in Him. I know, and knew as Laura's struggles intensified, that He gave His Son to take away my sins and give me eternal life – I stood on solid ground.

He provided me with the Holy Spirit to aid in asking God for help and understanding, even though I did not know how to ask. He gave me a way out as I was tempted by circumstances and my own feelings to react and respond in sin. I knew, at least intellectually, that God gave me whatever I needed when I needed it to deal with every situation in life – a belief that grew over time.

I am certain of this - I would never have survived without God's daily, immediate demonstrations of grace. He is all I needed to survive and prosper.

The LORD is gracious and merciful,

slow to anger and abounding in steadfast love. (Psalms 145:8)

Knowing that His grace extended to me at all times brought me hope. This did not always make it easy for me to accept His grace. Like most men, I wanted to be self-sufficient. Besides, my strength was my ability to fix problems. I held tight to the idea that I did not need any help from anyone, including from God. Learning to accept God's grace and rely on His faithful execution of it is a lifelong journey, and each day, I need the Holy Spirit to remind me to accept God's grace.

God never stops teaching me about His Grace. The lesson He has repeated, because my pride gets in the way of waiting on Him, is that His grace is sufficient. Paul wrote about grace in a way with which I connect:

> So to keep me from becoming conceited because of the surpassing greatness of the revelations, a thorn was given me in the flesh, a messenger of Satan to harass me, to keep me from becoming conceited. Three times I pleaded with the Lord about this, that it should leave me. But He said to me, "My grace is sufficient for you, for my power is made perfect in weakness." Therefore, I will boast all the more gladly of my weaknesses, so that the power of Christ may rest upon me. For the sake of Christ, then, I am content with weaknesses, insults, hardships, persecutions, and calamities. For when I am weak, then I am strong. (2 Corinthians 12:7-10)

I had to be regularly reminded of the reality that His grace would be sufficient enough to help me deal with all the challenges resulting from Laura's illness.

His grace is sufficient enough to help me to pray. His grace is sufficient enough to give me some kind of peace. His grace is sufficient enough to strengthen my faith in Him. His grace is sufficient enough to deal with my pain. His grace is sufficient enough to secure my marriage. His grace is sufficient enough to give me strength in my weaknesses. His strength and grace are sufficient enough to carry my burdens. His grace is sufficient enough to sustain and grow my faith. His grace is sufficient enough to provide me with friends who care for me. His grace is sufficient enough to give me hope. Maybe most importantly, His grace remained abundantly sufficient enough for me to continue to love Laura, as He wanted me to love her.

Absent the sufficiency of God's grace, I would be a complete wreck. I have found that God's grace is necessary for me every minute of every hour of every day of every year. God's grace through Jesus Christ saved me and rescued me from all my burdens and cares. So I accept this reality and trust in His grace.

After Laura's first suicide attempt and continuing for years afterward, God used her struggles with depression and anxiety to teach me about myself. I saw my own shortcomings and my own strengths. God showed me that my strength comes from Him.

My desire is that you learn from my experience about what God did for me and to me. By pointing out the strengths He gave me and my weaknesses, God made me a better man. The key thing that I learned about myself during this process is that I am nothing without God's grace working in me and involved in all that I do.

I Thought I Could Do it Myself

Prior to Laura's suicide attempt, I believed my efforts would be sufficient to help her solve her problems because I loved her so very much. I thought I could fix her if she cooperated. In the beginning, most of the time I thought very little about seeking God to find the solution. I felt self-sufficient, capable of dealing with it on my own.

The way I saw it, all we had to do was find the right doctor and use our own intellect, reason, and experience to overcome her depression. I believed that if we found the right therapy supported by the right medicine, Laura would get over it and everything would return to normal. Certainly, I thought to myself, *I love Laura, and love can overcome so much and I will do everything I can to help her.*

Her suicide attempt changed everything.

Both of us worked long hours right from the beginning of our marriage. We enjoyed our work and we enjoyed its fruit with a nice home, living comfortably though conservatively. Laura liked nice clothes but preferred muted colors, feeling they most accurately reflected her vision of herself (this would become an increasingly difficult issue as she questioned the value of her life). On shopping trips, I encouraged her to buy bright clothes and greatly enjoyed seeing her dress in them. I loved her and I loved how she looked.

Each year we made it a point to take vacations. We had learned how to travel cheaply, often traveling abroad during the off-season. Even as her depression worsened, we set aside time to travel. As long as she stayed on her medications, we enjoyed our time together. We loved Disneyland and Disneyworld and took many trips overseas. Prior to knowing about her depression, one-year Laura suggested we invite my parents along – Laura loved my dad as the father she never had – and went to Norway and other European cities. After my father died sometime later, I believe it became part of the trigger that started Laura's slide into clinical depression.

Each year we would travel to Seattle to spend time with her parents. Because of their abuse of alcohol, and the many tough years Laura had spent in their home, these trips would bring a change in her. She would mask her symptoms, become careful and withdrawn, and she insisted that we would never share her depression diagnosis with her parents. One Saturday morning during a trip to Seattle, after a few years of her battle with depression, she refused to get out of bed. She did not want to face the day. Once she finally got out of bed, I made her coffee just the way she liked it. Her father noticed something was wrong, saying, "You look really tired. You should lay back down." He had no idea she had been suffering an anxiety attack.

Around noon she finally got up and got dressed. We went for a ride, and she was able to settle down. That was the last year we stayed with her parents, opting instead for a nearby hotel on future trips. Watching her suffer, and the extent to which she went to hide her depression from her parents, was tough. I had hoped it would be otherwise.

God used this time of stress to teach me about true love. We find a practical definition of love throughout the Bible, but especially in 1 Corinthians 13:4-8.

> Love is patient and kind; love does not envy or boast; it is not arrogant or rude. It does not insist on its own way; it is not irritable or resentful; it does not rejoice at wrongdoing, but rejoices with the truth. Love bears all things, believes all things, hopes all things, endures all things. Love never ends. As for prophecies, they will pass away; as for tongues, they will cease; as for knowledge, it will pass away.

The Love Chapter is familiar to most Bible readers. It might be the most-read passage of Scripture at weddings. Familiarity is a good thing, but seeing it through the eyes of a trial like ours brings it to life. I had read it many times in my life, but after Laura's suicide attempt, I began questioning whether I practiced its teachings. I gained a new perspective.

Up to that point in time during our married life, I believed I was kind. I did not envy. I was not arrogant or rude. I was not resentful. I thought I did a pretty good job of bearing and enduring all things. God showed me that when there is very little to bear or endure, it is easy to bear and endure. I had always been an optimist. This made believing and hoping all things pretty easy. By nurture and nature, the idea came easily to me that my love for Laura meant loving her forever.

I struggled with patience and had a propensity to be boastful. I had a selfish streak. Too often, I showed myself to be irritable.

One of the greatest attributes of Scripture is how it acts like a mirror – displaying our true nature by comparison with God's desire for us. God never quits showing us how to become more like Him.

I Corinthians 13:6 is particularly difficult for me. "…[love] does not rejoice at wrongdoing, but rejoices with the truth." I struggled mightily with this one. *How do I apply this now?* I asked God. I especially did not want to rejoice in wrongdoing, and how could I? Yet, *how am I to deal with, support, and help a person I love who harms herself?* I believe this was the hardest part of my struggle trying to make sense out of what Laura had done, and bring some level of order and peace in my own life. *What should I say or not say, or what should I do or not do?*

I loved Laura and believed I needed to express my unhappiness with her behavior for her own good, but did I need to do more, and if so, what did I need to do, and how was I to do it? Frankly, I am still not able to answer these questions clearly – I have more to learn. I trusted God to help me as these situations occurred, and still do.

I have come to the conclusion that the taking of one's own life is a sin. The sin of suicide is not an unforgivable one nor is the attempting of suicide. In this context Christians use many proverbs to explain their actions and attitudes. "Love the sinner and hate the sin," is often quoted. I had to face the practicality of trying to apply this proverb. *What happens when the sin could lead to death, or more specifically, when Laura intended it to end her life?* I asked myself whether I properly loved Laura, and had to answer *no, because I am not Jesus and He is the only one who can love perfectly.* I did everything that I could possibly do from talking and praying with her to just short of tying her down to help her deal with her suicidal ideations. However, the reality is that ultimately every individual makes his or her own decision about whether or not to sin.

God used Laura's suicide attempt to stress to me the importance of prayer. Laura's illness showed me my helplessness. In my helplessness, God reached out to me. The Holy Spirit urged me to pray for her and for myself. I had no idea what to say in those prayers, but God knew what I needed to say – He knew what I needed without me asking.

As my prayer life deepened, I became more amazed at the fact that God sent His Holy Spirit to intercede with God in my prayers.

> Likewise, the Spirit helps us in our weakness. For we do not know what to pray for as we ought, but the Spirit Himself intercedes for us with groanings too deep for

words. And He who searches hearts knows what is the mind of the Spirit, because the Spirit intercedes for the saints according to the will of God. (Romans 8:26-27)

How amazing it is that God gives us His Spirit so that we can effectively communicate with Him!

After Laura had attempted suicide for the first time, I started to doubt that my Abba Father was really faithful all of the time. After all, I watched as Laura continued to go to her doctor's appointments and attempted to deal with her depression, but as far as I could see, she did not seem to be changing. She did not seem to be getting better.

Once again, I began to wonder where was God in all of this. How did He show Himself faithful to her or to me? I kept thinking that if Laura did what she needed to do, then God was obligated to heal her – that made sense to me. Yet, I saw that God did not heal her, and that made me think that He must not be faithful. God led me to this verse in the Psalms: "Your faithfulness endures to all generations; You have established the earth, and it stands fast." (Psalms 119:90) This verse showed me that God keeps His covenants. He would bless me out of His steadfast love because He is forever faithful.

Trusting My Abba Father

When as a Christian husband I saw my depressed wife in a hospital after she attempted suicide, the question of trusting God quickly surfaced. I addressed this in some detail in an earlier chapter when I talked about God being in control of everything. As I saw Laura in the hospital, I did believe that I could trust God because He is holy and just and He loves me. God is truthful and unchanging.

I spent time wrestling with the fact that God is unchanging. What does this mean, and how did it apply to my present predicament?

God helped me to understand that His character never changes, but is certain. Through my prayer and meditation, He revealed to me I could trust Him to be the same today and tomorrow - forever.

God will never do anything inconsistent with His character, and His mercy and graciousness are a part of His character. Grasping a sense of His unchangeable nature helped me to better understand His plan for my life. I eventually came to see that God reveals His mind and refrains from judgment as a response to our prayer and repentance, and it is consistent because of His unchangeable nature.

Knowing that God never changes means that His promises and grace will always stand strong because they are part of His character. This helped me understand during those times when it seemed as if God might be changing His mind. I came to better understand He was actually revealing His intended purpose to me. This helped me to see how prayer makes a difference. It helped me see that encouraging Laura could make a difference in her life.

What does it mean that God is unchanging and why is it important? What did God teach me about His unchanging nature during my trials?

My Abba Father Does Not Change!

God's nature is fixed – He does not evolve or devolve. He has not become better or worse. He has not become more or less loving. He has not become more or less faithful. He has not become more or less ever-present, all-knowing, or all-powerful. Nothing about Him has changed.

I read some Scripture passages that suggest He changes His mind about what He chooses or not chooses to do. I will discuss those passages later.

> Of old You laid the foundation of the earth,
> and the heavens are the work of Your hands.
> They will perish, but You will remain;
> they will all wear out like a garment.
> You will change them like a robe, and they will pass away,
> but You are the same, and Your years have no end.
> (Psalms 102:25-27)

This Psalm showed me that God's creation will perish over time, and so will we, but God will never change. He will always be the same.

The world is constantly changing. We see it in earthquakes, volcanoes, avalanches, hurricanes, and other natural phenomena. We also see it in human tragedies. I believe that God is the one doing the changing of the world. This is evidence of God's sovereignty. "For I the Lord do not change; therefore you, O children of Jacob, are not consumed." (Malachi 3:6)

Because God does not change, He does not consume the children of Jacob – Israel – in His wrath, despite their egregious sin. God made a covenant with Abraham concerning Israel, and God will keep it, though Israel sinned. It is because of His unchanging mercy that He spared Israel, just as it is because of His unchanging mercy that He has given salvation to all those who believe in Jesus.

James reminds me that everything that is good and perfect comes from God, and this fact rests on the reality that He does not change. In God, there are no variations or shadows. "Every good gift and every perfect gift is from above, coming down from the Father of lights with whom there is no variation or shadow due to change." (James 1:17) I find it amazing that because God does not change, I can receive good and perfect gifts.

> "The counsel of the Lord stands forever,
> the plans of His heart to all generations."
> (Psalms 33:11)

Wow! Because God is unchanging, His counsel and plans never change. I can trust His Word. I can trust His promises. I can trust that He is in control.

Isaiah 46:8-11 is rich with facts about God and His immutability. As I listened to Him during the trials Laura and I faced, He reminded me often of this reality – "I AM, and do not change."

God still calls me to remember His nature. I see in this passage that He is God and there is none like Him. Let that sink in for a moment. He is the beginning and the end. His counsel shall stand and it will accomplish all His purposes. Once again, we see a strong reminder that God is in control. He does not change. He has spoken and He will bring it to pass. He has purposed and He will do it. What an amazing God we serve. There is nothing too big or too small for Him and about this, He will not change.

Men Lie and Change Their Minds, But Not My Abba Father

> God is not man, that He should lie,
> or a son of man, that He should change His mind.
> Has He said, and will He not do it?
> Or has He spoken, and will He not fulfill it? (Numbers 23:19)

This passage created a dilemma for me. It is easy for me to understand that God is not a man, and unlike men, He could not lie. All men lie – some more than others – but God never does. But it also says that He does not change His mind. Yet we see in other passages that it appears at times and under certain circumstances, God seems to change His mind – so to speak. We see that there were times when He decided not to punish a group of people but spared them instead. So how can this passage so clearly state that God does not change His mind?

I look at the first part of that statement and consider that He is not like a man or the son of a man. I know a great deal about men. Men seem to change their mind at every whim and fancy. Men have favorites that outshine all other choices until something better comes along and becomes their new favorite thing. A man or woman is attracted to another person, and then yet another person gets their attention – even true among married people (to which the divorce rate attests). Yet, I also see that God does change His mind as He responds to the actions of others – this, too, is evidence of His unchanging nature. Perhaps in the bigger picture, He really never changes His mind, but what we see is a test of the people with whom He is dealing.

This passage also tells us that if God says it, it will be done. God's decision is final and absolute. There will be no change to it.

The Bible tells us that someday, God's mercy will come to an end. On that day, we will each face the consequences of our decision to have accepted or rejected Him. There will be no changing His mind at the Judgment Seat.

As I ponder this idea of God changing His mind, it occurs to me that maybe God does not actually change His mind although it looks that way to me. God does, however, reveal His plan, which may appear to us that He changes His mind.

Laura and I agreed at the beginning that our marriage was God's will for us. As we lived together, we saw that God allowed challenges to come into our lives. We understood His will for us in His unchanging nature, which revealed His plan to us. It was important to us to know and understand how and why God reveals His plans. We knew, however, that God does not change His mind based on numerous Scriptures.

> The Lord said to Moses, "I have seen this people, and behold, they are an obstinate people. Now then let Me

alone, that My anger may burn against them and that I may destroy them; and I will make of you a great nation."

Moses' Entreaty
Then Moses entreated the Lord his God, and said, "O Lord, why does Your anger burn against Your people whom You have brought out from the land of Egypt with great power and with a mighty hand? Why should the Egyptians speak, saying, 'With evil *intent* He brought them out to kill them in the mountains and to destroy them from the face of the earth'? Turn from Your burning anger and change Your mind about *doing* harm to Your people. Remember Abraham, Isaac, and Israel, Your servants to whom You swore by Yourself, and said to them, 'I will multiply your descendants as the stars of the heavens, and all this land of which I have spoken I will give to your descendants, and they shall inherit *it* forever.'" So the Lord changed His mind about the harm which He said He would do to His people. (Exodus 32:9-14) (NASB)

The first words of this passage strongly suggest that God intended to wipe out all of Israel, saving only Moses. As we read further in Exodus, of course, we know that God did not destroy Israel. Instead, God revealed His true plan to "relent from the disaster" that He had planned. So how and why did God reveal His true plan to Moses and the Israelites, and to us?

God accepted the prayers and faithfulness of Moses and then granted His mercy and forgiveness to Israel. He could have wreaked ruin on Israel as they deserved it. Yet God chose to be merciful to Israel because of Moses' intercession.

Laura and I deserved God's wrath, but despite our sins and failure, He showed us mercy.

Isaiah tells us more about how God reveals His plan.

In those days Hezekiah became sick and was at the point of death. And Isaiah the prophet the son of Amoz came to him, and said to him, "Thus says the Lord: Set your house in order, for you shall die, you shall not recover."

Then Hezekiah turned his face to the wall and prayed to the Lord, and said, "Please, O Lord, remember how I have walked before You in faithfulness and with a whole heart, and have done what is good in Your sight." And Hezekiah wept bitterly.

Then the word of the Lord came to Isaiah: "Go and say to Hezekiah, "Thus says the Lord, the God of David your father: I have heard your prayer; I have seen your tears. Behold, I will add fifteen years to your life. I will deliver you and this city out of the hand of the king of Assyria, and will defend this city." (Isaiah 38:1-6)

God heard Hezekiah's prayer, the prayers of a righteous man. God spared His life for 15 more years, and by this, He revealed His plan.

In Jonah we see an incredible expression of God revealing His plan in response to the humble faith and repentance of the Ninevites.

So Jonah arose and went to Nineveh according to the word of the Lord. Now Nineveh was an exceedingly great city, a three days' walk. Then Jonah began to go through the city one day's walk; and he cried out and said, "Yet forty days and Nineveh will be overthrown."

Then the people of Nineveh believed in God; and they called a fast and put on sackcloth from the greatest to the least of them. When the word reached the king of Nineveh, he arose from his throne, laid aside his robe from him, covered *himself* with sackcloth and sat on the ashes. He issued a proclamation and it said, "In Nineveh by the decree of the king and his nobles: Do not let man, beast, herd, or flock taste a thing. Do not let them eat or drink water. But both man and beast must be covered with sackcloth; and let men call on God earnestly that each may turn from his wicked way and from the violence which is in his hands. Who knows, God may turn and relent and withdraw His burning anger so that we will not perish."

When God saw their deeds, that they turned from their wicked way, then God relented concerning the calamity which He had declared He would bring upon them. And He did not do *it*. (Jonah 3:3-10) (NASB)

In this case God revealed His plan once the people of Nineveh repented and turned in faith to God.

Two Principles We Saw That Helped Us Move Forward

Laura and I saw that the Scriptures teach that God reveals His plans for two reasons: because of the prayers of a righteous person and repentance from sin.

God's righteous judgment condemns all sinners to eternal damnation. God, however, gave us a way to satisfy His righteous judgment by the death of Jesus Christ on the cross. Jesus took on Himself the sins of the world and delivered His blood to God to pay for them all. He satisfied God when He paid the penalty for all who believe on His Name. God gave us the ability to accept His grace and forgiveness. He reveals His plan for our lives and allows us to have eternal life. All praise be to God!

I learned to remember that God never changes – He is the same yesterday, today, and tomorrow. His unchanging nature gives me confidence to trust all His promises. I know His plan is the best for me. I am completely confident that all His attributes will always be the same for all eternity.

Yet We Faced Incredibly Difficult Challenges

God began teaching Laura and me tough lessons about love, faith, trust, honesty, and more. We believed that, at this point in our journey, we should keep confidential what was happening to her. At the same time, I know that James tells us to share our burdens with each other. I wanted and needed help and encouragement from others in the church. I also thought it was important that her parents and family knew what was happening, and I never liked keeping secrets from my family. Laura, however, had made her mental illness a taboo subject outside the two of us. I honored her request – at that time.

In hindsight, especially as I watched her illness begin to intensify, I'm not sure keeping it a secret was the best decision. I still cannot be sure we would have benefited from the help of others. At this point in time, though, we both believed her illness was unique and would improve in the months ahead. We did not yet understand that others in the body of Christ suffered in a similar manner.

Today, I am still unsettled about whether sharing the truth of her illness after her first suicide attempt would have helped either of us. I only know that I agreed with her to keep it private. Thus, we would suffer in private, while seeking God and His answers.

Soon we experienced greater trials.

CHAPTER 4

Second Suicide Attempt

Where is My Abba Father?

Laura's first attempted suicide had happened in September. I had hoped it would be the event that would trigger her healing. I saw that in some ways, her illness had opened the door to what I viewed as a time for a spurt of spiritual growth. Surely, I thought, she will begin to get a grip on her anxieties, and together, we would be able to set her on a course to mental health. We needed to do the right things and trust God for the results.

At the same time, I continued to pour myself into my work as a political party field-director. Political work is always time-consuming and does not conform to any common workday. I had to be ready to respond and reach out to party volunteers on short notice, plus pay attention to the direction of our political director. Stress is part of the job, but I enjoyed it. This meant, however, attending to the rigors of daily routines and what sometimes seemed like an endless stream of meetings.

As normal, about two months after Laura's first suicide attempt, I attended a regularly scheduled late night monthly meeting. The campaign season was in full swing and we had candidate requests flying at us, while local party leaders were anxious for our help. In the middle of these campaigns, time and financial resources are always lacking, and urgency is a present motivator. When not in meetings, I was preoccupied with countless tasks, all seemingly needing immediate action. I loved it!

Although I did not carry a constant sense of dread, Laura's illness often did weigh heavily on my heart and mind. As hard as I strove to focus on work, from time-to-time I would find myself wondering what and how she was doing. I had begun to wonder whether she would be drinking while I was away, or become overwhelmed by the challenges she faced. As much as I wanted to leave it all in God's hands, I must admit that I carried a good deal of worry in my heart.

As I headed to my car after a late evening meeting in December, my cell phone rang. As usual, I had planned to call Laura and let her know I was on my way home and assumed she was calling me. Calling her served several purposes, including letting her know I would be home soon which would help reduce anxiety for both of us. Hearing her voice and briefly chatting with her was a way I could check up on her, make sure she was okay, give her a sense of security and provide myself with some relief. Maybe, I thought, my calls would keep her from doing something rash.

When my cell phone rang that evening, I did not recognize the phone number on the caller ID. "Mr. Hansen, this is Officer Jones. Are you the husband of Laura Hansen?" I heard the voice say.

"Yes, yes I am," I answered, as my heart and mind began to race. "*What is going on?*"

"Your wife appears to have attempted suicide and is on her way to the hospital." As I heard his voice, I felt my world once again being shaken to the core. I sat stunned. *How could this be happening again? I thought we were making progress. God, help us – help Laura and preserve her life.*

During the previous 3½ months, my life had changed from a predictable normal to living with a major crisis, and I was now learning every sense of peace could blow up at any time. In those few months, Laura had gone from being as - I saw her - a completely well - adjusted and healthy woman to this new person who suffered from a difficult case of major depression. I didn't know what to think or feel. I didn't know what to do. Since her diagnosis, I found myself periodically feeling absolutely lost, hopeless, and alone.

I asked myself several questions. *Where can I go for help? What can I do to help her? What can I do to help me? Where is God in all of this? Will Laura get better? Do I need to accept the fact that I must deal with this for the rest of my life? Will Laura have to deal with this for the rest of her life?*

At the hospital that night I tried hard to be encouraging to Laura. Seeing her lying in bed, realizing that she had come close to death, left me mentally drained. Still, I knew enough to pray, even though my prayers expressed mixed sentiments. I prayed for Laura's safety and for recovery – permanent recovery. I prayed for myself, and I asked God for answers.

I began to feel pain – my own, of course, but more so, Laura's pain. As my heart and mind searched for meaning, I started to understand the oneness that God spoke about in Genesis. "Therefore, a man shall leave his father and his mother and hold fast to his wife, and they shall become one flesh. And the man and his wife were both naked and were not ashamed." (Genesis 2:24-25) The old King James Version called this idea of holding fast as being of "one flesh." As I saw Laura ache, I also began to ache.

"Where do I get help?" The answer to this question sent me to seek more intimacy with God. Growing closer to God helped me answer my other questions. As I asked God for answers, among other things, during the days and weeks that followed, He led me to godly men to seek and receive their counsel, comfort, and encouragement. By sharing my concerns – my heart – openly with these men, God revealed some of the other answers.

With my friends' help, God showed me there were actions I could take that would help both Laura and me. Some of those actions were quite simple, though profoundly important. I needed to be available, supportive, and understanding to and for Laura. I needed to show love to her in tangible ways. I needed to continue forgiving her. I needed to spend time with her to show her that I cared. I needed to do things with her that she wanted to do, not what I wanted to do. I needed to listen carefully to her and respond in a supportive manner. This fought against my normal tendencies as a problem solver, wanting to take charge, set up a strategy, and then lead her toward health. I had to concede the reality that I could not be in control, and instead be a servant to Laura.

One of the major personal issues with which I had to deal was that in most cases I felt, and indeed was helpless concerning Laura's illness. I could not heal her. I could not make her do what she didn't want to do. Thankfully, God stepped into my dilemma and reminded me, "I can do all things through Him (Christ) who strengthens me." (Philippians 4:13) Applying the all to our situation meant *all*, a concept that is hard to grasp when life is tough, but vitally important to receive spiritual and emotional help. So, it was with the help of the Holy Spirit that I continued to try my best to care for Laura and to provide for her needs.

The Holy Spirit directed me to better support Laura and attempt to relate to her illness. I needed to encourage her and assure her that it was possible for her to get better. I knew and observed that there were many times when Laura felt isolated and alone. I offered encouragement by reminding her that God was always with her, and not to rely on her feelings of abandonment.

For my own health, the Holy Spirit worked to teach me to, "Rejoice always, pray without ceasing, give thanks in all circumstances; for this is the will of God in Christ Jesus for you." (1 Thessalonians 5:16-18)

Saying that the Holy Spirit led and taught me is true, but He had to be extremely patient with me. I was not very good at any of those actions and had barely adopted these attitudes. It's difficult to be thankful when the person you love has twice tried to take her own life and is not doing well.

I tried my best but ultimately had to turn everything over to God to help me to be thankful no matter the situation. God had to become my source of joy, and this drove me to be able to rejoice in our tough circumstances. "The LORD is my strength and my shield; in Him my heart trusts, and I am helped; my heart exults, and with my song I give thanks to Him." (Psalms 28:7)

What about praying without ceasing? I concluded that I needed to be in constant communication with God. This did not require me to stop what I was doing, bow my head, close my eyes, and pray aloud in any formal manner. Instead, as Laura or a tough situation came to mind, I would whisper a short prayer. Sometimes that prayer was as simple as "God help me." By His grace He helped me, and continues to do so, in all areas of my life.

God Reminded Me That He Is in Control

After the second suicide attempt, I began to doubt whether God was in control though He had convinced me twice before of this fact. I saw that she was certainly not getting better and I felt myself becoming more frustrated. My Abba Father, in response, showed me His grace by pointing me to a verse in Psalms. "Our God is in the heavens; He does all that He pleases." (Psalms 115:3) However, this verse led me to another question.

I also wanted to know where God was in all this. I thought that if He was truly faithful, He should have been there to stop Laura. God showed me this passage in Psalms. It talks about how His faithfulness surrounds us. "O Lord God of hosts, who is mighty as You are, O Lord, with Your faithfulness all around You?" (Psalms 89:8) God showed me that wherever I go and whatever I do, He surrounds me with His faithfulness. Though I felt like He was not faithful, He was – He corrected my feelings of isolation, and replaced this with the truth of His Word. I gladly repented of my unbelief.

™"Where Is My Abba Father in All of This?"

Let me answer the two most difficult questions before I try to answer some of the others. I regularly struggled with these questions. *"Will Laura get better?" "Do I need to be resolved to deal with the issues of mental illness and Laura for the rest of my life or for the rest of Laura's life?"*

You may be disappointed by my answer, but the best answer is "Maybe." I came to this conclusion because I cannot know the future. At best, I could take comfort knowing that God knew the answers to both those questions. I left the answers to those questions in His hands, trying to learn to be content in the state of my life as it played out. Today, I continue to try to leave the answers in God's hands.

Now to the question *"Where is God in all of this?"* I asked God the question – often – and waited for His answer. For most people, God's answer to this question is difficult to accept. For me, I resolved to accept whatever answer God showed me through the Scriptures. One result is that I am writing this book and learning that God is in control of it and all facets of my life.

The second part of the answer is that He is always with everyone who believes in Him, everywhere, all the time. This is to say that God was with me in every aspect of my life at the same moment in time He was with Laura in every aspect of her life. I am not saying that I understand what He was doing, but I knew He never left us, nor did He ever forsake us.

Like understanding God's faithfulness, understanding that He is not subject to space or time is vitally important as I dealt with my trials. This meant that as I went through life with Laura, it comforted me to know that God was with her.

The notion of God always being present became even more important as I watched Laura struggle with depression. I knew that she needed God to be with her and to comfort and protect her. At the same time, I realized that I needed Him to comfort and give me strength. We both needed His presence at the same time, and praise be to God, He was always there for both of us at the same time even when at times we were hundreds of miles apart.

I will tell you that I continued to struggle. It's part of the human dilemma, where we want to believe and trust completely, but fight against what we can see, touch, and feel – what lies in front of our eyes. As a result, I constantly worried about Laura. I kept wanting to fix her myself, and often thought I could. Yet, regardless of my thoughts and my unfaithfulness to fully trust God's ability to be there for both of us, He continued to be faithful and never left us alone.

What does it mean that God is not subject to space or time, and why is it important? This is a hard concept to accept with my finite mind – God is totally everywhere all at once. This means that He is completely where I am and where you are as you read this sentence. I cannot comprehend how He can be completely in two places at the same time, but He said it, and I still believe it.

"Am I a God at hand, declares the LORD, "and not a God far away? Can a man hide himself in secret places so that I cannot see him?" declares the LORD. "Do I not fill heaven and earth?' declares the LORD." (Jeremiah 23:23-24)

So here God says He is at hand and He is far away at the same time. He asks a rhetorical question: "Can a man hide himself in secret places so that I cannot see him?" The answer is "No." Then He says He fills heaven and earth. He reinforces this concept in other scriptures.

> Can you find out the deep things of God?
> Can you find out the limit of the Almighty?
> It is higher than heaven—what can you do?
> Deeper than Sheol—what can you know?
> Its measure is longer than the earth
> and broader than the sea. (Job 11:7-9)

Scripture continues this theme. God showed me several other passages regarding His omnipresence. You can look at these on your own: 1 Kings 8:27and Psalm 139:7-10.

Clearly, Scripture teaches us that God is omnipresent – everywhere at the same time. But what about the question of His eternal nature? I have always thought that this is an even more difficult concept to grasp than His being in two places at one time.

God is everlasting and is not encumbered by time. He created time and He created the heavens and earth. "But do not overlook this one fact, beloved, that with the Lord one day is as a thousand years, and a thousand years as one day." (2 Peter 3:8)

When I saw Laura in some of her toughest days, I longed for the passage of time, so that her immediate suffering would end and she could recover. I often hoped for Christ's return so Laura's pain would end. God saw her as in an instant, both present and future, and remained in control.

God's eternal nature is often repeated in the Psalms.

> "Lord, You have been our dwelling place
> in all generations.
> Before the mountains were brought forth,
> or ever You had formed the earth and the world,
> from everlasting to everlasting, You are God." (Psalms 90:1-2)

So, God has always existed and will always continue to exist. The idea that to Him a day is as a thousand years demonstrates that time does not constrain Him from His purposes.

Why was God's omnipresence and eternal nature important to me as Laura and I struggled with her illness? It gave me comfort to know that when I could not be there for Laura, God was. At the same time, He was with me giving me grace and comfort. It provided me with deeper peace knowing that God gave all of Himself to Laura and me at the same time. Wow! That still blows my mind!

Knowing that God was with her all the time helped me to know that He was not going to allow Laura to be tempted beyond what she could resist. When she faced a struggle or temptation, He gave her a way out.

"No temptation has overtaken you that is not common to man. God is faithful, and He will not let you be tempted beyond your ability, but with the temptation He will also provide the way of escape, that you may be able to endure it." (1 Corinthians 10:13)

It is self-evident that we do not always choose the way out of temptation that God provides, yet He remains faithful and in control. I knew that God was not surprised with anything that Laura did. He was not surprised that she attempted suicide. He was not surprised that she used alcohol to alleviate her psychological pain. Even more amazing, God would not be surprised by any of her future actions because He was already there as well as being here.

Now She Was in The Hospital

Standing in that hospital room after her second suicide attempt, once again I found myself distressed by Laura's illness. *"Lord, save her life, please, and help her find healing."*

This time the doctors changed her medication and they recommended Electro-Convulsive Therapy (ECT). Their decision to treat her depression with (ECT) concerned me more than the drugs they now recommended.

"Electroconvulsive therapy (ECT) is a procedure, done under general anesthesia, in which small electric currents are passed through the brain, intentionally triggering a brief seizure. ECT seems to cause changes in brain chemistry that can quickly reverse symptoms of certain mental illnesses. It often works when other treatments are unsuccessful."

The doctors explained how they would administer my dear wife a general anesthesia and then send electric shocks through certain parts of her brain. As I understood it, they believed this treatment would help her forget the trauma that caused her depression. The doctors added that ECT could produce a negative, although usually temporary, side effect – not so with Laura. The doctors explained that Laura should expect some loss of short-term memory. We reasoned that we could live with this for a time, but instead, it affected her ability to perform her job.

After the ECT, she suffered enough short-term memory loss issues to cause her to struggle at work. The good news, though, is that it seemed to help with her depression – for a time. Upon reflection, I remain unconvinced that her loss of short-term memory was worth the minor improvement.

The hospital released Laura after 14 days and she came home with me. I remember feeling hopeful and thanking God for sparing her life. It also helped me recover some order in my life, as the political pace continued. I thanked God for the individuals with whom I worked, fellow Christians, who came alongside me and helped me manage my work requirements. I cherished their concern and prayers for Laura and me.

The doctors gave her instructions to decrease her works hours from the normal 50-60 to no more than 40 hours a week. Laura, however, worried about how her bosses would react to this work reduction, so she ignored her doctor's recommendation.

Over time, I came to see that Laura's decision to continue to work long hours negatively affected her long-term health. When I tried to convince her to follow her doctor's instructions, she refused. Once again, I saw that I had no control, and only scant influence over her choices. The decision to work more than 40 hours a week was hers, though I don't believe it was in her best interest and told her so. Her short-term memory loss also caused her difficulties in accomplishing her work tasks.

You may have picked up on this, but patience is not one of my strongest traits – quite the opposite. I want things done now, not later. God showed me in dealing with Laura's mental illness that I needed to learn to wait. Her medical and mental health tests required patience, and so did the hope for progress.

"But the fruit of the Spirit is love, joy, peace, patience, kindness, goodness, faithfulness, gentleness, self-control; against such things there is no law." (Galatians 5:22-23) This verse reminded me – and still does – that I needed to seek the Holy Spirit to help me deal with my impatience. The great thing is that God is patient with me so the Holy Spirit continues to teach me patience.

Bringing Others Into Our Lives

Finally, much to my relief, Laura decided that I could share some of our struggles with a small group of close Christian friends. She still did not want me to share her illness with our families. I disagreed with her wishes, but honored them at this time.

I started to share our struggles with her illness with some of my friends at church and two of the pastors. Their support and my sharing it with them were immensely helpful to me. It's why Scripture teaches us to "Bear one another's burdens, and so fulfill the law of Christ." (Galatians 6:2) This powerful verse pays immense dividends for Christians, but it comes with a caution. Paul warns that we should only share with skillful (i.e. mature and trustworthy) Christians, not necessarily with everyone. In fact, the judgment of other Christians, even though well-meant, would from time-to-time, become a stumbling block for Laura and me.

Sharing with fellow believers is powerfully therapeutic and gaining their prayerful support is immensely helpful. Finding that we were not alone and that others struggled with similar situations provided strength for us.

God never left me alone, and He gave me others to love and by whom I could be loved. Maybe I could call this God's ECT – Everlasting Covenant Therapy.

CHAPTER 5

Added Stress and Continual Struggles

My Abba Father Provides and We Learn to Trust Him

Shortly after the hospital released Laura after her second suicide attempt, the hospital and medical bills for her first visit showed up in our mailbox. My eyes immediately went to the column that showed our share of the bills remaining after the insurance company paid their portion and applied our deductible and co-pays. Our share of the bills was huge!

We owned a medical insurance plan that had limited coverage for mental illness. We had made that choice because neither of us thought we would face any mental health problems.

Earlier, when Laura and I talked about health insurance, we discussed mental health coverage, but at that time, Laura did not tell me of her struggles. She was in denial about her mental distress. I am not sure that at that time she felt it was as bad as it turned out to be. As far as I knew, she was doing well and the idea of choosing an insurance option for expanded mental health coverage did not cross my mind.

In retrospect, it is difficult to believe that Laura didn't know something was wrong, since she was already hiding her consumption of alcohol at the time when we chose coverage nine months prior to her first suicide attempt. The stigma, however, attached to mental illness is powerful and many people avoid discussing it.

Our medical insurance included coverage for mental health with a maximum of $5,000 per year. The hospital bill for the first stay exceeded $40,000. As I held that bill in my hand, I shook my head and wondered aloud, "How are we ever going to pay this?" Of course, I knew the bill for her second stay would be in our mail very shortly thereafter. Once the second bill arrived, our hospital debt approached $60,000.

Naturally, I became concerned with how to find the money to pay these bills. Laura became even more depressed. She saw the medical bills as a great burden she had created for us. Laura's increased anxiety in response to the bills compounded my sense of responsibility to figure out how to deal with our financial situation. The weight of these two profoundly difficult issues followed me around every minute of every day.

I found myself questioning why Laura had not discussed her emotional issues with me earlier so we could have at least protected ourselves against the financial risk of mental illness. I recognized, thanks to the Holy Spirit, that I needed to forgive Laura for keeping her condition secret. The next step for me could have been devastating, if blame would turn to bitterness. "See to it that no one fails to obtain the grace of God; that no 'root of bitterness' springs up and causes trouble, and by it many become defiled…" (Hebrews 12:15) These were powerful words to call to memory during times when I became frustrated and angry toward Laura.

When we first faced the reality of having to pay the medical bills, at least we knew we were close to the end of the health insurance plan year and could choose a new plan for the future. We chose to include more mental health service coverage going forward. This made us feel more secure about our financial future, at least to some extent. I calculated and strongly hoped that future spending related to her depression would be for therapy and not for additional emergency care.

With the new health insurance plan in place, we still needed to determine how to pay the almost $60,000 of medical bills already in hand. We went to the hospital and asked them for patience as we tried to figure out how to pay them. The hospital connected Laura with the county, suggesting the government might help us pay the medical bills.

After trying to figure out what to do financially on our own, I finally turned to God for His help. I still hadn't learned to seek God first to provide for our needs.

God, our provider, started to teach me about His desire to provide us with our needs. ""Ask, and it will be given to you; seek, and you will find; knock, and it will be opened to you. For everyone who asks receives, and he who seeks finds, and to him who knocks it will be opened." (Matthew 7:7-8) (NASB) As God called these verses to my mind, He told me to go ahead and ask Him, in faith, to meet our needs. I did.

He also reminded me of what Jesus said in Matthew 6:25-34.

> ""For this reason I say to you, do not be worried about your life, *as to* what you will eat or what you will drink; nor for your body, *as to* what you will put on. Is not life more than food, and the body more than clothing? Look at the birds of the air, that they do not sow, nor reap nor gather into barns, and *yet* your heavenly Father feeds them. Are you not worth much more than they? And who of you by being worried can add a *single* hour to his life? And why are you worried about clothing? Observe how the lilies of the field grow; they do not toil nor do they spin, yet I say to you that not even Solomon in all his glory clothed himself like one of these. But if God so clothes the grass of the field, which is *alive* today and tomorrow is thrown into the furnace, *will He* not much more *clothe* you? You of little faith! Do not worry then, saying, 'What will we eat?' or 'What will we drink?' or 'What will we wear for clothing?' For the Gentiles eagerly seek all these things; for your heavenly Father knows that you need all these things. But seek first His kingdom and His righteousness, and all these things will be added to you.
>
> "So do not worry about tomorrow; for tomorrow will care for itself. Each day has enough trouble of its own." (NASB)

Based on these two passages, I decided to ask God to provide for our financial needs and asked Him to take away my worry about our finances. God did provide.

God provides for us in many ways. In our case, He used the county, which paid all but $28,000 of the bill, and refinancing our home provided the rest. This lesson taught me regarding payment of our medical bills, that through the equity in our home, God had already made provision for them, and gave me confidence that we would be covered in the future. I have continued to depend upon God for my finances, and He has continued to meet my needs.

Laura's illness meant that she would need to start taking disability income. Instead of 60 or more hours a week of work as had been her habit, she worked far fewer hours and at lower income. Our household income, which had been based on our combined paychecks – and she generally earned as much or more than I did – dropped dramatically. Amazingly, we could meet our needs despite losing such a large share of our monthly income. God provided, as He said He would.

Earlier I mentioned that Laura had previously worked long hours, and as such, derived some of her self-worth from her ability to do so. Now, on disability and with a reduced ability to work, Laura experienced additional stress because she felt like she was not doing enough. This stress added to her deteriorating view of her value, further damaging her emotional state.

Addiction and Laura's Mental Health

During the next 18 months, I watched Laura continue to struggle with alcoholism. Also during this time, she began to cut herself. As I saw the cut marks on her body, I became more alarmed. I really did not understand how someone could choose to cut himself or herself. I could not associate how physical pain could dull emotional pain. It seemed absolutely illogical. However, God reminded me of a message I heard from Pastor Bob Ricker. He said, "Everything that a person does is logical in their own mind. Even if we do not think it is logical." I continue to try to comprehend the idea of cutting oneself.

I wondered if this was another suicide attempt that was badly done. Her psychologist would tell me that he did not believe it was a suicide attempt but rather it was about inflicting physical pain to relieve emotional pain.

My need to learn how to trust God more completely grew even more important. More than ever, I saw how I needed to commit Laura's life and health to God.

We made many attempts and employed several strategies to deal with Laura's alcoholism. Her new destructive behavior complicated those strategies.

First, Laura tried outpatient group therapy though Alcoholics Anonymous. Usually, after going to a group meeting, she would stop drinking for a day or two, then she would start drinking again. She would go back to AA, and stop drinking for a day or two. Then she would start again. The cycle repeated over the next several weeks. We saw it was obviously not successful.

Next, Laura tried inpatient treatment for alcoholism. Unfortunately, she was not yet ready to stop drinking. She looked for or created excuses to quit the program from the day she started.

Shortly after entering inpatient treatment, Laura found a way out. One of the other patients stole her CD player and CDs. She used this theft to justify leaving the program because she said she could not trust other people. This mistrust of others stayed with her for many years.

When outpatient and inpatient treatment failed to help Laura overcome alcoholism, her doctors decided to prescribe medication to stop drinking. Each day she took Antabuse. If she drank alcohol, she would become violently ill from the terrible side effects, including vomiting.

In hindsight, I see two flaws in this use of Antabuse in Laura's case.

Taking Antabuse did not change Laura's desire to have alcohol. I saw that in some ways, it caused her to desire alcohol even more. At least a couple times she took the pills and then decided to drink anyway – she became very ill. After a time, she decided to quit taking the pills and continue drinking instead.

During the time Laura took Antabuse, she began to express her depression by cutting herself. Her first attempt was small, a superficial cut, but it did cause pain. Cutting, as I understand it, is an attempt to take away or mask emotional pain. Though I understand the reason, I still don't understand the logic behind cutting oneself to experience physical pain to relieve emotional pain.

Cutting, however, makes sense to thousands of people who struggle with it daily. I heard one of my pastors say, "Everything a person does in their life is logical to the person who does it." To most people, it seems like a foolish way to deal with personal problems, but to the cutter, it seems a logical answer to emotional suffering.

As I saw Laura continue to struggle with her alcohol abuse and see the results of cutting herself, I again doubted if God was just. I did not see how Laura deserved to be struggling so much. It was unfair. In response to my doubt, God pointed me back to His Word and to this passage in Isaiah. "Therefore the Lord waits to be gracious to you, and therefore He exalts Himself to show mercy to you. For the Lord is a God of justice; blessed are all those who wait for Him." (Isaiah 30:18)

Finally...At Least We Hoped

Almost two years into her diagnosis of major clinical depression, Laura finally decided that she had to stop drinking. She recognized that she needed help. With this decision, I felt that finally we were going to make progress.

We enrolled her in a nationally known treatment facility for alcoholics. When I dropped her off at the facility that first day, we each believed and hoped she would come out clean after 28 days of treatment. We also both knew that I would have limited interaction with her since the program limited visits to Sundays.

As I drove away, I thanked God for His intervention, and I asked Him to cover Laura with His love and help her heal. I also asked Him to help me defeat the idea that perhaps this would fail. Hope, I knew, was an important part of my own mental, emotional, and spiritual need.

The program called for her to spend the first few days in isolation to go through withdrawal. Next, they moved her to a semi-private room with two other women. Now settled in, she began intensive inpatient treatment for alcoholism.

A few days after moving into the semi-private room, however, Laura cut herself with a razor blade. She had hidden it under the insole of her shoe. As a result, the treatment facility staff wanted to send her home. Before dealing with alcoholism, they said, she needed to be cured of her cutting behavior. Her psychologist, however, pleaded with the facility staff to allow her to stay, contingent on a thorough search of her personal effects and her room. The staff agreed and did not find any other razor blades or cutting tools in Laura's things. Thankfully, she successfully completed the treatment. Laura had become alcohol-free. I praised God for this important victory in her recovery.

During this time God taught me to trust Him more. Proverbs 3:5-6 became more meaningful to me.

> "Trust in the Lord with all your heart
> And do not lean on your own understanding.
> In all your ways acknowledge Him,
> And He will make your paths straight." (NASB)

Like most people who have been a believer for a long time, this Proverb was familiar to me. During Laura's inpatient treatment, however, I realized that I had not been putting it into practice. Instead, I continually relied on my own understanding and finding my ways to solve problems. I tried to show her more love by bringing her flowers or chocolates. I tried to be more affectionate toward her. I tried to encourage her that she could get better but she had to want to get better and try harder. None of these actions were done because I was trusting God; they were done because I thought they would make Laura better.

It makes perfect sense for believers to trust God in all our ways, and to lean on Him for understanding. Yet, it is common for most of us to try to make our own way, a lifetime challenge that is not easily overcome. I continue to fail to trust God in all things, but there are times, like when Laura and I were under stress, when this reminder – that we are to trust God to make our paths straight – came alive to both of us.

One reason it is so difficult to trust God, and instead, to trust myself, is because I am prideful. "Pride goes before destruction, and a haughty spirit before a fall." (Prov. 16:18) And "…God opposes the proud but gives grace to the humble." (1 Peter 5:5c)

I needed to know about and vigorously apply, "Humble yourselves before the Lord and He will exalt you." (James 4:10) Be assured of this – defeating pride is tough. After all, during most of my lifetime I could overcome adversity, respond under pressure, and find strategies not just to cope with situations, but to win. I knew I was good at what I did, but God showed me this did not translate into solving Laura's problems. He had given me talents and gifts to use in my work and ministry, but for Laura's mental illness, He had to take the reins, and I had to trust Him.

Trust Me

There is no lack of examples in Scripture to provide good reasons to trust God. There is no lack of commands in Scripture to tell me to trust God. I believe, however, that it's part of my human nature to refuse to give up control over my own circumstances.

As hard as it is to give up control over my own life and create my own understanding, how much more ridiculous is it for me to think I can control and understand someone else's life? However, when I fail to trust

God and His understanding, I am admitting that my pride and sense of worth is more valuable than His will and wisdom for me.

During this period of time in our struggles together, God showed me His will for me through numerous passages in Scriptures. Here are three of them.

- "I know that You can do all things, and that no purpose of Yours can be thwarted." (Job 42:2)
- "He is wise in heart and mighty in strength—who has hardened himself against Him, and succeeded?" (Job 9:4)
- "Let us then with confidence draw near to the throne of grace, that we may receive mercy and find grace to help in time of need." (Hebrews 4:16)

I see that God can do all things and that His purposes cannot be stopped, that He is wise in heart, that God is for us and no one can be against us, and that when we approach Him He is full of mercy and grace. Yet, I still struggle with trusting Him. I do not fully understand this, but I continue to believe these truths and attempt to internalize them in my own life.

God continued to teach and help me to understand the lessons He had begun to teach me earlier on in our struggles. God gave me plenty of things to work on during these times of testing. He wanted me to draw closer to Him and to Laura.

Even after her second suicide attempt, I had no way of knowing when, if ever, she would be victorious over her depression. I could, however, continue to take her to God and do whatever I could to help her deal with her illness.

I am thankful that God led me to start a support group for other men who were, like me, dealing with family members suffering from depression. I drew members for the group I started from men who attended my church, a congregation with about 1,000 attendees on an average Sunday morning. Statistics suggest that our church could have, at any one time, something like 100 men who had family members suffering from mental illness. To me, it appeared God would use me to reach dozens of men.

Once we launched the group we had three men, counting me, who participated. Those results, in my own understanding, were disappointing.

"Where are all the other men who need help?" I asked God. He, of course, had a different plan for the group.

He used these other two men in remarkable ways as I dealt with Laura's illness and they dealt with their own loved ones. The three of us built a strong, trusting bond. We encouraged others, prayed for each other, and together, searched God's Word for answers.

I found that these two men were essential to my ability to deal with Laura's illness and my response to it. To this day, I am not sure what I would have done without these men in my life. They provided much-needed encouragement to me at all times. They provided a source of strength as we walked together through our wives' mental illnesses. Our wives, too, appreciated that we were meeting, calling us "The Crazy Wives Club".

In His wisdom, providence, and unique understanding of Laura's and my needs – and of these other two couples – once again God showed Himself faithful, and that He remained in control. At least, I had hope that life would improve, as I understood improvement.

CHAPTER 6

Laura's First Outpatient Dialectical Behavior Therapy (DBT) Treatment

My Abba Father's Understanding of Marriage

Several months after Laura completed her inpatient alcohol treatment, the good news was that she had quit drinking. This gave me hope. At the same time she continued struggling with depression and anxiety and sadly, continued her cutting behavior and suffering suicidal ideation. Her psychologist added to her mental health record a diagnosis of Borderline Personality Disorder.

Laura's doctors decided that she should start participating in a Dialectical Behavior Therapy (DBT) group.

> Dialectical behavior therapy DBT treatment is a cognitive-behavioral approach that emphasizes the psychosocial aspects of treatment. The theory behind the approach is that some people are prone to react in a more intense and out-of-the-ordinary manner toward certain emotional situations, primarily those found in romantic, family and friend relationships. DBT theory suggests that some people's arousal levels in such situations can increase far more quickly than the average person's, attain a higher

level of emotional stimulation, and take a significant amount of time to return to baseline arousal levels.

People who are sometimes diagnosed with borderline personality disorder experience extreme swings in their emotions, see the world in black-and-white shades, and seem to always be jumping from one crisis to another. Because few people understand such reactions — most of all their own family and a childhood that emphasized invalidation — they don't have any methods for coping with these sudden, intense surges of emotion. DBT is a method for teaching skills that will help in this task.

The Four Modules of Dialectical Behavior Therapy

1. Mindfulness

    The essential part of all skills taught in skills group are the core mindfulness skills.

    Observe, Describe, and Participate are the core mindfulness "what" skills. They answer the question, "What do I do to practice core mindfulness skills?"

    Non-judgmentally, One-mindfully, and Effectively are the "how" skills and answer the question, "How do I practice core mindfulness skills?"

2. Interpersonal Effectiveness

    Interpersonal response patterns taught in DBT skills training are very similar to those taught in many assertiveness and interpersonal problem-solving classes. They include effective strategies for asking for what one needs, saying no, and coping with interpersonal conflict.

    Borderline individuals frequently possess good interpersonal skills in a general sense. The problems arise in the application of these skills to specific situations. An individual may be able to describe effective behavioral sequences when discussing another person encountering a problematic situation, but may be completely incapable of generating or carrying out a similar behavioral sequence when analyzing her own situation.

This module focuses on situations where the objective is to change something (e.g., requesting someone to do something) or to resist changes someone else is trying to make (e.g., saying no). The skills taught are intended to maximize the chances that a person's goals in a specific situation will be met, while at the same time not damaging either the relationship or the person's self-respect.

3. Distress Tolerance

Most approaches to mental health treatment focus on changing distressing events and circumstances. They have paid little attention to accepting, finding meaning for, and tolerating distress. This task has generally been tackled by religious and spiritual communities and leaders. Dialectical behavior therapy emphasizes learning to bear pain skillfully.

Distress tolerance skills constitute a natural development from mindfulness skills. They have to do with the ability to accept, in a non-evaluative and nonjudgmental fashion, both oneself and the current situation. Although the stance advocated here is a nonjudgmental one, this does not mean that it is one of approval: acceptance of reality is not approval of reality.

Distress tolerance behaviors are concerned with tolerating and surviving crises and with accepting life as it is in the moment. Four sets of crisis survival strategies are taught: distracting, self-soothing, improving the moment, and thinking of pros and cons. Acceptance skills include radical acceptance, turning the mind toward acceptance, and willingness versus willfulness.

4. Emotion Regulation

Borderline and suicidal individuals are emotionally intense and labile – frequently angry, intensely frustrated, depressed, and anxious. This suggests that borderline clients might benefit from help in learning to regulate their emotions. Dialectical behavior therapy skills for emotion regulation include:

- Identifying and labeling emotions
- Identifying obstacles to changing emotions
- Reducing vulnerability to "emotion mind"
- Increasing positive emotional events
- Increasing mindfulness to current emotions
- Taking opposite action
- Applying distress tolerance techniques"

My role with Laura's DBT was to drive her to her group and pick her up afterward. The evening after her first group meeting, as she settled into the car, she said, "Why are you still with me?"

Her question shocked me. More than that, I felt dismayed and perturbed. "Why are you asking me?" I responded.

"Because all of the spouses or significant others of people in my group have left them," she answered.

Her response shook me again. What I heard greatly troubled me.

I answered logically, confidently, but passionately. "On February 9, 1985, I stood before you, our families, and our friends and promised that I would be with you in sickness and in health as long as we both should live. So frankly, just because you're sick doesn't mean I am leaving you. It means you're still stuck with me." I hoped she would find that by reminding her of my public commitment to her, it would give her strength and confidence, but I had more.

"Secondly, and probably more importantly, my promise was not only to you but it was to God, who was there with us at the time. I am really more afraid of what He would do to me if I were to desert you because of your illness."

To my amazement, she giggled at that response. Trust me, after living for several years with a wife who hardly ever smiled, to hear her giggle was encouraging.

God used this new therapy to teach me about marriage. He taught me that it was a covenant relationship. He taught me that it was between one man and one woman. He taught me that it was a picture of the Gospel. He taught me that it was to be an example to others so that they might be drawn to God. He also taught me that it was the biggest battlefield in Satan's war against God. He taught me that His design for marriage is vitally important and it can still be saved in our modern society.

The Importance of My Abba Father's Plan for Marriage

God impressed on me the importance of including this discussion of marriage in this book, to share what He taught me about being married. He taught me about His plan and design for marriage. He taught me that it was the first institution He created. God designed man to be fruitful and multiply and subdue the earth.

God taught me that marriage provides the best human example of Christ's love for the Church. He taught me that anything we do to discredit Christ as the groom and the Church as His bride does great harm to our ability to share the Gospel. When God's design for marriage is distorted, then the picture God gave us about His relationship with the Church is also distorted. God reminded me during my time of learning that marriage is under siege in our culture and that each marriage is a spiritual battlefield.

What is My Abba Father's Design for Marriage?

Laura told me about others who were in her various support groups, and her stories motivated me to add this section to the book. She told me stories about spouses being abandoned because the husband or wife found the situation to be unbearable. Almost all the groups she attended included several individuals whose spouse or significant others could not deal with spousal depression and anxiety and, as a result, abandoned the marriage.

As I studied God's plan for marriage, I saw how it fit His creation plan in Genesis 1-2. God said marriage was between a man and a woman. He created Eve to be Adam's helper. He said that from the marriage bond, man should be fruitful and multiply and fill the earth. Marriage formed part of God's plan for man to subdue the earth.

Jesus reiterated God's design for marriage.

"Jesus answered, 'Have you not read that He who created them from the beginning made them male and female, and said, "Therefore a man shall leave his father and his mother and hold fast to his wife, and the two shall become one flesh"? So they are no longer two but one flesh. What therefore God has joined together, let not man separate.'" (Matthew 19:4-6)

When God created marriage, He established the first institution upon which all others depend. He designed marriage to serve to populate the earth. He designed men and women to work together to subdue the earth – to be stewards of God's creation. God used the family – a man joined to a woman along with their children – to take a central role in the care and nurture of nature.

God instructed Israel to use the family to teach the truth about Himself.

> Hear, O Israel! The Lord is our God, the Lord is one! You shall love the Lord your God with all your heart and with all your soul and with all your might. These words, which I am commanding you today, shall be on your heart. You shall teach them diligently to your sons and shall talk of them when you sit in your house and when you walk by the way and when you lie down and when you rise up. You shall bind them as a sign on your hand and they shall be as frontals on your forehead. You shall write them on the doorposts of your house and on your gates. (Deuteronomy 6:4-9) (NASB)

Once God created a male and female, and they became one flesh in marriage to each other, their union became the center point of the rest of His creation. God created marriage to be the foundational building block of all of society.

It should not be a surprise that Satan attacked marriage from the beginning. Satan would like nothing better than to destroy marriage as creation's foundational building block. Satan knows that if you remove or damage the foundation, everything built upon it will crumble.

The world sees marriage as a contract between consenting adults. It is, however, far more than a contract. Contracts can be altered or broken given a proper assent by the two parties to a court-mediated settlement. We call this divorce.

My Abba Father Taught Me the Importance of Wedding Vows

I am a Christian, and my faith in Christ was central to my decision to marry Laura. She, too, was a Christian. During our wedding ceremony, we repeated specific vows in front of a pastor, family, friends, and God. Those vows committed us to a covenant relationship before God. They were not a recitation of legal terms in a contract.

A sacred covenant is a much stronger bond than any worldly contract. A covenant is not to be broken. The marriage covenant, when it invokes God, is the "three-fold cord" of Ecclesiastes 12:4 that cannot easily be broken.

Like you, I have attended many weddings. Christian couples often recite vows on the order of the one I repeated at my wedding:

"I, James Hansen, take you Laura Wagner, to be my lawfully wedded wife to have and to hold, from this day forward, for better for worse, for richer or poorer, in sickness and in health, to love, cherish, and to obey, till death do us part, according to God's holy ordinance; and thereto I pledge thee my troth."

Laura repeated the vow back to me. These vows sealed our covenant to each other, with God as our witness. Most dictionaries define a covenant as a formal, solemn, and binding agreement.

Scriptural covenants are not to be broken. God promises to deal with those who honor or break a covenant. A covenant is not a simple little promise or a contract that can be easily broken – it is meant to be forever, or as long as the husband and wife will live, all of our lives.

Culture has Distorted Marriage

Nearly every culture has been trying to destroy God's design for marriage since the beginning of time. We saw this when Satan, as the snake, tempted Eve in the garden. After she and Adam gave in, God said to Adam, "I will put enmity between you and the woman, and between your offspring and her offspring..." (Genesis 3:15a)

During the twenty-first century, however, I believe we have seen the most major attack on marriage the world has ever known – even greater than the attack on marriage in the Roman Empire during the first to third Centuries, A.D.

For most of history, the primary assault on marriage resulted from infidelity and divorce, with divorce being the lesser of the two. Since the 1950s we have witnessed an increase in divorce. The no-fault divorce movement in America has basically made it impossible for one of the spouses to keep a marriage intact. All one of the spouses needs to say is that they believe there are irreconcilable differences and the court will award a certificate of divorce.

The increase in divorce has crept into the Church in alarming numbers as well. There is little difference between church members and the whole of society concerning divorce. Many American churches no longer stand for or protect the sanctity of marriage. Many modern churches overemphasize God's grace and ignore the call to the Lordship of Jesus and obedience to His Word.

Infidelity and cohabitation without marriage has become common and is increasing in numbers. It's hard to prove there is an increase in infidelity since it is no longer needed to get a divorce and most people will not admit to it. However, cohabitation, on the other hand, is also on the rise and many surveys show it to be true. American culture has accepted cohabitation as a norm and popular culture promotes it right alongside licentiousness, fornication, and adultery.

It is common in modern America to accept the idea that a couple should live together to try out their relationship before they get married. Besides compatibility, the couple can test out whether they please each other sexually. Cohabitation, it is erroneously thought, will weed out bad marriages before they happen.

Church members and Bible-believing Christians are not exempt from sexual sin, not by a long shot. We have witnessed many well-known Christian leaders who have fallen into sexual sin and violated their marriage covenant. More than leaders, however, are those who blend unseen into our congregations but have secret liaisons inside and outside the church body.

Far too many Christian families are struggling because one or more of their children are co-habiting with someone else. Unfortunately, we all probably have family members who no longer live up to God's expectations for marriage and sexuality. In our own hearts, where only God can see, most of us have failed to live up to God's standards if we were honest about it. Thank God that He is merciful and forgiving.

Roles

Not only has culture distorted marriage via sexual immorality and cohabitation, but culture is also distorting marriage based on God's designed roles for husbands and wives. Culture has distorted the husband's headship role and instead, talks about an equal partnership. God sees husbands and wives as equals, but He designed a different role for each, roles that are mutually and equally important.

Culture has also distorted parents' role in the lives of their children. Our family and human services laws – welfare – encourage single-parent families, so that many of our families no longer have a father in the home. Survey upon survey inform governments that children do better when they live in a stable home, with both a mom and a dad involved in their lives.

The culture has undermined the meaning of some key words relative to God's marriage design. The word "submit" has become untenable to most women. Paul, however, laid out a clear objective regarding love and submission in Ephesians 5:22-33 (we will explore it in a few paragraphs).

If you are a woman, let me ask you this question: If a man loved you as Christ loved His Church and gave His life up for it, would you have a problem submitting to him as your husband and following his leadership?

Let me ask men: How hard would it be to lead your wife if she submitted to you and respected you?

The modern context of submission between a husband and wife has been relegated too often to their sexual relationship. Or as many members of society see it, submission means subservience. In contrast, the love that God wants in a marriage is that which would cause someone to be willing to die for another person. God's concept of marital love is such that a person would do anything to make the other person better. God's love in a marriage is such that would always put the other's needs first. The kind of love that Paul referred to in Ephesians 5 is the kind of love that he wrote about in his first letter to the Corinthians.

> Love is patient and kind; love does not envy or boast; it is not arrogant or rude. It does not insist on its own way; it is not irritable or resentful; it does not rejoice at wrongdoing, but rejoices with the truth. Love bears all things, believes all things, hopes all things, endures all things.

> Love never ends. As for prophecies, they will pass
> away; as for tongues, they will cease; as for knowledge, it
> will pass away. (1 Corinthians 13:4-8)

Paul suggests in this passage that this is the kind of love by which we should live our lives among all people in all we do. My goal should be to treat my neighbors with this kind of love. God's love in Christ Jesus is the perfect example of His design for marriage, and His design for marriage is essential as we live out our lives before the world. It's also the perfect model for how to love our neighbors.

Do I Understand That My Marriage and Yours Is a Spiritual Battlefield?

Yes, our marriages are spiritual battlefields. I do not like admitting that I am battling spiritual enemies in my own marriage, but I want to be honest. Since Scripture tells us that marriage between a man and woman is an image of Christ's love for His Church, then it is logical that Satan wants to do everything he can to destroy marriage. Satan's attacks on our culture are simple to see, but it may not be as apparent in our marriages.

Satan is the great deceiver. Jesus said:

> "Why do you not understand what I say? It is because
> you cannot bear to hear my word. You are of your father
> the devil, and your will is to do your father's desires. He
> was a murderer from the beginning, and does not stand
> in the truth, because there is no truth in him. When he
> lies, he speaks out of his own character, for he is a liar and
> the father of lies. But because I tell the truth, you do not
> believe me." (John 8:43-48)

Knowing that Satan is a liar, based on the authority of the Scripture, why do I continue to listen to Satan as Adam and Eve did in the Garden of Eden? Satan is very good at spinning lies, and I am not very good at seeing through them. Satan tried to divide Laura and me. He wanted us to fail.

What do we do about the spiritual warfare that occurs in our marriages? What does God want us to do about it?

First, I must prepare for the battle. Paul placed his instructions about spiritual warfare in Ephesians 6 for good purpose – he knew we would need to read and act on it. Note that Paul included it close after the paragraphs in which he describes marriage and family relationships.Paul wrote about marriage because he knows that Satan is going to attack marriage and families. Paul, led by the Holy Spirit, knew that Satan had already been working to destroy marriages, as he wrote these words:

> Wives, *be subject* to your own husbands, as to the Lord. For the husband is the head of the wife, as Christ also is the head of the church, He Himself *being* the Savior of the body. But as the church is subject to Christ, so also the wives *ought to be* to their husbands in everything.
>
> Husbands, love your wives, just as Christ also loved the church and gave Himself up for her, so that He might sanctify her, having cleansed her by the washing of water with the word, that He might present to Himself the church in all her glory, having no spot or wrinkle or any such thing; but that she would be holy and blameless. So husbands ought also to love their own wives as their own bodies. He who loves his own wife loves himself; for no one ever hated his own flesh, but nourishes and cherishes it, just as Christ also *does* the church, because we are members of His body. For this reason a man shall leave his father and mother and shall be joined to his wife, and the two shall become one flesh. This mystery is great; but I am speaking with reference to Christ and the church. Nevertheless, each individual among you also is to love his own wife even as himself, and the wife must *see to it* that she respects her husband. (Ephesians 5:22-33) (NASB)

Just a few verses later, Paul writes:

> Finally, be strong in the Lord and in the strength of His might. Put on the full armor of God, so that you will be able to stand firm against the schemes of the devil. For our struggle is not against flesh and blood, but against the rulers, against the powers, against the world forces of

this darkness, against the spiritual *forces* of wickedness in the heavenly *places*. Therefore, take up the full armor of God, so that you will be able to resist in the evil day, and having done everything, to stand firm. Stand firm therefore, having girded your loins with truth, and having put on the breastplate of righteousness, and having shod your feet with the preparation of the gospel of peace; in addition to all, taking up the shield of faith with which you will be able to extinguish all the flaming arrows of the evil *one*. And take the helmet of salvation, and the sword of the Spirit, which is the word of God.

With all prayer and petition pray at all times in the Spirit, and with this in view, be on the alert with all perseverance and petition for all the saints, and *pray* on my behalf, that utterance may be given to me in the opening of my mouth, to make known with boldness the mystery of the gospel, for which I am an ambassador in chains; that in *proclaiming* it I may speak boldly, as I ought to speak. (Ephesians 6:10-20) (NASB)

As Satan stirred up trouble between Laura and me, why did I need to put on the whole armor of God, and how could I use it as I fought the battle? His armor gave me the strength I needed to fight the battle against Satan.

I had confidence I could stand against the Devil's schemes. Paul reinforced the concept of standing by reminding me I could withstand Satan's attack and then, having done all I could, I could remain standing.

The Gospel of peace made me ready to fight steadily and under control. I could exercise faith to extinguish Satan's attempts to attack me. By taking on the rest of the armor and praying, I was ready for battle.

A critical aspect of being covered with God's armor is to be alert all the time. I had to watch for – be discerning about – Satan's attacks. I needed to pray for others; I saw it as a mandate to pray for Laura. And if to tie up the last piece of armor, Paul exhorted me to share the Gospel with my spouse and others.

Imagine how different the world would be if, as believers, we represented Christ in our marriages as God intended. How many more opportunities would we have to share the Gospel? How much more encouraging would we be to others who witness our absolute commitment to our spouses? How many people would see and understand God's love for them because they see His love in our marriages?

Am I convinced that Satan wants to destroy marriage, not only my marriage, but also marriage as a whole? Should I pray for our nation because Satan appears to be winning the battle against godly marriages? Should I talk with my neighbors about God's plan for marriage?

Do I want to pattern my marriage after the model God created? This can only be done when I depend upon Him, and put on the whole armor of God every day – and recognize that God's armor is necessary to defeat Satan's attack on my marriage.

How Can a Marriage Survive?

I believe that the only way that our marriage survived before and during the turbulence created by Laura's illness is because of our understanding of the importance of the covenant relationship of marriage, which God taught me during those tough times. What is great about learning from God is that He also provided me the grace to fulfill my covenant. When God is made part of a covenant, He does not want it broken so He helps us not to break it.

At one point in time, I pondered divorce. God reached out to me in His grace, and the thought disappeared. God reminded me of the marriage covenant we had made between Him, Laura, and me.

It may sound simplistic, but I have heard of a statistic that shows when a couple faithfully pray together and for each other, the divorce rate for these couple drops to 1 in 1,156 according to the National Association of Marriage Enhancement. This makes sense.

Knowing that Satan was committing warfare against my marriage, I knew that praying together was a key element in our fight to win the battle. God also taught me the need for daily devotions both privately and together with my wife, even though I too often failed miserably at this.

I truly believe that any marriage can be preserved, and even when it seems shattered, can be saved. God does permit divorce when adultery is a factor, but He does not require divorce. I know several couples who have reconciled and rebuilt their marriages after an adulterous relationship. They claim their marriages are better now because they have recognized

God's role in their marriage. I am not suggesting you should experience trauma to strengthen your marriage. Trust me, marriage can be better without the trauma. What I am saying is that the marriage covenant between two people and God is always worth saving and improving.

We must take our marriage seriously. We must work hard on making it better and stronger. We must spend time in God's Word together with our spouse. We must pray together. We will be a great example to those around us as we share and demonstrate God's definition of marriage to the world around us.

Let us agree to end the silence about God's creative plan for marriage. Let us speak the truth with love and understanding, and demonstrate God's love to a world in which marriage is under siege.

CHAPTER 7

Laura's Eating Disorder
Treatment Program

My Abba Father Helps Me to Better Understand Mental Illness

Laura's behavioral changes continued to worsen as she struggled with depression and anxiety. Her psychologist had also diagnosed her with Borderline Personality Disorder. Over time, her self-injury behavior began to give way to eating disorders.

Instead of cutting herself, Laura started to overeat, particularly favoring candy and chocolate. She rapidly gained weight. Her weight gain added to her anxiety and depression, and in response, she began to starve herself, hardly eating anything. When sparse eating failed to meet her emotional needs, she added laxatives to purge her system before her body could absorb any food.

Because of her newfound anorexia, within a few weeks of weighing nearly 170 pounds, Laura fell back to 120 – her "normal" weight. Although she looked good, her rapid weight loss was terribly unhealthy and dangerous.

Laura's psychologist and psychiatrist recommended that she start receiving treatment for her eating disorder. She found a nearby program and began outpatient treatment, which included group meetings. The program did not accomplish much because Laura did not see her behavior as a problem – what she saw was that it helped relieve her depression and anxiety. Despite her skepticism, she continued to go to the outpatient treatment group for a time, but continued to eat very little and use laxatives to purge.

During those times when Laura attended meetings, I found myself grabbing hold of hope. Maybe these times of instruction and sharing would open her mind and feed her emotions; maybe she would find tools to help her overcome these unhealthy behaviors. Maybe we would see a healthy balance in our lives and a sense of peace.

After some time, however, her mental health team saw that the outpatient treatment groups had not helped, so they had Laura admitted to an inpatient program for those with eating disorders. The inpatient program included close and constant monitoring of her diet, forcing her to comply.

With her eating disorder at least under some control, Laura had no outlet to relieve her depression and anxiety and she once again resorted to self-injury. The facility made sure she had no access to razor blades or sharp objects, so she chose to burn herself with a curling iron. The self-injurious behavior resulted in Laura being expelled from the program with the hope she might return someday if she became more mentally stable.

When Laura began struggling with the eating disorder, I found myself resorting to doubt that God could be trusted to handle our lives. I began to think that God was no longer on our side. I felt deep frustration that Laura still struggled with her illness. I felt like we were on our own. Based on my feelings, I saw that God did not seem to be helping us.

Praise God He is not restricted by my feelings! God pointed me to a passage in Romans that proclaimed that not only was God on my side; no one could be against us.

What then shall we say to these things? If God is for us, who can be against us? He who did not spare His own Son but gave Him up for us all, how will He not also with Him graciously give us all things? Who shall bring any charge against God's elect? It is God who justifies. Who is to condemn? Christ Jesus is the one who died—more than that, who was raised—who is at the right hand of God, who indeed is interceding for us. Who shall separate us from the love of Christ? Shall tribulation, or distress, or persecution, or famine, or nakedness, or danger, or sword? As it is written, 'For Your sake we are being killed all the day long; we are regarded as sheep to be slaughtered.' No, in all these things we are more than conquerors through Him who loved us. (Romans 8:31-37)

Nearly three years had passed since I first became aware of Laura's mental illness. I had watched this happen and tried to help as she allowed me. I still struggled with the realization that I could not fix her, but had come to understand she needed professional help. During those three years, she had gone from being a normal person to an alcoholic who had attempted suicide twice, started cutting herself, and now had an eating disorder. My heart broke for her, but I also had my own issues. Mainly, I felt lost and helpless.

To deal with my own issues, I reasoned that I needed to become more patient and trust God more fully. You may have noticed a cycle in this narrative, where I draw closer to God, He teaches me, I watch Laura's life grow more troubled, I become discouraged, and then God reminds me of the lessons He wanted to teach me. Again, I determined to put into practice God's teaching in my life.

The lessons God taught me included a growing understanding of the inability of Laura to accept help from the mental health system. They were providing Laura with tools to overcome her illness. These tools were all based on changing her mind not her spirit. God also showed me some of the fallacies that church-goers hold regarding mental illness.

Mental Illness and the Secular Approach

By this time, I had learned some very important facts about mental illness, and particularly, Major Clinical Depression and Borderline Personality Disorder. More than this, my observation of how health professionals and some of my fellow Christians dealt with Laura showed me that both the world and the Church have a distorted view of mental illness. Like it or not, some Christians who want to love and support a person who suffers from mental illness attach a stigma to it. They see the mentally ill person differently from those with a more understood disease like cancer. In their attempts to love and support Laura, sometimes their helpful comments were hurtful.

When a secular mental health professional looks for answers and recommends treatment strategies, his or her perspective is that one can only treat the mind and body. Some professionals quickly turn to pharmaceuticals to treat the body, to try to create a calmer and more rational state of mind so that they can treat underlying causes. Then the professionals turn to talk therapy to attempt to perfect the patient's mind. Their approach makes sense to them, but they come at it without an understanding of man's spiritual nature, and they disregard man's need for a Savior.

Without recognizing man's sinful nature and need for a Savior, secular mental health professionals fall back on medications, stimulation treatments, one-on-one talk therapy, and group therapies. The secular counselor discounts the need each of us has for God's forgiveness and spiritual healing.

This is not to say that talk therapy and medications never provide relief or could open the door to healing – ample proof exists that these can be effective. What I am saying is the secular world does not believe in or may reject Biblical foundations regarding an individual's spirit. By failing to embrace and address a person's spiritual nature, secular counselors cannot appeal to a person's soul or engage God in the healing process – they will never be able to treat or help to heal the whole person, because they leave the person's spirit outside of the therapy strategies.

Mental Illness and the Church

As Christians, we are reminded often to share our burdens with others. Paul wrote, "Bear one another's burdens, and so fulfill the law of Christ." (Gal. 6:2) James instructed us to, "… confess your sins to one another and pray for one another, that you may be healed. The prayer of a righteous person has great power as it is working." (James 5:16)

Clearly, the Church is to play a major role in helping individuals deal with life's challenges, including mental illness.

Some in the Church, however, seem to believe that because the Bible never specifically defines depression, then it cannot be an illness. Too often, I heard well-meaning Christians identify Laura's illness as her sin problem. Christians did not mean to be hurtful or critical, but wanted to see Laura's mind and spirit healed. Too often they were hesitant to consider the physiological needs of her body and psychological needs of her mind.

Some Christians' approach to mental illness, I saw, relied primarily on counseling, Bible study, and prayer, enlisting the Holy Spirit to help bring conviction and healing to the person suffering from mental illness. Too often, this approach disregarded the physical aspects of mental illness.

My experience during Laura's illness taught me insights into both the secular and Christian approach to dealing with someone suffering from mental illness.

The secularist sees that man is, by nature, basically good and perfectible. He sees that man is evolving, believing that in the end, the fittest will survive and the fittest will be perfect. We know by observation that man is prone to trouble – we see evil in the world and it seems as if it is growing in nature and intensity. If man is good, why is there so much evil, and if perfectible, why so many human failures?

We know that talk therapy and pharmaceuticals only work some of the time and have limited application. If men are basically good or perfectible, then should we not expect these therapies to succeed most of the time? But we know their success rate according to National Association of Mental Illness (NAMI) is 80% for Bi-polar Depression, 60% for Major Depression, and 45% for Schizophrenia. Why? The secularist says that evil comes from society, and the need is there to work toward a more perfect society. If, however, society is made up of basically good and perfectible people, then how can society be evil? Secularists cannot answer these questions, and neither can I apart from Biblical truth.

Group meetings are a common therapy across all sorts of institutions. In the treatment of addiction and mental illness, group therapy is nearly always employed. This concept of using group dynamics to foster healing has always puzzled me. Consider how group therapy operates. A group of people who all have the same or similar unresolved issues come together to talk about getting better or their latest struggle, temptation, or failure. It is also used to encourage each other to stay the course of recovery. This is in some ways very similar to the small group in a church.

Like a church small group, each person participating in secular group therapy has unresolved issues that continue to trouble him or her, and no one in the group has the answer. In secular group therapy, then, what is the source of any useful solution that group members can appropriate? Solutions must come from the group leader, especially in a clinical setting, and it is hoped that the leader has a correct view of the nature of man. Unlike the church small group, secular therapy groups do not rely on The Bible for their source of truth. In failing to tie treatment to the Word of God and the work of the Holy Spirit in man's heart, it is hard to see the ability to cure the root problems of a person's mental illness.

When the group leader is a skilled, experienced clinician, he or she can direct the discussion in ways that might be helpful to some, at least in a limited fashion. Yet, without an understanding of man's spiritual nature or an understanding of God's sovereignty, how can a leader create any valuable discussion that works past the mind and into the heart of each person to help them mature and become whole?

A primary difficulty with the secular worldview in treating mental illness, however, and despite professionalism and experience, is its lack of understanding of an individual's spiritual nature. Secular therapists do not address any spiritual aspect of the illness. God created humans with a body, mind, and spirit, and successful treatment of mental illness requires dealing with all three parts of the person.

The secular world ignores the third and most important aspect of being human – the spiritual aspect – because it does not recognize it as such, seeing it instead as some complicated congregation of thoughts, emotions, experiences, and chemistry. If the therapist does not believe in the Biblical view of humans, but still recognizes man has a spiritual nature, their answer could be to appropriate spirituality apart from God. Satan, too, has a spiritual nature. Unfortunately, Laura and I found that the Christian psychologists that we met with never addressed our spiritual natures.

The Church also Limits Treatment of The Whole Person

As Laura and I continued to deal with her illness, we remained engaged in the local church. We looked to our church body as a place to give and receive comfort, understanding, love, and compassion. In general, the church helped us. As far as Laura's mental illness, however, I saw a misunderstanding of treating the whole person, and sometimes, it could be harsh and unkind.

I saw that some in the Church wants to deal with one or maybe two aspects of the individual. Many Christians with whom I interacted during Laura's illness saw mental illness only as a spiritual problem. Too often I heard them say that Laura had a sin problem, needed to pray more, or lacked enough faith. For certain, they saw that her behaviors were sinful. "…For the LORD sees not as man sees: man looks on the outward appearance, but the LORD looks on the heart." (1 Samuel 16:7b) God had forgiven Laura's sin when she accepted Jesus and God saw her as clean before Him, but this mental illness had moved her to harm herself – her behavior did not express the forgiveness of Christ.

We know that God did not design us to hurt our bodies – Paul called them the temple of God. Hurting one's own body is, in part, a sin problem. It may or may not have been Laura's personal sin problem, but it definitely is an original sin problem. When Adam sinned, it introduced illness and death to the human race.

In heaven, however, depression will have ceased. The consequences of Adam's fall will be gone forever. "He will wipe away every tear from their eyes, and death shall be no more, neither shall there be mourning, nor crying, nor pain anymore, for the former things have passed away." (Rev. 21:4)

It is clear to me that illness entered the world through Adam's sin. "Therefore, just as sin came into the world through one man, and death through sin, and so death spread to all men because all sinned–" (Romans 5:12)

It is also clear that just because someone falls ill, it is not necessarily because they sinned.

> "As He passed by, He saw a man blind from birth. And His disciples asked Him, 'Rabbi, who sinned, this man or his parents, that he was born blind?' Jesus answered, 'It was not that this man sinned, or his parents, but that the works of God might be displayed in him.'" (John 9:1-3)

It is clear that some illness or physical affliction is not caused by a person's sin – therefore, we must not assume that it is. Job's friends chided him for his sinful actions and beliefs, which they said caused his physical problems – but they were wrong.

I do not, however, discourage people from examining their lives to see if unconfessed sin exists and needs to be dealt with by confession, repentance, and a changed life. On the other hand, if a person confesses sin that contributes to illness, the confession does not necessarily mean that healing will somehow occur – it may or may not. Unconfessed sin, or willfully practicing sinful behaviors, may or may not be the cause of a mental illness – or any other illness.

When Laura attempted suicide, cut herself, or suffered from an eating disorder, some Christians said it was because she had unconfessed sin. They suggested that her sin caused it. I found that observation to be untrue, and it could be harmful. The conflict Laura endured included a sense that she had failed God, others, and herself by her lack of control over these behaviors. This could contribute to depression. Suggesting that her sin caused her mental illness showed a lack of a fuller understanding of the nature of mental illness.

Prayer is a powerful antidote to human failure, frustration, and lack of peace. The Bible is full of passages regarding prayer and its effectiveness. The passages about prayer are absolutely true. Consider 2 Corinthians 12:5-10:

> On behalf of this man I will boast, but on my own behalf I will not boast, except of my weaknesses—though if I should wish to boast, I would not be a fool, for I would be speaking the truth; but I refrain from it, so that no one may think more of me than He sees in me or hears from me. So to keep me from becoming conceited because of the surpassing greatness of the revelations, a thorn was given me in the flesh, a messenger of Satan to harass me, to keep me from becoming conceited. Three times I pleaded with the Lord about this, that it should leave me. But He said to me, "My grace is sufficient for you, for my power is made perfect in weakness." Therefore, I will boast all the more gladly of my weaknesses, so that the power of Christ may rest upon me. For the sake of Christ, then, I am content with weaknesses, insults, hardships, persecutions, and calamities. For when I am weak, then I am strong.

Paul showed me here that in a way, God does not always answer my prayers as I want them to be answered – rather He answers them in the way He wills to answer. In Paul's case, a thorn in the flesh troubled him enough that he prayed three times for God to remove it from him. God said "No." God answered Paul's prayer differently from what he wanted, instead desiring that Paul should see that His grace is sufficient, and Paul should be satisfied with it. Furthermore, Paul learned that God's power was made perfect through this thorn in the flesh – he does not tell us how, but he tells us it is true.

As I came to see Laura's illness, I am not sure that I would ever have truly understood the oneness of marriage without going through this trial with her. I would not have known God's grace, love, and power as I do today. Apart from Laura's illness, I doubt that I would have been able to withstand all that I have gone through in my life, nor would I have understood how His power still assists me in my weakness.

Pray More?

It struck me as ironic when someone would suggest that Laura or I did not pray enough or pray effectively. How can anyone know about another person's prayer life? Does anyone other than the individual who prays and God know how often someone prays? Can anyone other than God hear the words uttered during an intercessory prayer of a husband for a wife or a mentally ill person for personal healing?

I came to understand that it is unfruitful – and maybe hurtful – for me to suggest that another person needs to pray more often. As far as I can know, the other person may be praying without ceasing. "Rejoice always, pray without ceasing, give thanks in all circumstances; for this is the will of God in Christ Jesus for you." (I Thessalonians 5:16-18)

Christians are strengthened through personal and corporate prayer. Perhaps, instead of suggesting someone needs to pray more, a better idea is to ask, "Can we pray about this together, now?" or to promise to regularly pray for someone. "How can I pray for you during this next week?" is a good deal better than saying, "Let me know how God answers your prayers when we get together next Sunday." Once Christians make the commitment to pray for someone, then they must follow through on it.

More Faith

"Okay, I know you pray a lot, and that you do not walk in sin, but I wonder if you lack faith. Do you really believe God will heal you? If not, I am not sure that He will." Can you imagine these comments? I heard them and other similar comments from well-meaning people during the time of Laura's struggles.

Look again at what Paul wrote in 2 Cor. 12:5-10. Paul prayed earnestly and in faith that God would remove the thorn. He did not lack faith. God chose not to remove Paul's thorn because God's power could be shown to be perfect in Paul's weakness. Paul may have come to understand that despite his thorn, the fact that he remained committed to God helped others in their struggles with faith.

From Paul's example, I can have absolute confidence that God will answer my particular prayer, even in the way that I want it to be answered, but I also must have faith that God may answer in a way different from my desire. I prayed often, with passion, and in faith that God would heal Laura. God did not heal Laura in the way I had prayed. God's answer was, "Not now, and not in that way." God's answer is eternal in nature, not bound by our understanding and limitations of time.

God Gave Us a Body of Flesh and Blood

If one views mental illness as a purely spiritual problem, it ignores the reality that it can and often does have a physical cause. Yet, I had people tell me that there was no proof that Laura had a physical problem.

According to the Mayo Clinic, typically mental illness is diagnosed by a mental health professional who speaks to you about your symptoms. These symptoms are used to diagnose. At least for now, blood tests are not commonly used that shows a chemical imbalance in the brain that causes mental illness. Scientists can show that brain synapsis are misfiring or not firing at all in some cases. Brain malfunctions related to electrical pulsing may be the cause of mental illness, as mental illness is seen in how people behave.

Physicians perform scans that show a brain is not functioning as a normal brain should function. However, everyone's brain is different. Physicians can spot similarities in one individual's brain scan compared to someone else's, but they are never identical. To date, there is more evidence that a mentally ill person may have a physical issue that is causing the illness.

On the other hand, when there has been brain trauma, brain scans can show the areas that have been damaged, or in some cases, destroyed. From this, physicians can speculate with a certain degree of accuracy what type of behaviors will result. Even then, however, they can never be sure what therapy or medicine will provide the best possible outcomes.

Sometimes people would remind me, "A brain scan cannot necessarily prove that a physical problem has caused a person's mental illness." To this, they might add, "You know, if a scan does show brain damage or malfunction, that could be consistent with having a sinful mind that causes our brain to respond differently." The Bible, however, teaches us that we are all sinful and therefore, we all have a sinful mind. What would a normal, sin-free brain look like?

Because we have all sinned and all have experienced sinful thoughts, we might say there is a problem with everyone's mind. Paul wrote:

> I appeal to you therefore, brothers, by the mercies of God, to present your bodies as a living sacrifice, holy and acceptable to God, which is your spiritual worship. Do not be conformed to this world, but be transformed by the renewal of your mind, that by testing you may discern what is the will of God, what is good and acceptable and perfect. (Romans 12:1-2)

If I did not have some form of a problem with my mind, why would I need to renew it? Paul is writing about a core issue from which we all suffer – corrupt, unhealthy minds.

Individuals who suffer with mental illness have malfunctioning minds. Their mind-problems are greater than ours and could be physiological. The mind problems faced by a mentally ill person may be bigger than our own problems, but both are solved in the same way – by renewing of the mind. The question we want answered for Laura and others suffering from mental illness, is how do we renew our minds?

Renewing the Mind, No Matter the Cause

First, healing begins with confession of our sins and trusting God to help get our heart set on Him, instead of self. Secondly, we must confess our sins to another trusted person – not to the whole world. As it says in James 5:16: "Therefore, confess your sins to one another and pray for one another, that you may be healed. The prayer of a righteous person has great power as it is working." Public confession does not belong on Facebook. We can, however, pursue talking with trusted Christian friends or seek out a Christian spiritual advisor. Thirdly, we must seek God's answers to our challenges, found in His Word. This is how I would attack the spiritual aspect of mental illness.

There is also great value in talk therapy with a qualified Christian counselor. I suggest only seeing a Christian counselor who uses the Word of God as a primary resource. God's Word speaks to both the mental and spiritual aspects of mental illness.

Why seek out a Christian counselor? A Christian counselor's point of view will evaluate feelings and emotions from a biblical perspective. God has gifted many good Christians so they can help others. The Christian counselor will also better understand the whole person – mind, body, and spirit.

Do not, however, ignore the physiological basis of mental illness. In my opinion, a Christian psychiatrist provides the best hope to address the whole person. He or she might recommend medications, diet changes, talk therapy, or other therapies – but all of them will start from a Biblically-based, spiritual perspective. They will have an understanding that all men are sinners and need a Savior. God has given them a gift to do their job, and they will come with the perspective that mental illness could have a basis in the spirit, soul, or body – the whole person. They become part of the team that includes family, trusted friends, and other professionals working to care for someone you love who suffers from mental illness.

CHAPTER 8

Laura's Third Suicide Attempt

My Abba Father Teaches Me About Love, Fear, Strength, and Refuge

Nearly four years passed since Laura had attempted suicide. As far as I could tell, she continued to make progress in dealing with her depression, and we were making progress in our marriage. Many nights, I laid my hands on her back and prayed for her. Prayer gave me hope and seemed to give strength to her. I knew that both of us had a personal relationship with God through Jesus Christ, and this meant hope for eternity.

Contending with the potential for a relapse would from time to time cause me concern. I had learned that her illness could flare up without warning and further complicate our lives. My concern followed me to work, and I would find myself wondering how she was doing, and if she was safe. Yet, in the midst of all this, we had some great and wonderful times together.

Early in our marriage we had discovered how to travel to somewhat exotic sites around the world, but keep our expenses down by traveling in the off-season. Though our lives changed dramatically after her suicide attempts, we still kept our commitment to travel together. We visited Paris, Bruges, Belgium, and Salzburg, Austria, and continued to Vienna. Laura stayed on her medication during these trips, and we had a wonderful time. Each successful trip built my hope that over time, she would continue to improve. Perhaps someday we would return to a more normal life.

Then one day at work, my phone rang and the call shattered my sense of peace about Laura.

"Mr. Hansen, this is Anne Smith,[3] one of Laura's DBT counselors," I heard her say. At first, I thought she would be giving me a routine report.

"Yes," I answered.

"I'm sorry to have tell you this, but Laura has attempted suicide again. She is on the way to the hospital," she said.

My heart sank as my countenance fell. I cried out to God as I drove to the hospital, and as I replayed memories from the previous two attempts. Tears filled my eyes as I asked God, *Why?* I kept reviewing the last several weeks, looking for situations that could have triggered this new tragedy.

I found Laura in an exam room in the emergency department. I didn't know what to say, but tried to offer comfort and assure her I loved her. I felt helpless as the doctors admitted her, and my sense of helplessness increased over time, as they decided on a course of treatment. Her fate, at that point, was out of my hands, and we had to rely on the medical and mental health professionals to make wise decisions. I cried out to God to give wisdom to her caregivers.

Once again, we faced a long hospitalization, with inpatient ECT treatments, medication changes, and additional group therapies.

I began repeating my previous questions. *Why doesn't God heal Laura? When will this be over? Does God really love us?*

The first two questions, of course, were closely linked. If God healed Laura, then our struggle would be over, and we could move forward. Yet, even if God healed her, I recognized it might not be immediately. His timing and ours is often different. I sensed that God answered, "Not yet."

I believe that God can heal anyone of anything at any time. I also believe that God is sovereign, and if it is His plan, He does not have to heal anyone of anything at any time, at least healing in the way we see it, meaning free from illness or injury. So ultimately, Laura's healing would be a matter of timing and in a manner God would ultimately decide.

> But do not overlook this one fact, beloved, that with the Lord one day is as a thousand years, and a thousand years as one day. The Lord is not slow to fulfill His promise as some count slowness, but is patient toward you, not wishing that any should perish, but that all should reach repentance. (2 Peter 3:8-9)

---

[3] A pseudonym.

God reminded me of the truth that His timing is different from mine to comfort me, to put my soul at rest – to give me peace.

My Abba Father's Love is Certain

Does God really love us? I needed a clear answer to this question. As I meditated on this and searched His Word, I became convinced that God loved us because "God is love," and it would be out of character for Him not to love us.

What does it mean that God is love? How does His love help me during the tough times?

The reality that God is love makes it possible for me to abide in God. What an amazing thought – that the God of the universe wants to abide with me, a sinner. "So, we have come to know and to believe the love that God has for us. God is love, and whoever abides in love abides in God, and God abides in him." (1 John 4:16) The idea of abiding in God is a mystery greater than I can completely comprehend, yet several other Scriptures refer to this phenomenon. John 14 and John 15 come to mind.

Because God loved me first, and because He *is* love, I am able to love others. "Anyone who does not love does not know God, because God is love." (1 John 4:8) God's love for me empowers me to love others.

Living with Laura as she suffered from mental illness created many challenges for both of us. As the husband, to whom Paul admonished, "… love your wives as Christ loves the church," (Eph. 5:25), I knew I wanted to love her, and had an obligation to do so. The fact that God loved me, and empowered me to love her, made it possible for me to continue to have hope for her, and to help her in any way I could. When I considered that God loved me despite all of my shortcomings, knowing me better than I knew myself, *how could I not love Laura?* Jesus loves the Church, His bride, despite all of our sin and failings, and He gave me the ability and responsibility to love Laura.

When Laura stopped taking her medicine and there seemed to be nothing I could do to convince her otherwise, I also knew it could mean another suicide attempt. She suffered immeasurably from her suicide attempts, making it extremely difficult during those times in which I met her in the emergency room or the hospital admitted her for long periods of time. It took all of God's love for me during these times to look on her with love, and continue to have hope for her healing.

And Then, Well-Intentioned Others

God's love also extended to dealing with others.

People who were close to Laura and me, and many others who knew us as acquaintances, did their best to reach out to console or encourage us. They knew the hospital had admitted her, and wanted to, in their own way, express hope or concern, or perhaps, help me understand what was happening. Often – actually, too often – these good people would say things like, "She needs to pull herself up by her own bootstraps. There is actually no proof that there is some kind of physical issue. After all, you cannot see the problem with a blood test."

Others said, "If you would just pray more or believe more she would get better," or, "God will heal her if you just believe."

I love Scripture, and when fellow Christians use it wisely, in the right context, and for the right reasons, it lifts the spirit, provides hope, and reminds us of God's love. On the other hand, when used without understanding the context or seeing events through the eyes of another person, even though well meant, it can be stinging. This verse, for instance: "And we know that for those who love God all things work together for good, for those who are called according to His purpose." (Romans 8:28) Yes, what Paul wrote is the truth, and it can be a tough truth, yet in the circumstances Laura and I faced, it was not encouraging – rather it was hurtful when those who were not among our closest friends would say these things. When you fall into a swamp and are fighting for your life, even though you know God can use your stinking situation for His glory and your good, you are focused on getting out of the swamp. But oftentimes this passage is taken out of context. The context is that of the Holy Spirit helping us in our weakness in miraculous ways as He intercedes on our behalf. It is the start of a reassurance of the promise that we will be conformed in the image of Christ, be justified and finally glorified when God calls us home to live with Him in eternity. It is not meant to comfort those who are struggling with an earthly trial in which that particular trial in and of itself will be good. But in most cases, well-meaning people do not apply it in the context of the chapter. When you look at Romans 8:29, "For those whom He foreknew He also predestined to be conformed to the image of His Son, in order that He might be the firstborn among many brothers ...", we see that the reason God uses difficulties in our life is so that we become conformed to the image of His Son; to me that is comforting.

Paul wrote to Timothy: "All Scripture is inspired by God and profitable for teaching, for reproof, for correction, for training in righteousness; so that the man of God may be adequate, equipped for every good work." (2 Timothy 3:16-17) (NASB)Using Scripture to comfort and encourage a fellow Christian is powerful and appropriate, and we welcomed it, yet too often, it felt to us like judgment or discouraged us. Scripture needs to be used tactfully to be effective.

Christians sometimes quote Scripture in such a way that it sounds like an empty platitude. "Rejoice in the Lord always; again I will say, rejoice," (Phil. 4:4) is perhaps an insensitive use of Scripture when a man's wife has just attempted suicide. I can rejoice in God's love to know He is in control, but I am not sure I want to be encouraged to exclaim "Praise the Lord" while my wife struggles for life.

What Laura and I needed on her darkest days was to see, hear, and feel God's love, and when a fellow believer expressed it in a wise manner, it served as a balm to our spirits. Instead, I had to often draw on God's love to forgive a fellow believer for his or her insensitivity.

What are the words you can use to encourage a person caught in the grips of depression? Perhaps, "Jim, I cannot imagine what you are experiencing, but I can love you, pray for you, and help you. Is there anything I can pray for or do?" Sometimes the best thing a person can do is listen and not say much.

The fact is that God's love was and continues to be a great source of comfort.

Paul also wrote:

> "and hope does not put us to shame, because God's love has been poured into our hearts through the Holy Spirit who has been given to us. For while we were still weak, at the right time Christ died for the ungodly. For one will scarcely die for a righteous person—though perhaps for a good person one would dare even to die—but God shows His love for us in that while we were still sinners, Christ died for us." (Romans 5:5-8)

What a great love that God showed me in Jesus Christ's sacrifice for my sins. The thought that God sacrificed His only Son so that I, a sinner, could be saved moves me to want to love as He loved me. Christ's sacrifice for me – for sinners – gives me the ability to love others even when they are not worthy of love, and none of us are completely worthy of love.

Ponder this wonderful passage:

> "Who shall separate us from the love of Christ? Shall tribulation, or distress, or persecution, or famine, or nakedness, or danger, or sword? As it is written,
>
> 'For Your sake we are being killed all the day long; we are regarded as sheep to be slaughtered.'
>
> No, in all these things we are more than conquerors through Him who loved us. For I am sure that neither death nor life, nor angels nor rulers, nor things present nor things to come, nor powers, nor height nor depth, nor anything else in all creation, will be able to separate us from the love of God in Christ Jesus our Lord." (Romans 8:35-39)

The reality is that once we accept God's love through faith in Jesus Christ, nothing can separate us from His love – this truth might be the most comforting verse in Scripture – for certain it was to me during our darkest days.

Nothing can separate me from God. I do not have to worry about losing His love or losing my salvation. I can rest in His loving arms and He will care for me. He will help me to love others. I knew that God held Laura close to Him, too, and Jesus Christ's sacrifice had sealed her unto Him.

His grace, His jealousy, and His mercy are a result of His Love. I could count on God's love, even when I felt unlovable. There were many times when what I needed to remember was that God loves me. During these times, I turn to Psalm 136 "…For His steadfast love endures forever!" (Psalms 136:1ff)

God Reminds Me that He Wants to Have a Relationship with Me

After Laura had attempted suicide for the third time, I needed God to remind me that He cared for me and wanted a relationship with me. I had found myself angry with God because He had not healed Laura.

God showed me that, despite my anger over Laura's ongoing illness, I needed to understand and internalize the reality that the most important thing in my life was not Laura, but it was God. I needed God to remind me of His covenant with me just as Israel needed to be reminded of God's covenant with them. "Take care, lest you forget the covenant of the LORD your God, which He made with you, and make a carved image, the form of anything that the LORD your God has forbidden you. For the LORD your God is a consuming fire, a jealous God." (Deut. 4:23-24)

Jesus explained that God does not sit idly by, waiting for us to turn ourselves around. Oh no! He sought me out to rescue me, a profound truth shown in the story Jesus told about the 99 and one sheep.

> "What man among you, if he has a hundred sheep and has lost one of them, does not leave the ninety-nine in the open pasture and go after the one which is lost until he finds it? When he has found it, he lays it on his shoulders, rejoicing. And when he comes home, he calls together his friends and his neighbors, saying to them, 'Rejoice with me, for I have found my sheep which was lost!' I tell you that in the same way, there will be *more* joy in heaven over one sinner who repents than over ninety-nine righteous persons who need no repentance. (Luke 15:4-7) (NASB)

God's continued pursuit of me, and His loving acceptance when I returned to Him, made possible the lessons He planned to teach me. I knew that I had failed to find a church to actively attend, I hardly ever spent time in His Word, and I did not pursue God.

God Reminds Me That He is Just

During my time of despair after Laura's suicide attempts, I found myself thinking that God really was not just. After all, I am a Christian and I do not deserve to have a wife that wants to take her own life – and I am human, so self-pity came easily. What kind of a just God would put me through this situation? The Lord led me to this passage in Ezra which showed me that God *was* just, but even though I was a redeemed sinner I did not deserve special treatment. God's grace alone could be the single source of my hope for His intervention in our marriage and Laura's illness. "O Lord, the God of Israel, You are just, for we are left a remnant that has escaped, as it is today. Behold, we are before You in our guilt, for none can stand before You because of this." (Ezra 9:15)

Coming to Grips with Fear

Laura's illness created a sense of fear in me. I feared that I would never be at peace while I was away from Laura. I feared that Laura would never get better. On my darker days, I feared that somehow God had abandoned us, although I knew better – "I will never leave you nor forsake you." (Heb. 13:5b)

Several places in Proverbs we are taught to fear God – the good kind of fear. Biblical fear means standing so much in awe of God, knowing that we deserve death but instead, He gives us grace that it causes us to tremble. The good kind of fear of God leads us to wisdom and understanding.

God, however, began to teach me about the bad kind of fear, the kind of fear that comes from Satan. Satan used fear to separate me from God or paralyze me to prevent me from moving forward.

I decided to search the Scriptures to find out more about fear. I wanted to know about the fear that comes from God, and puts us in good stead with Him. I also wanted to know about the kind of fear that separates us from God, obviously emanating from something else – perhaps from Satan. First, God pointed me to 1 John.

> "So we have come to know and to believe the love that God has for us. God is love, and whoever abides in love abides in God, and God abides in him. By this is love perfected with us, so that we may have confidence for the Day of Judgment, because as He is so also are we in this world. There is no fear in love, but perfect love casts out fear. For fear has to do with punishment, and whoever fears has not been perfected in love. We love because He first loved us." (1 John 4:16-19)

This Scripture teaches that God is love and there is no room for fear in love. I concluded that the kind of fear I was experiencing could not come from God.

What I had hoped to find, and soon discovered does not exist, is a Bible passage that says something like, "The fear men know in this world comes from [_____]." I began to lay out a path through Scripture relating to the sources of fear.

"Let no one say when he is tempted, 'I am being tempted by God,' for God cannot be tempted with evil, and He Himself tempts no one. But each person is tempted when he is lured and enticed by his own desire. Then desire when it has conceived gives birth to sin, and sin when it is fully grown brings forth death." (James 1:13-15)

First, this passage confirms that fear does not come from God – rather, it comes from within me. I saw that the sin of fearfulness comes about when my own desires give birth to it.

I believe Satan plays a significant role in causing me to fear. I believe Satan planted thoughts in my mind that caused me to think improperly. "You are of your father the devil, and your will is to do your father's desires. He was a murderer from the beginning, and has nothing to do with the truth, because there is no truth in him. When he lies, he speaks out of his own character, for he is a liar and the father of lies." (John 8:44) Satan is the father of all lies.

Since Satan is the father of lies and I found myself fearing, which is a lie, then at some point, Satan plays a role in unholy fear. *How do I protect myself from ungodly fear?* I asked myself. "Put on the full armor of God, so that you will be able to stand firm against the schemes of the devil." (Ephesians 6:11) (NASB.) Here, Paul wrote that I needed to be prepared for battle, and to prepare for that battle I need to "put on the whole armor of God."

James wrote, "Submit yourselves therefore to God. Resist the devil, and he will flee from you. Draw near to God, and He will draw near to you. Cleanse your hands, you sinners, and purify your hearts, you double-minded." (James 4:7-8) In these two verses I found the way to combat ungodly fear: Put on the whole armor of God and resist the devil. That sounds simple and easy. If you are like me, however, you know that it's easier said than done.

The power of the Holy Spirit in me will help me put on the armor of God and resist the devil. The problem, however, is that I'm not always willing to accept His help, and He will not force His help upon me. When I am experiencing ungodly fear, it's a sign that I have not appropriated the power of the Holy Spirit, which God so willingly offers to me.

There are several passages in Scripture that encourage me while dealing with ungodly fear. These passages give me comfort, make me promises, and instruct me on what to do.

"...for God gave us a spirit not of fear but of power and love and self-control." (2 Timothy 4:7)

"I can do all things through Him who strengthens me." (Philippians 4:13)

"Even though I walk through the valley of the shadow of death,
I will fear no evil,
for You are with me;
your rod and Your staff,
they comfort me." (Psalms 23:4)

My Abba Father is My Strength

The next lesson God taught me during this time is that He is my strength. I learned that when I was too weak to do what needed to be done, God gave me strength to do it. Once again, I found Scripture to help me understand about God's strength. "Have I not commanded you? Be strong and courageous. Do not be frightened, and do not be dismayed, for the LORD your God is with you wherever you go." (Joshua 1:9) Not only is God my strength, but because He is my strength I did not need to be frightened.

Then there is this:

"Three times I pleaded with the Lord about this, that it should leave me. But He said to me, 'My grace is sufficient for you, for my power is made perfect in weakness.' Therefore, I will boast all the more gladly of my weaknesses, so that the power of Christ may rest upon me. For the sake of Christ, then, I am content with weaknesses, insults, hardships, persecutions, and calamities. For when I am weak, then I am strong." (2 Corinthians 12:8-10)

While this passage reminded me of the strength that God gives to me, it also served as a reminder that, like Paul, I faced a long battle. I needed to realize that God continued to show His strength to me at all times. I also needed to understand that His grace was sufficient and His power was shown through my weakness.

My Abba Father is My Refuge

When I experienced the most difficult trials of loving Laura in the midst of her mental illness, there were times I wanted to hide from the world. These times were more acute while she was hospitalized, although my concern for her remained my first priority. Yet, I wanted to shed the pain I felt for her and for our relationship and needed a refuge, where I could feel totally at peace and at rest. My first impulse was to search for a physical place to hide.

God showed me that the only refuge that met my needs happened when I looked to Him as my hiding place – my refuge.

> "God is our refuge and strength,
> a very present help in trouble." (Psalms 46:1)

And Psalm 91:

> He who dwells in the shelter of the Most High
> will abide in the shadow of the Almighty.
> I will say to the LORD, "My refuge and my fortress,
> my God, in whom I trust."
> For He will deliver you from the snare of the fowler
> and from the deadly pestilence.
> He will cover you with His pinions,
> and under His wings you will find refuge;
> his faithfulness is a shield and buckler.
> You will not fear the terror of the night,
> nor the arrow that flies by day,
> nor the pestilence that stalks in darkness,
> nor the destruction that wastes at noonday...
> Because you have made the LORD your dwelling place—
> the Most High, who is my refuge—
> no evil shall be allowed to befall you,
> no plague come near your tent.

For He will command His angels concerning you
to guard you in all your ways.
On their hands they will bear you up,
lest you strike your foot against a stone.
You will tread on the lion and the adder;
the young lion and the serpent you will trample underfoot.
"Because He holds fast to me in love, I will deliver him;
I will protect him, because He knows my name.
When He calls to me, I will answer him;
I will be with him in trouble;
I will rescue him and honor him.
With long life I will satisfy him
and show him my salvation."' (Psalms 91:1-6,9-16)

When I felt fear creeping into my spirit, I learned to press into the arms of my Lord and Savior and take refuge in Him – in this I found relief.

Enjoying God's refuge did not shield me from the reality of Laura's illness, but rather it provided me with the ability to trust God with my worries and concerns about Laura and her illness. I cast those concerns on Christ. These were the times when Jesus' words in Matthew 11 came alive in my spirit:

"Come to me, all who labor and are heavy laden, and I will give you rest. Take my yoke upon you, and learn from me, for I am gentle and lowly in heart, and you will find rest for your souls. For my yoke is easy, and my burden is light." (Matthew 11:28-30)

As I took refuge in Christ, it made it possible for me to forgive myself for all my failures as I struggled to learn what God taught me. Finding refuge in God is still the only place where I truly am at peace today.

Still Struggled with Fear

Even after all of this, I must confess that I still struggled with fear. I struggled with the fear that every time I was somewhere else than with Laura, I might not see her alive again. So, every time I went to work, I was afraid. Every time Laura went out by herself, I was afraid. Every time I left her to do something with friends, I was afraid. It was no fun living that way but I did.

CHAPTER 9

Laura's Fourth Suicide Attempt

Abba Father Teaches Me about Answered Prayer, Mercy, and Grace

Two tough years passed after Laura's third attempt to commit suicide. Now that this had happened three times, it became harder for me to put it out of my mind. Trusting God to care for her – and me – became a regular theme of daily life, and the idea she may try again lingered in my spirit. We still took trips, and to our mutual relief and joy, they went well. Laura stayed on her medications, and we were able to relax and enjoy God's creation.

Yet, Laura continued to struggle with depression, anxiety, and borderline personality disorder. This put additional strain on our relationship, as I tried to find ways to show my ongoing love for her. I hung on to the hope for her healing.

Laura questioned why God would not bless us with children. She believed her barren womb meant God didn't love her. I wondered whether God would give us children while she suffered from mental illness. Perhaps God would give us children to help to heal her troubled mind. Thoughts like this came and went as we both struggled for answers.

Side effects from Laura's treatment for depression added to her frustration and anxiety. Her ongoing struggle with short-term memory loss was particularly frustrating and ultimately caused her to leave her job as a medical assistant at an assisted living facility. She found it impossible to remember all the tasks she was supposed to do and became afraid that she would forget something vital to the health and safety of her patients. Laura decision to quit working at the assisted living facility only added to her depression as she felt it reduced her self-worth.

In response to her depression and frustration, Laura continued to abuse her body through cutting behavior and eating disorder. Laura made several trips to the emergency room to treat the damage caused by her self-inflicted cuts. Most of those were treated in the ER, but occasionally the hospital admitted her. Her therapists, friends, and I pleaded with her to eat a healthy diet, but to no avail. Laura's refusal to accept and act on our advice added to my own frustrations as I watched her suffering increase.

To her credit, Laura continued to regularly see her psychologist, although each visit was a struggle. One of the strategies her psychologist used was to have Laura sign a contract agreeing that she would refrain from killing herself in between their counseling sessions. These contracts adequately restrained Laura because she would not violate her promises. However, when she felt the need to abuse herself once again, she would do so.

Trying to Remain Active

Laura and I continued to socialize and remain active as much as possible. We felt it might relieve some of her symptoms. Sometimes we would be alone, and at other times, go to events with friends. We attended orchestra concerts, plays, baseball games, visits to the zoo, trips to foreign countries, walks in the park, and other activities. These ventures would often provide temporary relief, and at times, could be quite enjoyable. At other times, Laura's inability to enjoy herself could add to our mutual frustration.

One night, two other couples, Pastor Bob and Donna, and Tom and Leann, joined Laura and me for dinner and a show at the Chanhassen Dinner Theater in Chanhassen, Minnesota. That evening, Laura greatly enjoyed herself, and seemed to revel in being together with friends and me. The music and actors lifted her spirit, and she enjoyed the food and sounds of people laughing. It was the happiest I had seen her in six years. The following week, the other couples that attended the dinner with us commented on how they noticed Laura seemed better – happier, and enjoying herself. We all wondered and hoped that our socializing with her had finally started to yield fruits of joy, and some level of healing from her depression. We all thought Laura had finally turned the corner and was on her way to recovery. We wondered if more social outings, like this one, should be planned.

As her husband, I suffered from times when I wondered whether she ever would be healed. That night, and the week that followed the joy she showed at the dinner theater lit a flame of hope in me.

Six days after the dinner theater experience, Laura drove to the medical center for an appointment with the psychologist. After she found a parking place in the ramp and parked her car, she took an overdose of pills. A doctor who had never seen her prescribed the drugs.

She got the prescription and purchased these pills on the Internet.

After taking the pills, Laura got out of her car and walked to the psychologist's office. As her counseling session ended and she rose to leave, she became very unstable. The pills had begun to have an effect on her. Laura did not expect the pills to affect her that quickly or in such a dramatic manner.

The psychologist saw her lose balance, and called for a hospital employee to quickly bring a wheelchair and transport her to the emergency room in another part of the building. He was told that they do not provide that kind of transports for patients that are not already admitted to the hospital. So he found a wheelchair in the clinic and personally delivered her to the hospital emergency room.

"Mr. Hansen, this is Laura's psychologist," I heard him say when he called me. "I just took Laura to the emergency room," and he explained why.

This was Laura's fourth attempt to take her own life.

As I drove to the hospital, I called Pastor Bob Oehrig to let him know what Laura had done. At the emergency room the triage nurse told me to go to the waiting room while the doctors worked on Laura. Pastor Bob arrived shortly after I did and joined me in the waiting room. I am forever grateful for the love of this brother in Christ to comfort me as I sat there, struggling with the difficult truth that Laura had done it again. After two or three hours, the doctors had stabilized Laura enough to send her to the Intensive Care Unit (ICU) where Pastor Bob and I could see her.

"Mr. Hansen," Laura's ICU doctor said, "Your wife is in a battle for her life." His words stunned me.

At this point, I no longer cared whether Laura wanted me to tell others about her condition. She needed prayer - I needed prayer. I called most of my friends and told them what had happened. I asked them to pray for Laura and me. Pastor Bob continued to be there with us, sharing scriptures of comfort, encouragement, and forgiveness.

Prayer for the Staff

After I finished calling my friends, I suggested to Pastor Bob that we should pray for the medical team that provided care to Laura. Shortly after our discussion, her nurse came into Laura's room to check on her. We asked if we could pray for her. "Yes," she answered. Pastor Bob prayed that God would provide her with the wisdom, knowledge, and ability to more effectively care for Laura.

As we finished praying for the nurse, she saw that the doctor had ordered another IV for Laura. We watched as the nurse pulled out the necessary equipment to start the IV. We saw and appreciated her professional ability to insert the needle and start the IV.

As far as we could see, starting an IV was routine for this nurse. The nurse, however, told us it was a surprise for her. She explained that she had neuropathy in her fingers and had not been able to feel a vein in a patient's arm for the last six or seven years – except she readily felt Laura's vein. This made it possible to insert the needle quickly and easily.

"This is the first time in 30 years of nursing anyone asked if they could pray for me," she explained. As surprised as she was by our prayer, she was more amazed at the result. She joined with us in believing that God had answered our prayers for Laura's medical care providers.

Close to Death

Bob and I kept a vigil at Laura's bedside. Around 11:00 PM, seven hours after I had arrived, the doctor came into the room to check on Laura. "Doctor, do you think it would be okay if I went home to get some sleep?" I asked.

"I don't think that is a good idea yet," the doctor said. "Your wife is still in a very precarious condition and appears to be close to death." We waited another two hours until the doctor told us that he felt she was stable enough for us to be able to leave.

Laura remained in the ICU for the next two days, after which the doctor had her transferred to the psychiatric ward.

The fact that once again Laura's illness put her in a psychiatric ward triggered many emotions in me. I felt anger at both Laura and God that I was once again in this position. I felt discouraged that the illness had persisted so long. I had a sense of abandonment knowing that Laura would rather die than to be with me.

On the other hand, I experienced joy seeing God work with the ICU nurse. I had peace deep within me, knowing that God was in charge. I felt comfort knowing that the Holy Spirit was working in my heart to provide me with that comfort. I felt joy because Laura still lived, and there is always hope for the living.

Once again, God had lessons He wanted to teach me during this new trial. He taught me that He answers prayer. He taught me that He is merciful. And He taught me about His grace – God's unearned love and favor.

My Abba Father Answers Prayer

As I thought about the current crisis, God reminded me of how He helped the ICU nurse to start Laura's IV. I saw it as a miracle. This brought to mind one of my favorite passages from the book of John. "Whatever you ask in my name, this I will do, that the Father may be glorified in the Son. If you ask me anything in my name, I will do it." (John 14:13-14)

God taught me to pray with expectation that He would answer my prayers. Yet, I also needed to learn that sometimes His answer is different from how I would have answered my own request.

Sometimes His answer is "No." Consider again how Paul recorded the answer God gave him concerning Paul's thorn in the flesh:

"So to keep me from becoming conceited because of the surpassing greatness of the revelations, a thorn was given me in the flesh, a messenger of Satan to harass me, to keep me from becoming conceited. Three times I pleaded with the Lord about this, that it should leave me. But He said to me, 'My grace is sufficient for you, for my power is made perfect in weakness.' Therefore, I will boast all the more gladly of my weaknesses, so that the power of Christ may rest upon me. For the sake of Christ, then, I am content with weaknesses, insults, hardships, persecutions, and calamities. For when I am weak, then I am strong." (2 Corinthians 12:7-10)

Paul prayed that God would remove the thorn from his flesh. God said "No, because I want to show you how My power can be displayed working through your weakness." Paul's predicament instructed me to consider why God was answering the prayers Laura and I offered as He did. Perhaps God wanted to show His power to others and to us through our own weaknesses. This is not to claim equality with Paul's suffering, but only to show how I began thinking about how God answered our prayers for healing. I wondered if we were able to trust God enough so He could be shown acting through us in our times of weakness.

Sometimes God's answer to our prayers is "Not yet." Peter writes,

> "But do not overlook this one fact, beloved, that with the Lord one day is as a thousand years, and a thousand years as one day. The Lord is not slow to fulfill His promise as some count slowness, but is patient toward you, not wishing that any should perish, but that all should reach repentance. But the day of the Lord will come like a thief, and then the heavens will pass away with a roar, and the heavenly bodies will be burned up and dissolved, and the earth and the works that are done on it will be exposed." (2 Peter 3:8-10)

God showed me that my timeline is not necessarily His timeline. His answers will come in His time and not mine. I needed to be patient.

Sometimes God's answer to our prayer is immediate and "Yes." This is what Pastor Bob and I saw when God aided the ICU nurse just after we prayed for her.

When I prayed, whether alone or with others, God showed me that no matter His answer – No, Yes, or Not Yet – I still could trust that He would answer my prayers. This required me to have faith in Him and His Word. I saw how I could trust the Holy Spirit to help me understand prayer and the answers God gave to me. This reminded me that God has a long view of time, and in contrast, my priorities usually call for immediate resolution.

My Abba Father is Merciful

The fact remained that since the day Laura first attempted suicide, I saw nothing to indicate she had changed for the better, or hope that she would if given enough time. The reality of her lack of progress – in many regards, continuing in a downward spiral – sometimes caused me to be angry toward Laura and God. By now you have certainly noticed the cycle of human emotions from which I suffered and my periodic journeys between trust and lack of trust. I could at least take comfort in the examples God shows us with Israel, and know that He never abandoned them, though they often quit trusting Him. Having God as a sure refuge is a great comfort when going through trials.

When I prayed, *"Have mercy on me, Oh Lord,"* I saw that I needed to understand the nature of God's mercy. I needed God's mercy because of my failure to trust Him, and I needed to show mercy toward Laura. When she failed to follow her doctor's orders, failed to take her medications, and I failed to see improvement in her mental health, I needed to show her mercy, not anger. Now that she had made a fourth attempt to commit suicide, I needed to extend greater mercy to her.

During the darkest times of Laura's illness, I would often become angry with God. *"God, we keep praying for healing, but it's getting worse. Why?"* Oftentimes I wouldn't even ask *why,* but would let my anger boil over. At times, I felt that I did not trust Him or believe He was in control. At other times, when I at least acknowledged that He was in control, I let Him know I did not agree with how He was handling our situation. As I saw it, I knew that there had to be a better way.

God is so patient with us. He knows our needs. He knows our hearts. He loves us, even when we don't love Him.

God showed me many times that I was wrong about Him, and I needed His mercy for my own sin. Just to know that He knew me and still accepted me reminded me of His mercy. I saw that what was happening to us, no matter how awful it seemed, was better than we deserved. Like Moses, I needed to understand God's mercy:

> "The LORD passed before him and proclaimed, 'The LORD, the LORD, a God merciful and gracious, slow to anger, and abounding in steadfast love and faithfulness, keeping steadfast love for thousands, forgiving iniquity and transgression and sin, but who will by no means clear the guilty, visiting the iniquity of the fathers on the children and the children's children, to the third and the fourth generation.'" (Exodus 34:6-7)

As I came to the point of understanding the need to receive God's mercy, I learned that He was always there, willing and faithful to give it to me. "Let us then with confidence draw near to the throne of grace, that we may receive mercy and find grace to help in time of need." (Hebrews 4:16) When I found myself angry toward God, I also saw that all I needed to do was approach Him and accept His mercy. The mercy He gave me, when I was willing to accept it, comforted me. It removed my stress and worry – at least until I once again failed to accept it. This reminds me of one of Laura's favorite hymns, written by C. Austin Miles in 1912.

"In the Garden."

I come to the garden alone,
While the dew is still on the roses,
And the voice I hear falling on my ear,
The Son of God discloses . . .

And He walks with me, and He talks with me,
And He tells me I am His own,
And the joy we share as we tarry there,
None other, has ever, known!

He speaks and the sound of His voice,
Is so sweet the birds hush their singing,
And the melody that He gave to me,
Within my heart is ringing . . .

And He walks with me, and He talks with me,
And He tells me I am His own,
And the joy we share as we tarry there,
None other, has ever, known!

And the joy we share as we tarry there,
None other, has ever, known![4]

---

[4] Public domain

This cycle of growing angry with God and with Laura followed by my humble acceptance of God's mercy extended to me, repeated itself during her illness. In fact, it continues today. Praise God, for He remains merciful.

I came to understand that God's mercy stems from His great love for me – for each of us. Because He loved us, He extended mercy toward Laura and me. He has withheld the wrath and damnation we deserve, and replaced it with His love. Paul writes:

"What if God, desiring to show His wrath and to make known His power, has endured with much patience vessels of wrath prepared for destruction, in order to make known the riches of His glory for vessels of mercy, which He has prepared beforehand for glory—even us whom He has called, not from the Jews only but also from the Gentiles?" (Romans 9:23-24)

Furthermore, in Ephesians Paul says:

"But God, being rich in mercy, because of the great love with which He loved us, even when we were dead in our trespasses, made us alive together with Christ—by grace you have been saved—and raised us up with Him and seated us with Him in the heavenly places in Christ Jesus, so that in the coming ages He might show the immeasurable riches of His grace in kindness toward us in Christ Jesus." (Ephesians 2:4-7)

God showed His mercy to us from the beginning. "For the LORD your God is a merciful God. He will not leave you or destroy you or forget the covenant with your fathers that He swore to them." (Deuteronomy 4:31) My God, the only true God, is a God of mercy, who loves us beyond all we can comprehend.

God Reminds Me of Past Lessons about Fear

After Laura had attempted suicide for the fourth time, I found that I was losing hope that she would ever get better. I feared that there would be a next time, and the fact that I found myself thinking about a "next time" added to my frustration. It had gotten to the point that every time I left the house I feared I would come home to a dead wife. I had that same fear every time that Laura left home – I wondered if she would return alive. I knew that living with these fears conflicted with what I knew I believed. I asked, *How can I get rid of these fears and feelings of hopelessness?*

God again brought me back to His Word, and reminded me that He was holy and because of that I could always have hope. "This is the message we have heard from Him and proclaim to you, that God is light, and in Him is no darkness at all." (1 John 1:5)

"…in hope of eternal life, which God, who never lies, promised before the ages began." (Titus 1:2)

I saw that no matter how hopeless I thought life had gotten, God would bring light into my darkness and hope into my soul.

As powerful as hope is, however, it did not take away my fear. God needed to remind me that in perfect love there is no fear. He needed to remind me that no matter what happened, I did not need to fear – He has a plan and His plan is perfect. God sent me to His Word, and I found these two passages. "Fear not, for I am with you; be not dismayed, for I am your God; I will strengthen you, I will help you, I will uphold you with my righteous right hand." (Isaiah 41:10)

"Peace I leave with you; my peace I give to you. Not as the world gives do I give to you. Let not your hearts be troubled, neither let them be afraid." (John 14:27)

Even as, from time to time, I continued to struggle with hopelessness and fear, I could look to these passages and many others that God had shown me, and renew my faith in Him and His plans for me.

God Reminded Me of Past Lessons about God Working in His Time

I reverted to another recurrent theme, wondering why God had not healed Laura yet, and wondered if she would ever be well. I felt worried and upset. I felt lost once again. My Abba Father pointed me to the Psalms.

> "Wait for the Lord;
> be strong, and let your heart take courage;
> wait for the Lord!" (Psalms 27:14)

Grace Activated in Us

After Laura's fourth attempt at suicide and during her earlier attempts, the easiest thing I could have done, so it seemed at the time, was to walk away. Actually, I am not really sure that walking away would have been the easiest thing for me to do. Had I walked away, I am sure that I would have experienced a tremendous amount of guilt and remorse. Yet compared to the agony of suffering – mine, and hers as I watched it happen – the idea of walking away sometimes seemed enticing. God said, however, "I will never leave you nor forsake you."

The grace God extended to us during this time provided me with the ability to get through each day. His grace extended hope to Laura, and as she continued to relapse into her struggles, God's grace became more powerful and important to both of us.

God's grace toward Laura, who had many years earlier prayed in faith to trust Jesus Christ for her salvation, gave me the assurance that someday, she and I will be reunited in heaven when both of us had died or Christ returns. Without God's grace, Laura and I would be lost forever. "But we believe that we will be saved through the grace of the Lord Jesus, just as they will." (Acts 15:11)

God's grace made it possible for me to see His hand in my circumstances. When you are in pain it is hard to see God working, but He helps us to see Him: "And the Word became flesh and dwelt among us, and we have seen His glory, glory as of the only Son from the Father, full of grace and truth." (John 1:14)

By trusting in God's promise of salvation, extended to me as a free gift out of His grace, I became able to see past my pain and problems to set my eyes on Christ.

God's grace made it possible for me to become who I am. God's grace through my trials molded me into a man of faith. His grace helped me to accept my past, present, and future circumstances as part of His plan for me. "But by the grace of God I am what I am, and His grace toward me was not in vain. On the contrary, I worked harder than any of them, though it was not I, but the grace of God that is with me." (1 Corinthians 15:10)

As did Paul, by the grace of God, I continue to strive to make a difference for God in our culture and society. It is why I wrote this book.

God's grace assures me that I have an intercessor with God, even Jesus Christ, Who understands my pain and my needs.

"Since then we have a great high priest who has passed through the heavens, Jesus, the Son of God, let us hold fast our confession. For we do not have a high priest who is unable to sympathize with our weaknesses, but one who in every respect has been tempted as we are, yet without sin.

Let us then with confidence draw near to the throne of grace, that we may receive mercy and find grace to help in time of need." (Hebrews 4:14-16)

Knowing that Jesus Christ suffered far greater than I have suffered or ever will suffer, gives me greater confidence to ask His help whenever I need Him – constantly. I know He will answer "Yes," "No," or "Not yet," and it will be His will for me. Knowledge of God's grace and mercy toward me helps me to accept whatever He decides for me.

God answers my prayer. God is merciful. God extends His grace to me every day. As a result, my faith in Him continues to grow. I have come to see that one of God's spiritual gifts to me is the gift of faith.

So far, with each step I have taken, and especially those steps Laura and I took together – and separately – God has made me the man I am today and He continues to teach me more each day. As hard as it was – and remained – to go through those tough days with Laura, without those trials I am sure that I would not be who I am today.

Who I am today is a man closer to God than I was yesterday, but far from what I will be when He calls me, by His grace, to His heaven.

CHAPTER 10

Laura's Struggles Continue

My Abba Father Provides Again

After her doctors released her from the hospital weeks after her fourth suicide attempt, Laura continued to struggle with depression and her eating disorder. I had wanted to be strong in my faith and extend confidence to her. Watching her struggles continue, however, once again left me losing hope and patience, like I was at the end of my rope. At this point, I doubted that Laura would ever get better and this thought – or reality acceptance, I am not sure – was tough to accept. I found myself hurting as I watched her hurt.

In my mind, I began to visualize how I would have to deal with her illness the rest of my life. What I saw in our future discouraged me and caused me to question whether I had real faith in God. And as before, I sometimes wondered where God was in all of this.

God used this low point in my life to teach me that He was going to sustain me and would never leave nor desert me. He also continued to teach me that there was hope even when I had given up. He reminded me that He would provide all my needs, and thankfully, He continues to do so today.

My Abba Father, the Burden-Bearer

God led me to several scriptures to assure me that He would sustain me through this trial. "Cast your burden on the Lord, and He will sustain you;

He will never permit the righteous to be moved." (Psalms 55:22) "Never" makes a strong promise.

"And my God will supply every need of yours according to His riches in glory in Christ Jesus." (Philippians 4:19) "Every" covers a lot of needs.

"For nothing will be impossible with God." (Luke 1:37) "Nothing" covers a lot of situations.

"The steadfast love of the Lord never ceases; His mercies never come to an end; they are new every morning; great is your faithfulness." (Lamentations 3:22-23) "Never" is a long time. "Great" is an incredible measurement of His provision.

Finally, He reminded me about two of my favorite scripture verses. "I can do all things through Him who strengthens me." (Philippians 4:13) "All" is immense breadth.

With these wonderful truths from Proverbs, God reminded me that He was in the process of carving out my future path.

"Trust in the Lord with all your heart

And do not lean on your own understanding.

In all your ways acknowledge Him,

And He will make your paths straight." (Proverbs 3:5-6) (NASB)

As God directed me to these verses, at least most of the time, I knew that He was going to sustain Laura and me. Times of doubt and fear, however, continued to dog me. I am grateful that God does not require me to be perfect, but accepts me as I am.

My Abba Father, My Helper

As God showed me through His Word that He was not going to leave me nor forsake me, I gathered some strength to face each day. I relied principally on these verses from Hebrews to convince me of this truth.

"Keep your life free from love of money, and be content with what you have, for He has said, "I will never leave you nor forsake you." So we can confidently say,

"The Lord is my helper;

I will not fear;

what can man do to me?" (Hebrews 13:5-6)

"Confidently say," meaning in my heart I could know with certainty that God helped Laura and me.

My Abba Father, the Source of Hope

God clarified and helped me better understand hope. First, He showed me that He is the source of hope, not the doctors who treated Laura, or Laura herself. "...remember that you were at that time separated from Christ, alienated from the commonwealth of Israel and strangers to the covenants of promise, having no hope and without God in the world." (Ephesians 2:12)

"For whatever was written, in former days, was written for our instruction, that through endurance and through the encouragement of the Scriptures we might have hope." (Romans 15:4) God reminded me that His Scriptures provide the best place to understand and appropriate His hope.

God showed me that since He *is* love, He provides me with hope. Hope is part of the definition of love. So, God loves me to instill hope within me.

"Love is patient and kind; love does not envy or boast; it is not arrogant or rude. It does not insist on its own way; it is not irritable or resentful; it does not rejoice at wrongdoing, but rejoices with the truth. Love bears all things, believes all things, hopes all things, endures all things." (1 Corinthians 13:4-8)

God taught me that it is by placing my hope in Him that I could endure. My ability to effectively function as a husband, have personal peace, and perform the requirements of my job, rested on His enduring hope. I had to grab onto and internalize this reality, that God is the source of hope. Isaiah wrote beautifully and powerfully about this:

> "but they who wait for the Lord shall renew their strength;
> they shall mount up with wings like eagles;
> they shall run and not be weary;
> they shall walk and not faint."(Isaiah 40:31)

Of all the individuals about whom we read in the Bible, certainly no one better demonstrates the need for enduring hope in God than Job.

> "Though He slay me, I will hope in Him;
> yet I will argue my ways to His face. (Job13:15)
> "For there is hope for a tree,
> if it be cut down, that it will sprout again,

and that its shoots will not cease.
Though its root grow old in the earth,
and its stump die in the soil,
yet at the scent of water it will bud
and put out branches like a young plant. (Job 14:7-9)

I thought about Job. I realized that if Job could speak with hope after all that he had lost, then I should also be able to have hope. Like Job, I acknowledged that my hope was in God and not in myself, the doctors, or Laura.

My Abba Father, My Planner

God reminded me that I could hang on to hope because He had a plan for my life. It is hard to understand that God has a plan for us when life does not conform to our own plans, or His plan includes elements we would never have included.

God used this point in time to remind me of the lessons He had begun to teach me when I first encountered Laura's depression. I thought I had learned that God was in control, but needed to continue in this lesson, and pull it closer to me. "For I know the plans I have for you, declares the Lord, plans for welfare and not for evil, to give you a future and a hope." (Jeremiah 29:11) Is this not a powerful and motivating verse that speaks so strongly of holding onto hope?

He reminded me that because Christ died for me, I have complete access to God. God showed me that Jesus Christ is my anchor in a time of trials and provides hope. "We have this as a sure and steadfast anchor of the soul, a hope that enters into the inner place behind the curtain," (Hebrews 6:19) Furthermore:

"For God is not unjust so as to overlook your work and the love that you have shown for His name in serving the saints, as you still do. And we desire each one of you to show the same earnestness to have the full assurance of hope until the end, so that you may not be sluggish, but imitators of those who through faith and patience inherit the promises." (Hebrews 6:10-12)

God showed me that hope is part of His nature – a characteristic of God. It is not because of who I am but rather because of Who He is.

"Trust in the Lord, and do good;
dwell in the land and befriend faithfulness.
Delight yourself in the Lord,
and He will give you the desires of your heart.
Commit your way to the Lord;
trust in Him, and He will act.
He will bring forth your righteousness as the light,
and your justice as the noonday.
Be still before the Lord and wait patiently for Him;
fret not yourself over the one who prospers in His way,
over the man who carries out evil devices!" (Psalms 37:3-7)

Paul wrote about hope in Romans, reminding me that hope is part of God's nature. "Now may the God of hope fill you with all joy and peace in believing, so that you will abound in hope by the power of the Holy Spirit." (Romans 15:13) (NASB) As a result, I can "Rejoice in hope, be patient in tribulation, be constant in prayer." (Romans 12:12)

The truths God showed me about hope are more than words. God used them to lift my spirit and energize me so I could continue in my daily walk. As I faced daily challenges, when I felt my spirit falling and hope being dashed, I began to claim God's promise of hope. It is only by His grace that I can rest in the hope He provides, because on my own I would be a complete failure.

God Reteaches Me about His Righteousness

When Laura continued to struggle with her self-destructive behavior, I struggled with understanding how a righteous God could allow her to continue to suffer. How could it be right that one of His children would be in so much pain when He, from my point of view, had been doing nothing, or at least had not been doing enough? So again, God pointed me back to His Word, to this passage in Psalms.

"For the Lord is righteous;
he loves righteous deeds;
the upright shall behold His face."
(Psalms 11:7)

I had to once again be reminded that it is not about what I believed or how I felt that led to truth; it was His Word that was true. My opinion did not matter.

We Pressed On

As Laura and I continued on our journey together, God provided for our needs financially, for which we were both thankful. Most certainly, we did not need additional stress from financial challenges. God also ministered to our emotional and spiritual needs. He continually reminded me to:

> "Trust in the Lord with all your heart
> And do not lean on your own understanding.
> In all your ways acknowledge Him,
> And He will make your paths straight. (Proverbs 3:5-6) (NASB)

God used Jesus' words in Matthew as strong medicine to lift our spirits. "'Ask, and it will be given to you; seek, and you will find; knock, and it will be opened to you. For everyone who asks receives, and he who seeks finds, and to him who knocks it will be opened. Or what man is there among you who, when his son asks for a loaf, will give him a stone? Or if he asks for a fish, he will not give him a snake, will he? If you then, being evil, know how to give good gifts to your children, how much more will your Father who is in heaven give what is good to those who ask Him!'" (Matthew 7:7-11) (NASB)

In 2001, after the terrorist attack on 9/11, the musical trio Selah recorded and released the song, *Press On* as part of an album of that same name. The lyrics can bring strength to individuals faced with trials like what Laura and I experienced.

Press On

> When the valley is deep
> When the mountain is steep
> When the body is weary
> When we stumble and fall

When the choices are hard
When we're battered and scarred
When we've spent our resources
When we've given our all

In Jesus' name, we press on
In Jesus' name, we press on
Dear Lord, with the prize
Clear before our eyes
We find the strength to press on

In Jesus' name, we press on
In Jesus' name, we press on
Dear Lord, with the prize
Clear before our eyes
We find the strength to press on
To press on[5]

God Reminds Me of His Holiness and My Sinfulness

As I said earlier, I am an inpatient man, wanting to get tasks done and out of the way, to move on to the next thing. Living with and loving a person suffering from depression does not sit well with impatience or an unforgiving spirit. At times, I found myself being short with Laura and not treating her in a loving way. I would behave badly in word and actions. Thankfully, God pointed me to these three Scripture verses. "And I am no longer in the world, but they are in the world, and I am coming to You. Holy Father, keep them in Your name, which You have given me, that they may be one, even as we are one." (John 17:11)

> "...but as He who called you is holy; you also be holy in all your conduct..." (1 Peter 1:15)

[5] PRESS ON (AKA "EN CRISTO YO VENCERE"), Words and Music by DAN BURGESS, © 1983 BELWIN-MILLS PUBLISHING CORP.
All Rights Administered by ALFRED PUBLISHING CO., INC, All Rights Reserved, Used By Permission of ALFRED MUSIC

These verses reminded me that if I love Jesus with all my heart, mind, and soul, I could live a holier life. I would have a better chance to keep His commandments.

"If you love me you will keep my commandments..." (John 14:15) I used to think that this commandment required me to keep God's commandments in order to love Jesus. However, as I read it more closely and mediated on it, I came to understand that if I love Jesus, He will give me the ability to keep His commandments. To be holier, love Jesus more.

My Abba Father Provides a New Resource

God made it possible for me, through my work, to visit Focus on the Family's headquarters in Colorado Springs, Colorado.

As I left for Focus, I worried about leaving Laura home alone – she promised me that she would not do herself any harm. Try as I might I still reverted back to wondering why God had not healed Laura and if she would ever get better. I noticed that I had become weary with my life. I needed my strength renewed and more courage to continue this massive battle. My Abba Father sustained me by pointing me to this passage in Isaiah.

> "...but they who wait for the LORD shall renew their strength;
> they shall mount up with wings like eagles;
> they shall run and not be weary;
> they shall walk and not faint. (Isaiah 40:31)

I am surprised that I did not learn this lesson sooner. Each time I looked at a wall in our bedroom I saw this verse in an embroidery hanging on the wall. Who knows why a verse you have seen almost every day for 20 plus years suddenly connects in your heart and you are willing to accept it? During my trip to Focus, the verse finally penetrated my heart. God made it real to me.

During the time I spent at Focus, I had the opportunity to meet a gentleman from the counseling department. Soon, I found myself explaining to him the situation that Laura and I faced. I asked him for advice and about Christian-based options for treating Laura. The counselor told me about an eating disorder treatment facility outside of Chicago that was connected to a very reputable Christian counseling organization.

Upon returning home from Colorado Springs, I told Laura about this new option that could provide effective treatment for her. Her psychologist agreed to explore this new option and others as he struggled to find effective therapy to help her.

Together we explored options outside of Minnesota for Laura. We narrowed the options down to a facility in Houston and the one outside of Chicago. Houston did not offer a Christian treatment perspective, and I did not like that. Chicago offered much the same treatment, but with a Christian perspective.

After considering health insurance coverage, we agreed that Laura would go to the Chicago facility. Thankfully, in addition to the Christian perspective, the insurance coverage was better for Chicago.

God continued to provide me with encouragement through His Church. The men's group that I had started continued to build into me, and this provided much-needed strength. My pastor friends at the local church I attended joined with me in praying for us.

Others I knew at work continued to pray for us, and gave me words of encouragement. I often reflect on whether I would have made it through my trials without the love and help of the godly men I met through my work. I won't know the answer to this question until I enter Heaven. For sure, though, I believe it was part of God's plan for me to use these Christian brothers to help me along the way.

Remarkably, during the years of Laura's mental illness, I had three different jobs. The third job provided me with the greatest spiritual counsel that I needed and at just the right time. The job put me in contact with hundreds of pastors in Minnesota and across the country, many of whom prayed regularly for us and a few became spiritual helpers. Yes, God had a plan for me that He bathed in hope and His enduring love.

CHAPTER 11

Laura's Second Eating Disorder Treatment

My Abba Father Reveals More Truth to Me

Laura and I discussed and prayed about seeking care for her at the Chicago-area eating disorder treatment facility. We both agreed it offered a positive opportunity and gave us some hope she could learn to deal with this illness, even though Laura seemed somewhat reluctant.

On the day we were to leave, Laura and I woke up at our normal time. We had decided to drive to Chicago a day before she was to enter the treatment facility.

Laura had done most of her packing the prior day, but finished up that morning. I packed an overnight bag, intending to drive home the middle of the day she settled into the treatment center. I planned to spend the night with my mom at her home on the way back.

We enjoyed a good breakfast together, took care of last-minute details, and I packed our car for the trip. I opened the door for Woody, our dog, to jump into the backseat; then the three of us were off to Chicago, about a six-hour drive. We had favorable weather as we departed, but knew we likely would run into snow along the route.

About two hours down the highway we ran into light snow. Soon, however, it turned into heavy, wet snow. The roads became slick and we had to drive slowly. The road conditions worsened the farther we drove. I saw Laura tensing up.

"Let's turn around and go home," Laura said. The way I took her request is that going back home had nothing to do with the weather – the road wouldn't be any better on the way home, since we would be driving back through heavy snow. Instead, I believed she wanted to turn around because she really didn't want to enter another treatment facility.

I stayed firm, reminding her that we had already decided she should enter the treatment program. I continued driving toward Chicago. What had started out to be a six-hour trip ended up being nearly ten hours. Finally, we safely arrived at our Chicago-area hotel; both of us were physically and emotionally drained from the drive. We found a fairly nice restaurant close by and had a good dinner – she ate well. I remained hopeful that, despite the trial of driving through a snowstorm, Laura was headed to the right place at the right time. After dinner, we returned to the motel room, watched some television, and went to sleep.

The next morning, as we began to get ready for the day, I noticed that Laura seemed to be pensive and uneasy about entering the treatment center. I sensed that she felt like she was being forced to go, rather than being truly interested in going.

As I watched her that morning, I became concerned that the treatment was not going to work. How could it, if Laura did not seem fully convinced that she wanted to go. I thought that without her really buying into the idea, she was not going to be successful.

After eating breakfast at the hotel, we drove to the treatment facility. We arrived a few minutes early for her admission appointment, and then together attended the orientation session. A staff member explained to us what was going to happen and the rules at the facility.

I realized even though Laura voluntarily agreed to admit herself, the sleeping rooms were in a locked facility from both the inside and outside. This gave me a sense of security, hoping that Laura would be closely watched and protected from harming herself.

The facility seemed clean and pleasant. It sat on a secluded wooded lot that included a few ponds. To me, it looked to be a place where Laura could enjoy some outside time whenever it was warm enough. It gave me hope that being outside in God's beautiful creation would provide her with some joy and a sense of peace.

Each woman in the facility shared a sleeping room with another woman. Each housing section in the facility included a common area where residents could enjoy various activities, either alone or with another, or in a group.

The commons area included a television, DVD player, books, games to play, and materials for doing crafts. The dining room was in a separate building.

I noticed that some of the women in the facility were Laura's age, but the clear majority of them were younger, including several teenagers. The teenagers lived in a separate building from the adult women, and for the most part, had their own groups.

Laura and I finished her orientation, and I helped her unpack and settle into her room. As I helped her unpack, I found myself feeling more hopeful, though I still felt unconvinced that this was going to work. All I could do was hope she would come around after getting into the treatment routine.

I watched her closely as we went through the day. Laura still appeared to be apprehensive. It seemed she was doing this out of duty, not out of a real desire to get better. I had come to understand that part of her lack of motivation to get better was because she believed she did not deserve to get better.

Laura feared meeting new people and living with strangers. As I thought about it later, I believe she was putting on a good face for me, but deep down, she did not want to go through this treatment. I don't think she ever believed it would help her, or maybe she did not want it to help. These conflicts are common to people suffering from depression.

After unpacking, Laura walked me to the door of the facility. I gave her a kiss and a hug. We lingered there for quite a long time before I said goodbye. I said, "I'll be praying for you, and we can talk on the phone next time you can receive phone calls." She looked sad.

The aide let me out of the facility. I got into the car and began driving to my mom's house in Harmony Minnesota, about four hours away.

Woody and I drove toward my mother's home, knowing Laura would be gone for a while – which ended up being three months. I prayed for Laura as I drove away. I asked God to help her to become open to the treatment and to touch her heart. I asked God to make this time be the time that would heal her. I prayed He would give me peace and a sense of hope, even as I reverted to troubling thoughts of yet another failure.

I drove through Galena, Illinois, birthplace of President Ulysses S.

Grant, on the way home. This piece of history helped distract me from my concerns for Laura.

Woody and I spent the night at Mom's and returned home the next day.

Unusual Emotions

Upon arriving home, I started to feel emotions that I had not previously felt. I felt a sense of relief. I felt like I could get better rest. I knew Laura was safe and that I did not have to worry as much about her. Unfortunately, that began to lead me to think I might actually be better off without Laura. It confounded me that I had these mixed emotions – and that I should even consider such a negative idea.

Yet, the fact was that with her secure in the treatment facility, I did not have to worry about her safety. This helped me relax, much more so than when she was at home. My feelings of relief were probably normal, yet I started to feel guilty about them, especially considering the idea that I would be better off without Laura. At first, as usual, I tried to work out these contradictory feelings on my own. Then, thankfully, I turned to God in prayer and His Word, looking for answers.

I knew that some great benefit accrued to me being able to find rest and relief, at least temporarily – stress is tough on the body. For quite some time, I had been getting tired and had become short with and insensitive to Laura. The tiredness and my moodiness were, at least in part, a result of trying to self-manage my problems rather than to seek God's grace, mercy, and peace.

The Holy Spirit worked in my heart and led me back to Scripture where God reminded me again that I needed to turn my burdens over to Him.

> At that time Jesus declared, 'I thank You, Father, Lord of heaven and earth, that You have hidden these things from the wise and understanding and revealed them to little children; yes, Father, for such was Your gracious will. All things have been handed over to me by my Father, and no one knows the Son except the Father, and no one knows the Father except the Son and anyone to whom the Son chooses to reveal him. Come to me, all who labor and are heavy laden, and I will give you rest. Take my yoke upon

you, and learn from me, for I am gentle and lowly in heart,
and you will find rest for your souls. For my yoke is easy,
and my burden is light.' (Matthew 11:25- 30)

I saw that God had made provision for my own needs by finding the
inpatient treatment center for Laura, located so many miles away. This
gave me a chance to rest and be rejuvenated. I knew that the care center
protected Laura and offered hope to her, so it relieved me of daily worry
and caring physically for her.

My Abba Father Reminds Me that I Must Continue to Wait on Him

With Laura in Illinois and me at home alone, I started to wonder if this
was finally the treatment that would help heal Laura. I wondered whether
our trials would soon be coming to an end. However, deep in my spirit I
really doubted that God would heal Laura. I had once again lost my faith
that God would end our agony. Still, God remained faithful to me and
pointed me to this passage in Lamentations. Here God encouraged me to
trust Him and wait for His timing.
"The Lord is good to those who wait for Him,
to the soul who seeks Him. It is good that one should wait quietly for
the salvation of the Lord." (Lamentations 3:25-26)

Am I Better Off, I Wondered

What challenged me greatly were the persistent thoughts and feelings
that I would be better off without Laura. As I found myself thinking about
this, I experienced guilt and shame. Once again, God brought me back
into His Word to help me understand my feelings.
About the idea that I would be better off without Laura, God took me
to Genesis and Matthew. "Then the Lord God said, 'It is not good that
the man should be alone; I will make him a helper fit for him.'" (Genesis
2:18) God reminded me that in my case, being alone did not fit His plan
for me. He showed me that Laura was my helper and an integral part of
my life. I needed her.

God showed me where Jesus talks about marriage and divorce, saying;

> And Pharisees came up to Him and tested Him by asking, 'Is it lawful to divorce one's wife for any cause?' He answered, 'Have you not read that He who created them from the beginning made them male and female, and said, "Therefore a man shall leave his father and his mother and hold fast to his wife, and the two shall become one flesh'? So they are no longer two but one flesh. What therefore God has joined together, let not man separate."' They said to Him, 'Why then did Moses command one to give a certificate of divorce and to send her away?' He said to them, 'Because of your hardness of heart Moses allowed you to divorce your wives, but from the beginning it was not so. And I say to you: whoever divorces his wife, except for sexual immorality, and marries another, commits adultery.' (Matthew 19:3-9)

As I understood Jesus' teaching, as a Christian husband I had no grounds to abandon Laura or seek a divorce from her. Our situation did not fit the narrow provisions for divorce.

God convinced me that even though Laura was sick and we faced difficult times and some severe trials, He preferred us to stay together. I felt grateful that He knew I needed rest and this time of separation would restore me emotionally and physically.

God brought Laura and me together for His purpose. He used our relationship to make me a better man. This temporal struggle I faced helped me become more mature in my faith in Him.

Shedding Guilt

Guilt haunts a man who wants relief from his trials by any means – it weighed me down. I knew God wanted Laura and me together, and yet, I had let myself contemplate separation. God, in His loving kindness and with endless patience, began to teach me more about guilt and how to deal with it.

My soul was troubled. I needed to understand guilt. God showed me the difference between the guilt that comes from the loving conviction of the Holy Spirit and the guilt that comes from Satan's lies.

Jesus described the role of the Holy Spirit in our lives in John.

"And when He (Holy Spirit) comes, He will convict the world concerning sin and righteousness and judgment: concerning sin, because they do not believe in me; concerning righteousness, because I go to the Father, and you will see me no longer; concerning judgment, because the ruler of this world is judged." (John 16:8-11)

It is clear to me that the Holy Spirit played a critical role in causing me to feel conviction about my sin. God gives the Holy Spirit to us for our good. When the Holy Spirit convicted me of sin, it was a reminder of God's love for me.

The Holy Spirit convicted me for what I already plainly saw as my sin.

> For the wrath of God is revealed from heaven against all ungodliness and unrighteousness of men, who by their unrighteousness suppress the truth. For what can be known about God is plain to them, because God has shown it to them. For His invisible attributes, namely, His eternal power and divine nature, have been clearly perceived, ever since the creation of the world, in the things that have been made. So they are without excuse. For although they knew God, they did not honor Him as God or give thanks to Him, but they became futile in their thinking, and their foolish hearts were darkened. Claiming to be wise, they became fools, and exchanged the glory of the immortal God for images resembling mortal man and birds and animals and creeping things. Though they know God's righteous decree that those who practice such things deserve to die, they not only do them but give approval to those who practice them. (Romans 1:18-23, 32)

The fact that I have a sense of right and wrong is because God's law is written on my heart.

> "For when Gentiles, who do not have the law, by nature do what the law requires, they are a law to themselves, even

though they do not have the law. They show that the work
of the law is written on their hearts, while their conscience
also bears witness, and their conflicting thoughts accuse
or even excuse them on that day when, according to my
gospel, God judges the secrets of men by Christ Jesus."
(Romans 2:14-15)

Because God's law was written on my heart, my conscience tells me
when I do something wrong. As a follower of Jesus Christ, the Holy Spirit
works within me to emphasize those wrongs, and show me a way to repent
and commit to trusting God, and doing right. After the Holy Spirit convicts
me of my sin and I repent, God remembers my sin no more.

And every priest stands daily at his service, offering
repeatedly the same sacrifices, which can never take away
sins. But when Christ had offered for all time a single
sacrifice for sins, He sat down at the right hand of God,
waiting from that time until His enemies should be made
a footstool for His feet. For by a single offering He has
perfected for all time those who are being sanctified.

And the Holy Spirit also bears witness to us; for after
saying,

'This is the covenant that I will make with them
after those days, declares the Lord:
I will put my laws on their hearts,
and write them on their minds,'
then He adds,
'I will remember their sins and their lawless deeds no
more.' (Hebrews 10:11-17)

What an incredible truth! In God's eyes, I am no longer guilty for
my sin! I can quit seeing myself as guilty, but instead, accept the fact
that Jesus Christ paid my penalty for sin. Then, as I live my life before
God, I am without condemnation for my sin. "There is therefore now no
condemnation for those who are in Christ Jesus. For the law of the Spirit
of life has set you free in Christ Jesus from the law of sin and death."
(Romans 8:1-2)

My experience had shown me that knowing I am forgiven and that God sees me as guiltless is different from the reality that sometimes, I still *feel* guilty. What is it that caused me to still feel guilty? At times, I continued to find myself thinking about being better off without Laura, even after I had confessed this as sinful. These sinful thoughts, I realized, were the Devil's lies. The Devil is the Father of Lies. "You are of your father the devil, and your will is to do your father's desires. He was a murderer from the beginning, and does not stand in the truth, because there is no truth in him. When he lies, he speaks out of his own character, for he is a liar and the father of lies." (John 8:44)

The Devil continued lying to me, trying to make me forget God. I saw this clearly in 1 Peter. "Be sober-minded; be watchful. Your adversary the devil prowls around like a roaring lion, seeking someone to devour." (1 Peter 5:8) I saw in this verse that when I found myself thinking these lying thoughts, I needed to submit myself to God and resist the Devil's lies – then he would flee. "Submit yourselves therefore to God. Resist the devil, and he will flee from you." (James 4:8) My struggle with these unwanted thoughts did not suddenly end. I still struggle, but I am doing better.

Progress, But Another Roadblock

The mental health professionals at the Chicago treatment center began working with Laura using what was to us a new approach – Eye Movement Desensitization and Reprocessing (EMDR).[6] From my point of view, the

---

[6] EMDR (Eye Movement Desensitization and Reprocessing) is a psychotherapy that enables people to heal from the symptoms and emotional distress that are the result of disturbing life experiences. EMDR therapy shows that the mind can in fact heal from psychological trauma much as the body recovers from physical trauma. The brain's information processing system naturally moves toward mental health. If the system is blocked or imbalanced by the impact of a disturbing event, the emotional wound festers and can cause intense suffering. Once the block is removed, healing resumes. Using the detailed protocols and procedures learned in EMDR therapy training sessions, clinicians help clients activate their natural healing processes.

EMDR therapy is an eight-phase treatment. Eye movements (or other bilateral stimulation) are used during one part of the session. After the clinician has

EMDR therapy seemed to be helpful, better than talk and group therapy had been. However, as with other therapies that seemed to help, Laura chose a therapist who was not trained to use EMDR despite acknowledging it made her feel better when she returned home.

Laura, as had happened previously, did not follow through because she believed that she did not deserve to feel better.

As her time at the treatment center moved along, day by slow day, Laura continued to struggle with her depression but made progress overcoming her eating disorder. As I sat in Minnesota, separated from her, I felt myself once again having hope. However, I had my doubts that Laura had progressed enough. I feared that she had not fully bought into the need for healthy eating or had concluded that she deserved to feel good. So I continued to flee to God seeking more patience, and my need to trust Him with my circumstances increased yet again.

Truthfully, the longer this new treatment continued and I saw Laura making minimal progress, the harder it seemed to get. The time of her inpatient treatment seemed to last forever. I missed Laura being at home, together with me, but I was fearful that the treatment would only be a temporary fix.

---

determined which memory to target first, he asks the client to hold different aspects of that event or thought in mind and to use his eyes to track the therapist's hand as it moves back and forth across the client's field of vision. As this happens, for reasons believed by a Harvard researcher to be connected with the biological mechanisms involved in Rapid Eye Movement (REM) sleep, internal associations arise and the clients begin to process the memory and disturbing feelings. In successful EMDR therapy, the meaning of painful events is transformed on an emotional level. Unlike talk therapy, the insights clients gain in EMDR therapy result not so much from clinician interpretation, but from the client's own accelerated intellectual and emotional processes. The net effect is that clients conclude EMDR therapy feeling empowered by the very experiences that once debased them. Their wounds have not just closed, they have transformed.

CHAPTER 12

Laura's Third Eating Disorder Treatment

My Abba Father Continues to Help

Laura completed her treatment at the Chicago-area clinic and was ready to come home. I planned to drive down to pick her up on the weekend, but she really wanted to get home as soon as possible. She told me she was struggling with a new roommate and as a result, decided to fly home. The treatment facility staff arranged for a ride to Midway Airport. It made me nervous to think she would be on her own even during this short time. I prayed that all would go well, and she told me when she landed that the flight went well, and she had been comfortable, looking forward to being home.

Although I felt glad she was home, I also felt concern that the treatment would not stick, as had been our previous experience. I reminded myself that treatment had helped her finally stop drinking and was thankful for that.

When I first saw Laura at the Twin Cities' airport, I felt some relief. She looked healthy and more vibrant than she did when I left her at the clinic several weeks earlier. Her spirits seemed good. She was well dressed as usual and her cheeks were fuller and rosier than they had been for the last several years. Her appearance gave me hope.

From what I could see at first after Laura returned home from the Chicago treatment center, she seemed to be doing fairly well. She ate well and was not purging her food.

Her positive and healthier behavior continued during the following several weeks. Then I noticed a sudden change and she began to regress. I noticed that she started to eat less. Then the purging behavior started, and she started to cut herself. My heart sank, and I felt frustrated. It looked like we had made one step forward, and we were about to take two steps back. I wondered if this cycle would ever stop.

As I saw it, Laura deserved to feel better and be healthier, but she still could not believe this fact. I searched my mind and heart, wondering if I could do anything to help her realize she was a person of great value to God, to me, to our friends. I was again at a loss.

For the next several months, I witnessed Laura's destructive behavior of eating and purging. Eventually, she consumed nearly 100 laxatives a day, and her weight fell below 100 pounds.

When I tried to talk to Laura about this behavior and what I saw, she seemed to go blank. She told me that I did not understand what she was going through and that I didn't understand she was not worthy of living. She continued to insist that she did not deserve my love or God's love.

None of us *deserve* to be loved either by God or by someone else. The only reason why we are loved is because God first loved us and He gives us the ability to love each other despite all our shortcomings. However, I could not get Laura to fully believe or understand that principle – and here again, I found myself trying to fix her.

Laura's psychologist got her to agree to try another eating disorder treatment program. This one was in the Twin Cities area. As I thought about it later, I am not convinced she went because she wanted to get better, based on how I observed her behavior at the clinic. She resisted the program's requirements. She acted belligerently and defied the staff's instructions, fighting them on every turn up to the point of being kicked out of the program.

My Patience with My Abba Father Runs Thin, But He is Faithful Still

As I witnessed Laura continuing to struggle with her eating disorder, and once again faced the reality that she would be admitted to yet another eating disorder treatment center, I became angry with God. My anger with God, after all He had brought us through, created great conflict within me. Why had I not overcome my anger and frustration? Yet I did not understand why God would not heal Laura. He again pointed me back to His Word and showed me that my relationship with Him was not where He wanted it to be. Laura had once again become more important to me than God was, and He would not accept this attitude. God used the nation of Israel as an example to show me my weakness and draw me back to Him.

"And the LORD drove out before us all the peoples, the Amorites who lived in the land. Therefore, we also will serve the LORD, for He is our God. But Joshua said to the people, 'You are not able to serve the LORD, for He is a holy God. He is a jealous God; He will not forgive your transgressions or your sins. If you forsake the LORD and serve foreign gods, then He will turn and do you harm and consume you, after having done you good.'" (Joshua 24:18-20)

Feeling Helpless And Turning to My Hope

Christians have this incredible advantage of being able to turn toward our Abba Father any time for any reason to seek Him and find answers. I know that, for me, knowing that God loved me and was ready to hear and answer my prayers made it possible for me to continue moving forward each day. With Laura's self-destruction occurring before my eyes, I continuously asked God to intervene in her life and mine.

God reminded me often during the seven plus years since Laura's illness first showed itself, that there were men in the Bible who faced terrible trials, and their stories could give me strength. King David and Job in particular, each faced very difficult trials, and with God's help, came through them. Their stories encouraged and strengthened me, although I do not mean to suggest that my trials were anywhere nearly as tough as theirs were – and certainly, they displayed far more faithfulness to God than I ever have. I knew, however, that by studying about David and Job and how they responded to God, I could be made better.

Job – Incredible Faith and Trials

About Job, God said to Satan, "The Lord said to Satan, 'Have you considered My servant Job? For there is no one like him on the earth, a blameless and upright man, fearing God and turning away from evil.'"

(Job 1:8) (NASB) Imagine the magnitude of that statement: God called Job blameless and upright. I am far from blameless and upright, but if God would allow a man like Job to be tested by Satan, who am I to believe that I should not be tested as well?

God allowed Satan to test Job, and Satan did what he does – took almost everything away from the man. Satan took or killed all of Job's livestock. He killed Job's children. Ravaged Job's wealth. Satan left Job with two servants only so they could report to Job what had happened to his family. Satan let Job's wife survive, and eventually she ended up begging him to denounce God.

Job's response to Satan's savage attacks? "He said,

> "Naked I came from my mother's womb,
> And naked I shall return there.
> The Lord gave and the Lord has taken away.
> Blessed be the name of the Lord." (Job 1:21) (NASB)

God showed me that it was possible to offer praise to Him even during my worst times because all that this world offered me is temporary. "Through all this Job did not sin nor did he blame God." (Job 1:22) (NASB)

As I studied Job – God's view of him and his view of his circumstances – I asked myself, "Is it possible for me to respond in this same way?" With the help of the Holy Spirit and trusting God's Word, in my heart this is how I wanted to respond. The desire of my heart was to trust God and seek His Will, and this helped remind me how to deal with my circumstances.

Satan saw that Job did not lose his faith and that he held on to an eternal perspective and continued to trust God. As he saw Job cling to his faith in God, Satan went back to Him. God said:

"The Lord said to Satan, 'Have you considered My servant Job? For there is no one like him on the earth, a blameless and upright man fearing God and turning away from evil. And he still holds fast his integrity, although you incited Me against him to ruin him without cause.'" (Job 2:3) (NASB)

God saw Job's heart, but Satan only saw external evidence that Job had not yet cracked under the major losses he had suffered.

"Satan answered the Lord and said, 'Skin for skin! Yes, all that a man has he will give for his life. However, put forth Your hand now, and touch his bone and his flesh; he will curse You to Your face.' So the Lord said to Satan, 'Behold, he is in your power, only spare his life.'" (Job 2:4-6) (NASB)

After that brief conversation, Satan attacked Job's body, rendering him a victim of terrible pain and suffering. Satan placed enmity between Job and his wife. Job's wife said:

> Then his wife said to him, "Do you still hold fast your integrity? Curse God and die!" But he said to her, "You speak as one of the foolish women speaks. Shall we indeed accept good from God and not accept adversity?" In all this Job did not sin with his lips (Job 2:9-10) (NASB)

The only enmity between Laura and me was caused by her mental illness. It brought both of us great pain. Like Job, only not with the same level of courage, I continued to trust God. If Job could remain committed to God while undergoing suffering, even with a discouraged and angry wife, so could I.

As I continued reading the book of Job, God showed me many verses to encourage me. These are some:

> "Let the day perish on which I was to be born…"
> (Job 3:3) (NASB)

This helped me know that I could feel sad and still be okay with God.

> "Why is light given to him who suffers,
> And life to the bitter of soul, Who long for death, but there
> is none,
> And dig for it more than for hidden treasures,
> Who rejoice greatly,
> *And* exult when they find the grave?" (Job 3:20-22) (NASB)

Laura could suffer from deep depression, even be suicidal, and still be okay with God.

> "What is my strength, that I should wait?
> And what is my end, that I should endure?" (Job 6:11) (NASB)

Even though at times I became impatient, I could still be okay with God.

What is man that You magnify him,
And that You are concerned about him,
That You examine him every morning
And try him every moment?
"Will You never turn Your gaze away from me,
Nor let me alone until I swallow my spittle?
"Have I sinned? What have I done to You,
O watcher of men?
Why have You set me as Your target,
So that I am a burden to myself?
"Why then do You not pardon my transgression
And take away my iniquity?
For now I will lie down in the dust;
And You will seek me, but I will not be.
(Job 7: 17-21) (NASB)

I can feel like all is hopeless, and I am still okay with God.
"In truth I know that this is so;
But how can a man be in the right before God?
If one wished to dispute with Him,
He could not answer Him once in a thousand *times*." (Job
9:2-3) (NASB)

I can ask God "why?" questions, and still be okay with Him.
"For though I were right, I could not answer;
I would have to implore the mercy of my judge." (Job 9:15)
(NASB)

What is happening in my life is not necessarily because I
am not right with God.
"In whose hand is the life of every living thing,
And the breath of all mankind?" (Job 12:10) (NASB)

I am in God's hands and therefore I am okay with Him.
"Though He slay me,
I will hope in Him." (Job 13:15a) (NASB)

> As for me, I know that my Redeemer lives,
> And at the last He will take His stand on the earth.
> "Even after my skin is destroyed,
> Yet from my flesh I shall see God;
> Whom I myself shall behold,
> And whom my eyes will see and not another.
> My heart faints within me!
> "If you say, 'How shall we persecute him?'
> And 'What pretext for a case against him can we find?'
> "*Then* be afraid of the sword for yourselves,
> For wrath *brings* the punishment of the sword,
> So that you may know there is judgment." (Job 19:25-29)
> (NASB)

The reality is that my Redeemer still lives no matter my situation, and because of that I am okay with God.

> "But He knows the way I take;
> *When* He has tried me, I shall come forth as gold." (Job
> 23:10) (NASB)

I know that when my trial is over, whenever that will be, I will be better than I was before it began, and because of that I am okay with God.

> "But He is unique and who can turn Him?
> And *what* His soul desires, that He does.
> "For He performs what is appointed for me,
> And many such *decrees* are with Him.
> "Therefore, I would be dismayed at His presence;
> *When* I consider, I am terrified of Him." (Job 23:13-15)
> (NASB)

I fear God, and because of that, I am okay with God.

Job, in his agony and suffering, offered a long lament to God in which he accused God of abandoning him, among other things. After God responded to Job's accusations by describing His own nature, Job responded twice. Job's responses to God helped me to understand my response to God.

"Behold, I am insignificant; what can I reply to You?
I lay my hand on my mouth.
"Once I have spoken, and I will not answer;
Even twice, and I will add nothing more." (Job 40:4-5) (NASB)

I know that You can do all things,
And that no purpose of Yours can be thwarted.
'Who is this that hides counsel without knowledge?'
Therefore I have declared that which I did not understand,
Things too wonderful for me, which I did not know."
'Hear, now, and I will speak;
I will ask You, and You instruct me.'
"I have heard of You by the hearing of the ear;
But now my eye sees You;
Therefore I retract,
And I repent in dust and ashes." (Job 42:2-6)

Job admitted the limits of his understanding of God's nature and His Will. I wanted to similarly respond, so that at some point I would quiet myself and accept my lot in life – this required me to repent from my wrong ideas about God and His role in my circumstances.

David, Blessed of Jehovah

God, using the prophet Samuel, hand-picked David to be Israel's second king. The Bible tells his story in relatively unblemished language with many highs and lows, but God still loved him.

As I studied the Biblical accounts of King David, I saw a man who started out as a simple shepherd. As he served King Saul, he had many great military victories. During the time King Saul chased after him, David showed great depth of character by not retaliating against King Saul. As King, he had great successes followed by great sins followed by great suffering. Despite his failures, David became known as a man after God's own heart. I learned a great deal from King David.

God directed Samuel to anoint David as the king.

Now the Lord said to Samuel, "How long will you grieve over Saul, since I have rejected him from being king over Israel? Fill your horn with oil and go; I will send you to Jesse the Bethlehemite, for I have selected a king for Myself among his sons."

So he sent and brought him in. Now he was ruddy, with beautiful eyes and a handsome appearance. And the Lord said, "Arise, anoint him; for this is he." [13] Then Samuel took the horn of oil and anointed him in the midst of his brothers; and the Spirit of the Lord came mightily upon David from that day forward. And Samuel arose and went to Ramah. (1 Samuel16:1, 12-13) (NASB)

David found the Philistines disregard for Israel, King Saul, and God to be repugnant. He killed Goliath with a single shot from his sling.

And there came out from the camp of the Philistines a champion named Goliath of Gath, whose height was six cubits and a span. He had a helmet of bronze on his head, and he was armed with a coat of mail, and the weight of the coat was five thousand shekels of bronze. And he had bronze armor on his legs, and a javelin of bronze slung between his shoulders. The shaft of his spear was like a weaver's beam, and his spear's head weighed six hundred shekels of iron. And his shield-bearer went before him. He stood and shouted to the ranks of Israel, 'Why have you come out to draw up for battle? Am I not a Philistine, and are you not servants of Saul? Choose a man for yourselves, and let him come down to me. If he is able to fight with me and kill me, then we will be your servants. But if I prevail against him and kill him, then you shall be our servants and serve us.'

Then Saul clothed David with his armor. He put a helmet of bronze on his head and clothed him with a coat of mail, and David strapped his sword over his armor. And he tried in vain to go, for he had not tested them. Then David said to Saul, "I cannot go with these, for I have not tested them." So David put them off. Then he took his staff in his hand and chose five smooth stones from the brook and put them in his shepherd's pouch. His sling was in his hand, and he approached the Philistine.

Then a champion came out from the armies of the Philistines named Goliath, from Gath, whose height was six cubits and a span. *He had* a bronze helmet on his head, and he was clothed with scale-armor which weighed five thousand shekels of bronze. *He* also *had* bronze greaves on his legs and a bronze javelin *slung* between his shoulders.[7] The shaft of his spear was like a weaver's beam, and the head of his spear *weighed* six hundred shekels of iron; his shield-carrier also walked before him. He stood and shouted to the ranks of Israel and said to them, "Why do you come out to draw up in battle array? Am I not the Philistine and you servants of Saul? Choose a man for yourselves and let him come down to me. If he is able to fight with me and kill me, then we will become your servants; but if I prevail against him and kill him, then you shall become our servants and serve us."

Then Saul clothed David with his garments and put a bronze helmet on his head, and he clothed him with armor. David girded his sword over his armor and tried to walk, for he had not tested *them*. So David said to Saul, "I cannot go with these, for I have not tested *them*." And David took them off. He took his stick in his hand and chose for himself five smooth stones from the brook, and put them in the shepherd's bag which he had, even in *his* pouch, and his sling was in his hand; and he approached the Philistine. (1 Samuel 17:4-9, 38-40) (NASB)

The women sang as they played, and said,

"Saul has slain his thousands,
And David his ten thousands."" (1 Samuel 18:7) (NASB)

King Saul, seeing his bravery, made David a commander in his army. "Therefore Saul removed him from his presence and appointed him as his commander of a thousand; and he went out and came in before the people." (1 Samuel 18:13) (NASB)

Saul became fearful and jealous of David, and issued orders to kill him. "Now Saul told Jonathan his son and all his servants to put David to death." (1 Samuel 19:1a.) (NASB)

David, instead of acting out of anger or to gain power, spared Saul's life even as the King had been trying to hunt him down to kill him.

> Then Saul took three thousand chosen men from all Israel and went to seek David and his men in front of the Rocks of the Wild Goats. He came to the sheepfolds on the way, where there *was* a cave; and Saul went in to relieve himself. Now David and his men were sitting in the inner recesses of the cave. The men of David said to him, "Behold, *this is* the day of which the Lord said to you, 'Behold; I am about to give your enemy into your hand, and you shall do to him as it seems good to you.'" Then David arose and cut off the edge of Saul's robe secretly. It came about afterward that David's conscience bothered him because he had cut off the edge of Saul's *robe*. So he said to his men, "Far be it from me because of the Lord that I should do this thing to my lord, the Lord's anointed, to stretch out my hand against him, since he is the Lord's anointed." David persuaded his men with *these* words and did not allow them to rise up against Saul. And Saul arose, left the cave, and went on *his* way. (1 Samuel 24:2-7) (NASB)

King David committed adultery with Bathsheba.

> Now when evening came David arose from his bed and walked around on the roof of the king's house, and from the roof he saw a woman bathing; and the woman was very beautiful in appearance. So David sent and inquired about the woman. And one said, "Is this not Bathsheba, the daughter of Eliam, the wife of Uriah the Hittite?" David sent messengers and took her, and when she came to him, he lay with her; and when she had purified herself from her uncleanness, she returned to her house. The

woman conceived; and she sent and told David, and said, "I am pregnant." (2 Samuel 11:2-5) (NASB)

Caught in adultery, David made his sin far worse by having Uriah killed.

Then David sent to Joab, *saying*, "Send me Uriah the Hittite." So Joab sent Uriah to David. When Uriah came to him, David asked concerning the welfare of Joab and the people and the state of the war. Then David said to Uriah, "Go down to your house, and wash your feet." And Uriah went out of the king's house, and a present from the king was sent out after him. But Uriah slept at the door of the king's house with all the servants of his lord, and did not go down to his house. Now when they told David, saying, "Uriah did not go down to his house," David said to Uriah, "Have you not come from a journey? Why did you not go down to your house?" Uriah said to David, "The ark and Israel and Judah are staying in temporary shelters, and my lord Joab and the servants of my lord are camping in the open field. Shall I then go to my house to eat and to drink and to lie with my wife? By your life and the life of your soul, I will not do this thing." Then David said to Uriah, "Stay here today also, and tomorrow I will let you go." So Uriah remained in Jerusalem that day and the next. Now David called him, and he ate and drank before him, and he made him drunk; and in the evening he went out to lie on his bed with his lord's servants, but he did not go down to his house.

Now in the morning David wrote a letter to Joab and sent *it* by the hand of Uriah. He had written in the letter, saying, "Place Uriah in the front line of the fiercest battle and withdraw from him, so that he may be struck down and die." So it was as Joab kept watch on the city, that he put Uriah at the place where he knew there *were* valiant men. The men of the city went out and fought against Joab, and some of the people among David's servants fell; and Uriah the Hittite also died. (2 Samuel 11:6-17) (NASB)

Nathan, the prophet, confronted King David about his murderous and adulterous behavior.

Then the Lord sent Nathan to David. And he came to him and said,

> "There were two men in one city, the one rich and the other poor.
> The rich man had a great many flocks and herds.
> But the poor man had nothing except one little ewe lamb
> Which he bought and nourished;
> And it grew up together with him and his children.
> It would eat of his bread and drink of his cup and lie in his bosom,
> And was like a daughter to him.
> Now a traveler came to the rich man,
> And he was unwilling to take from his own flock or his own herd,
> To prepare for the wayfarer who had come to him;
> Rather he took the poor man's ewe lamb and prepared it for the man who had come to him."

> Then David's anger burned greatly against the man, and he said to Nathan, "As the Lord lives, surely the man who has done this deserves to die. He must make restitution for the lamb fourfold, because he did this thing and had no compassion."
> Nathan then said to David, "You are the man! (2 Samuel 12:1-7a) (NSAB)

As a result of David's sins, God pronounced judgment upon him. David tore his clothes, repented, and sought forgiveness – God granted forgiveness, but David still had to endure suffering as a result of his actions.

> Thus says the Lord God of Israel, 'It is I who anointed you king over Israel and it is I who delivered you from the hand of Saul. I also gave you your master's house and

your master's wives into your care, and I gave you the house of Israel and Judah; and if *that had been* too little, I would have added to you many more things like these! Why have you despised the word of the Lord by doing evil in His sight? You have struck down Uriah the Hittite with the sword, have taken his wife to be your wife, and have killed him with the sword of the sons of Ammon. Now therefore, the sword shall never depart from your house, because you have despised Me and have taken the wife of Uriah the Hittite to be your wife.' Thus says the Lord, 'Behold, I will raise up evil against you from your own household; I will even take your wives before your eyes and give *them* to your companion, and he will lie with your wives in broad daylight. Indeed you did it secretly, but I will do this thing before all Israel, and under the sun.'" Then David said to Nathan, "I have sinned against the Lord." And Nathan said to David, "The Lord also has taken away your sin; you shall not die. However, because by this deed you have given occasion to the enemies of the Lord to blaspheme, the child also that is born to you shall surely die." So Nathan went to his house. (2 Samuel 12:7b-15) (NASB)

David's child with Bathsheba, conceived in adultery, died. "But when David saw that his servants were whispering together, David perceived that the child was dead; so David said to his servants, "Is the child dead?" And they said, 'He is dead.'" (2 Samuel 12:19) (NASB)

Bathsheba gave birth to a second son fathered by David. They named him Solomon.

"Then David comforted his wife Bathsheba, and went in to her and lay with her; and she gave birth to a son, and he named him Solomon. Now the Lord loved him" (2 Samuel 12:24) (NASB)

David suffered deadly division in his own home among his own children. His son, Absalom, conspired against the King to take the throne by force.

But Absalom sent spies throughout all the tribes of Israel, saying, "As soon as you hear the sound of the trumpet, then you shall say, 'Absalom is king in Hebron.' Then two hundred men went with Absalom from Jerusalem, who were invited and went innocently, and they did not know anything. And Absalom sent for Ahithophel the Gilonite, David's counselor, from his city Giloh, while he was offering the sacrifices. And the conspiracy was strong, for the people increased continually with Absalom. (2 Samuel 15:10-12) (NASB)

During a battle against David's men, Absalom's long hair got entangled in the branches of a tree. Contrary to King David's orders, Joab, the King's chief military commander, killed Absalom.

Now Absalom happened to meet the servants of David. For Absalom was riding on *his* mule, and the mule went under the thick branches of a great oak. And his head caught fast in the oak, so he was left hanging between heaven and earth, while the mule that was under him kept going. When a certain man saw *it*, he told Joab and said, "Behold, I saw Absalom hanging in an oak." Then Joab said to the man who had told him, "Now behold, you saw *him*! Why then did you not strike him there to the ground? And I would have given you ten *pieces* of silver and a belt." The man said to Joab, "Even if I should receive a thousand *pieces of* silver in my hand, I would not put out my hand against the king's son; for in our hearing the king charged you and Abishai and Ittai, saying, 'Protect for me the young man Absalom!' Otherwise, if I had dealt treacherously against his life (and there is nothing hidden from the king), then you yourself would have stood aloof." Then Joab said, "I will not waste time here with you." So he took three spears in his hand and thrust them through the heart of Absalom while he was yet alive in the midst of the oak. (2 Samuel 18:9-14) (NASB)

David mourned Absalom's death.

Behold, the Cushite arrived, and the Cushite said, "Let my lord the king receive good news, for the Lord has freed you this day from the hand of all those who rose up against you." Then the king said to the Cushite, "Is it well with the young man Absalom?" And the Cushite answered, "Let the enemies of my lord the king, and all who rise up against you for evil, be as that young man!"

The king was deeply moved and went up to the chamber over the gate and wept. And thus he said as he walked, "O my son Absalom, my son, my son Absalom! Would I had died instead of you, O Absalom, my son, my son!" (2 Samuel 18:31-33) (NASB)

As I considered David's life, I found myself amazed to see the depth of his love and faithfulness to God – even given his sins – and God's faithfulness to David. What a testimony to me to see that God would be so faithful to a man who sinned against Him in so many ways. David's profound depth of repentance set him apart from most men I have known – and certainly from me.

"Against You, You only, have I sinned
and done what is evil in Your sight,
so that You may be justified in Your words
and blameless in Your judgment.
Create in me a clean heart, O God,
and renew a right spirit within me.
Cast me not away from Your presence,
and take not Your Holy Spirit from me.
Restore to me the joy of Your salvation,
and uphold me with a willing spirit.
Then I will teach transgressors Your ways,
and sinners will return to You." (Psalms 51:4, 10-13)

Like all humans, King David was a sinner, and in the eyes of most people who knew the truth about him, David committed major sins – adultery and murder.

I then considered David's behavior and attitudes in the context of his relationship with God as evidenced in the 75 Psalms he wrote that are given to us in the Bible. Clearly, David knew God intimately, and God knew and loved him intimately.

I took comfort in David's Psalms because they assured me that I, too, could have a special relationship with God during my trials and for the rest of my life. Along with Psalm 51 quoted above, these are some of my favorite Psalms of David. They ministered to my spirit each time I considered them – and still do.

> "Arise, O Lord!
> Save me, O my God!
> For You strike all my enemies on the cheek;
> you break the teeth of the wicked.
> Salvation belongs to the Lord;
> your blessing be on Your people!" (Psalms 3:7-8)

> "Answer me when I call, O God of my righteousness!
> You have given me relief when I was in distress.
> Be gracious to me and hear my prayer!
> Be angry, and do not sin;
> ponder in your own hearts on your beds, and be silent."
> (Psalms 4:1,4)

> "what is man that You are mindful of him,
> and the son of man that You care for him?" (Psalms 8:4)
> "if the foundations are destroyed,
> what can the righteous do?" (Psalms 11:3)

> The fool says in his heart, "There is no God."
> They are corrupt, they do abominable deeds,
> there is none who does good.
> The Lord looks down from heaven on the children of man,
> to see if there are any who understand,
> who seek after God.
> They have all turned aside; together they have become corrupt;
> there is none who does good,
> not even one. (Psalms 14:1-3)

Preserve me, O God, for in You I take refuge.
I say to the Lord, 'You are my Lord;
I have no good apart from You.'
The Lord is my chosen portion and my cup;
you hold my lot.
The lines have fallen for me in pleasant places;
indeed, I have a beautiful inheritance.
I bless the Lord who gives me counsel;
in the night also my heart instructs me.
I have set the Lord always before me;
because He is at my right hand, I shall not be shaken.
Therefore, my heart is glad, and my whole being rejoices;
my flesh also dwells secure.
For You will not abandon my soul to Sheol,
or let Your holy one see corruption.
You make known to me the path of life;
in Your presence there is fullness of joy;
at Your right hand are pleasures forevermore.
(Psalms 16:1-2, 5-11)

"I love You, O Lord, my strength.
The Lord is my rock and my fortress and my deliverer,
my God, my rock, in whom I take refuge,
my shield, and the horn of my salvation, my stronghold.
I call upon the Lord, who is worthy to be praised,
and I am saved from my enemies." (Psalms 18:1-3)

The law of the Lord is perfect,
reviving the soul;
the testimony of the Lord is sure,
making wise the simple;
the precepts of the Lord are right,
rejoicing the heart;
the commandment of the Lord is pure,
enlightening the eyes;
the fear of the Lord is clean,
enduring forever;
the rules of the Lord are true,

and righteous altogether.
More to be desired are they than gold,
even much fine gold;
sweeter also than honey
and drippings of the honeycomb.
Moreover, by them is Your servant warned;
in keeping them there is great reward.
Let the words of my mouth and the meditation of my heart
be acceptable in Your sight,
O Lord, my rock and my redeemer. (Psalms 19:7-11, 14)

"Some trust in chariots and some in horses,
but we trust in the name of the Lord our God." (Psalms 20:7)

The Lord is my shepherd; I shall not want.
He restores my soul.
He leads me in paths of righteousness
for His name's sake.
Even though I walk through the valley of the shadow of death,
I will fear no evil,
for You are with me;
your rod and Your staff,
they comfort me.
Surely goodness and mercy shall follow me
all the days of my life,
and I shall dwell in the house of the Lord
forever." (Psalms 23:1, 3-4, 6)

Prove me, O Lord, and try me;
test my heart and my mind.
For Your steadfast love is before my eyes,
and I walk in Your faithfulness." (Psalms 26:2-3)

The Lord is my light and my salvation;
whom shall I fear?
The Lord is the stronghold of my life;
of whom shall I be afraid?
One thing have I asked of the Lord,

that will I seek after:
that I may dwell in the house of the Lord
all the days of my life,
to gaze upon the beauty of the Lord
and to inquire in His temple.
I believe that I shall look upon the goodness of the Lord
in the land of the living!
Wait for the Lord;
be strong, and let your heart take courage;
wait for the Lord!" (Psalms 27:1, 4, 13-14)

"Sing praises to the Lord, O you His saints,
and give thanks to His holy name.
For His anger is but for a moment,
and His favor is for a lifetime.
Weeping may tarry for the night,
but joy comes with the morning." (Psalms 30:4-5)

"I will instruct You and teach You in the way You should go;
I will counsel You with my eye upon You." (Psalms 32:8)
"For the Lord loves justice;
he will not forsake His saints.
They are preserved forever,
but the children of the wicked shall be cut off." (Psalms 37:28)

so the wicked shall perish before God!
But the righteous shall be glad;
they shall exult before God;
they shall be jubilant with joy!"
"Blessed be the Lord,
who daily bears us up;
God is our salvation. *Selah*
Our God is a God of salvation,
and to God, the Lord, belong deliverances from death.
(Psalms 68:2b-3, 19-20)

Incline Your ear, O Lord, and answer me,
for I am poor and needy.

Preserve my life, for I am godly;
save Your servant, who trusts in You—You are my God.
Be gracious to me, O Lord,
for to You do I cry all the day.
Gladden the soul of Your servant,
for to You, O Lord, do I lift up my soul.
For You, O Lord, are good and forgiving,
abounding in steadfast love to all who call upon You.
Give ear, O Lord, to my prayer;
listen to my plea for grace.
In the day of my trouble I call upon You,
for You answer me.
But You, O Lord, are a God merciful and gracious,
slow to anger and abounding in steadfast love and
faithfulness. (Psalms 86:1-7, 15)

Bless the Lord, O my soul,
and forget not all His benefits,
who forgives all your iniquity,
who heals all your diseases,
who redeems your life from the pit,
who crowns you with steadfast love and mercy,
who satisfies you with good
so that your youth is renewed like the eagle's.
The Lord is merciful and gracious,
slow to anger and abounding in steadfast love.
As a father shows compassion to His children,
so the Lord shows compassion to those who fear Him.
(Psalms 103:2-5, 8, 13)

"For Your steadfast love is great above the heavens;
Your faithfulness reaches to the clouds." (Psalms 108:4)
"Though I walk in the midst of trouble,
You preserve my life;
You stretch out your hand against the wrath of my enemies,
and Your right hand delivers me.
The Lord will fulfill His purpose for me;
your steadfast love, O Lord, endures forever.

Do not forsake the work of Your hands." (Psalms 138:7-8)

O Lord, You have searched me and known me!
You know when I sit down and when I rise up;
you discern my thoughts from afar.
You search out my path and my lying down
and are acquainted with all my ways.
For You formed my inward parts;
you knitted me together in my mother's womb.
I praise You, for I am fearfully and wonderfully made.
Wonderful are Your works;
my soul knows it very well.
Search me, O God, and know my heart!
Try me and know my thoughts!
And see if there be any grievous way in me,
and lead me in the way everlasting! (Psalms 139:1-3, 13-14, 23-24)

"Teach me to do Your will,
for You are my God!
Let Your good Spirit lead me
on level ground!" (Psalms 143:10)

"O Lord, what is man that You regard him,
or the son of man that You think of him?
Man is like a breath;
is days are like a passing shadow.
Blessed are the people whose God is the Lord!" (Psalms 144:3-4, 15b)

"Great is the Lord, and greatly to be praised,
and His greatness is unsearchable.
The Lord is gracious and merciful,
slow to anger and abounding in steadfast love.
The Lord is good to all,
and His mercy is over all that He has made.
You open Your hand;
you satisfy the desire of every living thing.

The Lord is righteous in all His ways
and kind in all His works.
The Lord is near to all who call on Him,
to all who call on Him in truth.
He fulfills the desire of those who fear Him;
He also hears their cry and saves them. (Psalms 145:3,
8-9, 16-19)

Even while writing this book and laying out those great verses from the Psalms, I am encouraged by David's love and intimate relationship with God. I acknowledge that my relationship with God does not begin to approach David's, but I am grateful to God that I can seek it, and He will continue to commune with me.

As the days moved on and I watched Laura struggle, I know that I depended upon God for strength and peace. I tried to plant my feet on the foundation that God provided for me – Jesus Christ, my sure foundation.

I love those hymns, songs, and choruses that remind me of our foundational faith in Jesus Christ. One of my favorites is

"My Hope is Built on Nothing Less"

by Edward Mote, 1797-1874
My hope is built on nothing less
Than Jesus' blood and righteousness;
I dare not trust the sweetest frame,
But wholly lean on Jesus' name.
On Christ, the solid Rock, I stand;
All other ground is sinking sand.
When darkness veils His lovely face,
I rest on His unchanging grace;
In every high and stormy gale
My anchor holds within the veil.
On Christ, the solid Rock, I stand;
All other ground is sinking sand.
His oath, His covenant, and blood
Support me in the whelming flood;
When every earthly prop gives way,
He then is all my Hope and Stay.
On Christ, the solid Rock, I stand;

All other ground is sinking sand.
When He shall come with trumpet sound,
Oh, may I then in Him be found,
Clothed in His righteousness alone,
Faultless to stand before the throne!
On Christ, the solid Rock, I stand;
All other ground is sinking sand.[7]

I also find great comfort and encouragement from this old hymn.

Great is Thy Faithfulness
by Thomas Obediah Chisolm (1866-1960)

"Great is Thy faithfulness," O God my Father,
There is no shadow of turning with Thee;
Thou changest not, Thy compassions, they fail not
As Thou hast been Thou forever wilt be.
"Great is Thy faithfulness!" "Great is Thy faithfulness!"
Morning by morning new mercies I see;
All I have needed Thy hand hath provided—
"Great is Thy faithfulness," Lord, unto me!
Summer and winter, and springtime and harvest,
Sun, moon and stars in their courses above,
Join with all nature in manifold witness
To Thy great faithfulness, mercy and love.
"Great is Thy faithfulness!" "Great is Thy faithfulness!"
Morning by morning new mercies I see;
All I have needed Thy hand hath provided—
"Great is Thy faithfulness," Lord, unto me!
Pardon for sin and a peace that endureth,
Thine own dear presence to cheer and to guide;
Strength for today and bright hope for tomorrow,
Blessings all mine, with ten thousand beside!
"Great is Thy faithfulness!" "Great is Thy faithfulness!"
Morning by morning new mercies I see;
All I have needed Thy hand hath provided—

---

[7] Public domain

"Great is Thy faithfulness," Lord, unto me![8]

As Laura continued to struggle with her mental health issues, I found that I needed help as well. I was beginning to lose hope that Laura would ever get better. I was beginning to think that someday she would attempt suicide another time. I believed that if Laura were to attempt another time, she would be successful.

I continued to pray for Laura as much as I could and whenever the Holy Spirit would bring her to mind. However, I wondered if it was doing any good as Laura continued to struggle. In order to find some hope, I started to look at statistics about mental illness and suicide. In reading and researching facts about suicide I found that only 7% of people who survive a suicide attempt actually ultimately die by suicide. Like Laura only 23% actually try again.

---

[8] Public Domain

CHAPTER 13

Laura's Fifth Suicide Attempt

As Laura continued to struggle with her mental health issues, I found that I also needed help. I began to lose hope that Laura would ever get better. I began to think that someday she might once again attempt suicide and worse, that she would be successful.

I prayed for Laura whenever the Holy Spirit brought her to mind. Admittedly, I wondered if my prayers were doing any good – I could see that no matter the urgency or fervency of my prayers, Laura continued to struggle.

My analytical side took me to statistics about mental illness and suicide. I found that only 7 percent of people who survive a suicide attempt ultimately die by suicide. Like Laura, only 23 percent try more than once. I found hope in those numbers. As I sought God He pointed me to Psalm 39:7:

> "And now, O Lord, for what do I wait?
> My hope is in You."

My hope in the Lord helped me hope that Laura would get better, and besides, all the statistics were in her favor. She had *only* attempted suicide four times, and according to the American Association of Suicidology, there are 25 attempts for every successful suicide. I told myself that Laura likely had 21 more tries .

The evening of August 27, 2010, Laura told me she was going to go for a drive and spend some time writing in her journal. She did this frequently. This was a fairly normal activity for her. She would go for a drive to one of four or five places and would sit someplace and journal about her feelings and what was going on in her life. She would usually be gone for about an hour. She returned home about an hour later. We decided that we would go to the Minnesota State Fair the next morning.

We headed to the fair about 7 am where we started our day with a breakfast burrito at one of the fairground's restaurants. Then we headed to the animal barns, a favorite stop-off for us each year. We saw the cows and the back ends of the horses – they always face the horses head first into the stalls so all you see is their back end. We saw the chickens and the rabbits, goats and sheep, and finally we gaped at the largest sow in Minnesota that year. We spent the day visiting all of Laura's favorite places at the fair, which were many. We crammed a lot of walking and gazing into a short amount of time, but around 10:30 am as it started to get crowded and the temperature reached 89 degrees, we headed home. (We never could understand how some Minnesotans could go to the State Fair every day, no matter the weather.)

We came home and after doing a few chores, watched the Twins beat the Mariners. As we ate lunch, I thought about how this day felt so normal. Normal felt good. We enjoyed a pleasant dinner and settled back for a relaxing, normal evening. We basically just hung out together.

At about 7 pm, however, Laura said she wanted to go for another drive and do some more journaling. About an hour and a half after she left that evening, I began getting concerned.

I went to pick up the phone to call her when it rang. I heard Laura telling me goodbye. She had taken another overdose of pills and did not want me to worry about her. She would not tell me where she was. I called 9-1-1 and told the operator that Laura had a cell phone with her. They planned to locate her and call me back.

I immediately called Pastor Bob, and he dropped whatever he was doing and headed to my house. About 20 minutes later, the 9-1-1 operator called back and said they could not directly pinpoint her location because her cellphone was not GPS enabled. He did pinpoint the last cell tower from which Laura had made her call to me. This gave me a good idea where she was located. I informed the 9-1-1 operator that I thought I knew where she was and would go look for her. He asked me to call him back if I found her. I called Pastor Bob again and told him I was headed out to find Laura and where I was headed. "No, wait for me. I am about a minute away," he said. I saw Bob driving down the block as I walked out the door. We headed directly for the park below the University of Minnesota on the east bank of the Mississippi River.

As we pulled into the parking lot at the park, I saw Laura's car – I saw that she was not in it. "She's got to be down by the river someplace," I told Bob. As he and I ran toward the river, I called 9-1-1. Since I was now in the University of Minnesota area and had accessed a different emergency system, I had to explain what was going on as I ran. Bob ran ahead of me and ran straight to Laura, even though he never saw her until he was right on top of her. He felt her pulse and noted she was barely breathing. The police arrived within a minute of my phone call. The ambulance, however, took longer and had trouble finding the park.

They loaded Laura into the ambulance and drove her up the hill toward the University of Minnesota Hospital. I stood stunned and weeping, watching the ambulance drive away. The doctors in the Emergency Room pronounced her dead on arrival, though several spent time and effort trying to revive her, to no avail. The doctor noted the time of death as just before midnight on Saturday, August 28, 2010.

Laura's pain had ended. She now rested in the arms of her Lord and Savior Jesus Christ. When Laura confessed her faith in Jesus earlier in life, at that moment God fulfilled His promise to her of eternal life with Him. True, she committed suicide, but that did not cost her eternal life – Jesus' death and resurrection paid for it all. I look forward to the day when I can see her again as we walk together in Glory.

The loss of Laura devastated me, even though I was not totally surprised. Pastor Bob and I left the hospital for my home to pick up my dog, Teddy, and then drove to Bob's home where I would spend the night. "If I do not do something to help others in my situation, Laura would have died in vain", I said, reflecting on what had just happened and the months leading up to it. I had no idea what the something would be at the time, but over the many years that followed, God directed me toward several opportunities, including sharing my testimony in front of churches, developing a Bible study and video to help others help suicide survivors, and writing books on caring for a loved one suffering from mental illness, and now this one on surviving the suicide of a loved one. I look forward to what the next thing is that God will entrust me to do to help others like me.

As the days and months progressed following Laura's death, I started to have a lot of unanswered questions related to her suicide and my new life without her.

As I write this chapter it has been about seven years since Laura committed suicide, and over that time God has given me answers in part or in whole to the following questions:

Where is Laura now?

This is probably the most difficult question that anyone faces when they have a loved one who commits suicide. It is made more difficult because many Christians believe that suicide is an unforgivable sin. I disagree. I believe that the only unforgivable sin is the rejection of God's free gift of salvation through faith in Jesus Christ. In other words, the only unforgivable sin is the sin of unbelief. If this is not true, no one would know for sure whether they were saved or not saved at the end of their life. Suppose I am a believer but I committed a sin in which I have not asked for forgiveness and died without confessing it. Does this mean I would die in sin? If so, I would be judged guilty and sent to hell as opposed to heaven.

I believe that the Scriptures teach that once we have accepted Jesus as our personal Lord and Savior, all our sins are forgiven, past, present, and future. Therefore, our salvation does not depend upon whether I have asked for forgiveness for the last sin I commit before my death, but my salvation depends rather upon the promises of God.

God gave me a promise that when I believe and accept Jesus as my personal Lord and Savior my sins are forgiven. "There is therefore now no condemnation for those who are in Christ Jesus." (Romans 8:1)

Holding to this belief that God's promise of salvation is sure, I know that Laura today is in the arms of her Savior Jesus Christ in heaven.

On the other hand, I do believe that Laura's act of committing suicide was a sin. I do not know whether Laura asked God for forgiveness after she had taken the pills that caused her to die. We never had the chance for that discussion, as she lay unconscious when we found her. What I do know is that God is faithful to fulfill His promise-it is not because of Laura's faithfulness, but because of God's faithfulness, righteousness, and truthfulness.

My faith is built upon my belief that once a person accepts Jesus as his or her Lord and Savior, their salvation is secure – period. Salvation, if based on a sincere trust in Christ Jesus, cannot be lost. Many Christians call this eternal security. I have explained in some depth my basic belief in eternal security in an appendix to this book. If you do not believe as I do, I would encourage you to read the appendix and consider the argument I lay out.

How did Laura get to this point that suicide was the only viable option?

You have already read many of the details of our journey together. I can never be sure about the answers, but by piecing together some of what Laura told me, I have decided her story helps me – and you – understand. Laura's life story may shed some light on her desperation and feelings that ultimately led to her suicide.

Laura's Childhood

My telling of Laura's story depends entirely on what she shared with me. Some of the story she never shared. Laura was very secretive about her time alone all her life. However, the parts of her life I do know that occurred before we met, and what I learned during our time together is important related to her major clinical depression.

Laura was born in the Pasadena, California area to a loving father and mother. She had one older sister at the time of her birth, and several years later her parents had a son. This made Laura the middle child of three siblings. The family moved to Mukilteo, Washington when Laura was seven and remained there as she grew into adulthood. This had a profound effect on her.

Laura perceived that her parents loved her older sister and her younger brother more than her. She told a story about how her parents demonstrated this to her. Her brother, Donnie, got a tomahawk as a gift from someone. He proceeded to hack down some of his mom's flowers. Her parents blamed Laura because she was not watching Donnie. They did not get angry with her sister who was also at home during that time. Neither did she see them as angry with Donnie, the actual doer of the deed. This reinforced her belief that her parents loved her siblings more than they loved her.

From what I came to understand after seeing Laura's depression, I believe her parents as well suffered from depression. Their depression caused them to self-medicate with alcohol leaving them intoxicated virtually every night and all day on the weekends. Yet, despite the obvious evidence, both parents denied their depression and alcoholism.

Laura told me there was never any physical or sexual abuse in her family, and I have no reason to doubt that. However, I believe there was unintentional emotional abuse. This abuse occurred as a result of the continual state of her parents' intoxication. Laura said that even when she was successful at something, she never received her parents' encouragement or notice. When Laura felt happy and excited, her parents did not join in her joy. When Laura felt hurt or unhappy, when she cried, her parents showed no response. Through these repeated parental responses (or lack of response), Laura came to see that emotions did not matter – better not to display them, just keep them hidden.

Since emotions did not matter, Laura decided she would not have any. The reality of human beings, in contrast, is that God created us with emotions, and when we do not let them out we continue to store them up, stuffing them deeper into our soul. Eventually, however, emotions will surface, and often times in ways we cannot control or that cause us mental distress. When confronted by her deeply suppressed emotions, Laura presented with major clinical depression and borderline personality disorder.

In high school Laura showed some signs of depression early on, including low self-esteem and an eating disorder, but she received no help from anyone. Laura called herself a wallflower and pretty much lived as a loner, except for one girl friend named Sharon. To self-medicate her depression, she tried marijuana, drinking and smoking for a while. Laura also suffered from an eating disorder as a way to deal with her depression without professional help. Before I met her, she managed to get the eating disorder under control, and I had no inkling of it for many years. She used diet pills to keep herself thin. She ate very little. Yet it didn't occur to me that she suffered a disorder, only that she was thin, and I loved her. However, when she reverted to this behavior later in life, it frightened me.

Laura found and became active with Fish Net, a Christian teen group, while in high school – and this helped her greatly. At Fish Net she learned about God's love for all of us and for her. She accepted God's free gift of salvation and was born again. Her confession of faith, however, did not take away her bouts of depression. She continued to experience low self-esteem and thought less of herself than she should have. She did not see herself as God saw her, an individual of infinite value.

After graduating from high school, she chose not to go to college and "waste the money." She had a clear goal that did not require a college degree—a stay-at-home mom. In her mind the greatest calling God could give her would be that of being a wife and mother. As she saw it, there was nothing more important than raising children in a loving home and teaching them God's ways. So she found a job as a dental technician, making crowns. Tiring of being a crown-maker, she began looking for a job and hence, she came to my office. That is how we met.

At the time I owned a shoe store in Lynnwood, Washington. Two of my good friends who also knew Laura suggested that I hire her because I was looking for a salesperson. I didn't share my friends' enthusiasm for her as a salesperson – she did not have the bubbly personality one would expect of a sales person. However, my friends convinced me she could learn, and it would be good for her. Obviously, I am glad I listened to them. We met in March 1984, started dating in May, became engaged in September, and were married on February 9, 1985.

I saw Laura at work and outside of work with a group of mutual friends. Laura was nine years younger than me, and I was bothered by dating an employee, but God had a different idea.

Dealing with Childlessness

After several years of marriage, we remained childless. We were both disappointed, but Laura more so. All Laura had ever wanted to be when she grew up was to be a mom. Her decisions about going to school and having a career were predicated on her desire to be a mom. Her choice of jobs allowed her at some point in her life to stay home and raise children.

Laura and I went through many medical tests. Both of us had surgeries designed to increase our chances of a successful pregnancy. Laura also took some fertility medication, but it was to no avail. We were never able to get pregnant.

As we tried to face the reality of being childless, we looked into adoption. What we found was not hopeful. Private adoption was unaffordable. Adoption through government agencies in Washington State included some criteria that neither Laura nor I could agree to obey. In the early 1990s, we came to the conclusion that we would end up being childless. At the same time, we struggled to find a body of Christians with whom to associate, so we foundered trying to make peace with life without the help of others. We lost our enthusiasm for prayer, praying for meals but seldom anytime else.

Laura's reaction to going childless, in retrospect, was to be expected. She stuffed all her feelings about it deep inside. I believe this is when she began self-medicating her depression. I first learned of her problem with alcohol on August 19, 2002. I had no idea that she had started drinking back in the early 1990s. She hid her alcohol use from me for about 10 years.

During that time, it was not uncommon for us to have a glass of wine with dinner. I was unaware that when she went to bed, typically an hour before I did, she would continue to drink and consume a fairly large amount of brandy every night, from a bottle she hid under the bed.

The Death of my Father

About a year before doctors diagnosed Laura with major clinical depression, my dad died of colon cancer that had spread throughout his body, even to his brain. Laura had grown close to my dad, and she viewed him as a second father. In some ways she felt closer to him than her own dad. After my dad died she became more depressed.

When I learned of her problem with alcohol, it startled and disappointed me. It woke me up to the myriad of problems with which we dealt that eventually led to a diagnosis of severe Clinical Depression. We spent the next eight years struggling with Laura's newfound disease.

The Next 8 Years

During the next eight years, Laura ended up in a hospital or treatment facility 19 times, ranging in time from five days to three months. Cumulatively, Laura spent more than a full year in hospital or treatment facilities during that eight-year time frame. In addition to this inpatient time, on many occasions Laura ended up in an emergency room to care for wounds from cutting herself, and occasionally, remained hospitalized on a psychiatric hold.

During this eight-year period, Laura attempted suicide five times, with the fifth one successful. She transitioned from, or added to using alcohol to cutting to an eating disorder. Her psychologists changed her diagnosis to Clinical Depression with an underlying Borderline Personality Disorder. She enrolled in alcohol treatment programs three times – one outpatient and two inpatient, with the third one being successful. She enrolled in four eating disorder treatment programs, one outpatient and three inpatient programs; all were successful in the short term but none in the long term. In most cases she was fine while in treatment but reverted to old behaviors usually within a week of returning home or stopping the treatment.

I cannot remember how often her doctors changed her medications, as it was too many to remember. Often, after she had a new medication she would start to feel better, but because she believed she did not deserve to feel better she would stop taking her medication. All five of her suicide attempts occurred after she had stopped taking her medication.

Laura's Lack of Understanding

During these eight years I became acutely aware of Laura's struggles with many issues. She struggled from a low self-image. I believe she did not understand or accept that her image, just like all of ours, came from God. She failed to understand that God created her in His own image, and as such, saw her as having infinite value. She never understood the value that came from the spiritual and material gifts that God bestowed on her, and how God used those gifts to affect the lives of others. If only she could have heard, understood, and accepted what others saw in her, life might have been different.

Laura believed that God had cursed her; otherwise we would have had children. This multiplied her suffering. Any answers or rationale I tried to give her was rejected. God's Word makes it clear that He does not condemn individuals during this lifetime, but He does condemn for eternity everyone who does not trust in Jesus as their Savior. Paul wrote, "There is no condemnation for those who are in Christ Jesus." God may condemn a nation or a people group. This comes when that nation or people group wantonly rejects God and is hostile to Him. This form of condemnation does not come in our timing but only as God choses to inflict it.

Over several years with the support of other Christian friends, we were able to convince Laura that God did not curse her. Then she came to believe that God did not love her. This is patently wrong for all people. "For God so loved the world, that He gave His only Son, that whoever believes in Him should not perish but have eternal life. " (John 3:16) God does not say that He loves people who obey Him, but rather that He loves the world – that is all of us. There are several other passages that confirm God's love for the world, but there are specific passages dealing with God's love for those who believe in Jesus. Laura believed in Jesus. However, it took several years for her to accept the fact that God truly loved her.

"I understand that God loves me, but He does not like me as much as He loves others," she would say. She believed that success and God's blessings depended on how much He liked her. In a sense she was asking the question, why do bad things happen to good people? The only answer I had is because of sin – not personal sin, but original sin. This is the sin that led to God's curse on all creation about which we read in Genesis 3.

All of us experience bad things, if by this we mean things that we don't like or that hurt or cause our soul to be troubled. Some experiences are worse than others, and some people seem to suffer more than others, but the reason for this suffering is not necessarily because of our personal sin. John 9:1-3 tells the story of a blind man. "As he passed by, he saw a man blind from birth. [2] And His disciples asked Him, 'Rabbi, who sinned, this man or his parents, that he was born blind?' [3] Jesus answered, 'It was not that this man sinned, or his parents, but that the works of God might be displayed in him.'"

James wrote that bad things are allowed to happen to us so that we might get closer to God. "Count it all joy, my brothers, when you meet trials of various kinds, [3] for you know that the testing of your faith produces steadfastness. [4] And let steadfastness have its full effect, that you may be perfect and complete, lacking in nothing." (James 1:2-4) It is difficult for all of us to understand that when bad things happen to us, it might be to make us more perfect, complete and lacking in nothing.

I also want to make it clear that God does not cause bad things to happen to anyone but rather He allows them to happen for our own good. It says in James 1:13-15, "Let no one say when he is tempted, 'I am being tempted by God,' for God cannot be tempted with evil, and he Himself tempts no one. But each person is tempted when he is lured and enticed by his own desire. Then desire when it has conceived gives birth to sin, and sin when it is fully grown brings forth death."

So perhaps the better question for Laura to have asked was, because of her sinful nature, why are not more bad things happening to her? After all, as a sinner God is not obligated to do anything for us, but He has instead chosen to love us.

All of the beliefs so far were very difficult and played a huge role in Laura's mental health, but the most difficult belief that Laura had was that she believed that she was not worthy to feel better. As a result, every time she started to feel good, she would stop taking her medication. This would cause her to spiral down into a deeper depression. Some of the times either her doctors or I would figure it out and get her to take her medication again, but in five cases her deep depression would cause her to attempt suicide.

I believe ultimately that her belief that she did not deserve to feel better led to another wrong feeling that she had no hope. When a person gets to a point in their life that there is no hope, it leads to an understanding that they are no longer of any value to anyone. In fact, they come to the belief that everyone else would be better off without them. Because of this belief, Laura felt that it would be an act of love to me that she would take her life. Well, let me tell you that belief is wrong. I am not better off without Laura. In fact, there is a huge hole in my life. I will talk more about this hole later.

Laura's fateful decision

So, given the story above, Laura ultimately came to the conclusion that everything and everyone would be better off without her. She had lost all hope. She lost purpose for her life. She believed she was a burden to others, and therefore her family, friends and the world would be better off without her. To me this was a totally illogical decision but Bob Ricker, a former pastor of mine, once said, "Every decision a person makes is logical in their own mind." So, if you really think about it, even though Laura's decision was completely illogical to me, it was just the opposite for her.

Why did this happen?

I am not sure that I have a good answer for this as well. All I can understand is that ultimately all that I go through in my life is to give glory to God and that God's work might be seen through my life. See John 9:1-4.

I have also found that God uses everything in my life to make me perfect and complete, lacking in nothing, as it says in James 1:2-4, "Count it all joy, my brothers, when you meet trials of various kinds, ³for you know that the testing of your faith produces steadfastness. ⁴And let steadfastness have its full effect, that you may be perfect and complete, lacking in nothing." So if what I went through is to make me perfect and complete, I do not need the answer to this question. I just need the grace of God to help me to believe that it happened for my good.

God also reminded me that I am incapable of understanding His ways completely. Paul tells us in Romans 11:33, "Oh, the depth of the riches and wisdom and knowledge of God! How unsearchable are His judgments and how inscrutable His ways!" So I have come to the conclusion that if God wants to let me in on the complete answer, I will be willing to understand. However, if all I understand is what I understand today, I am good with that as well. After all, who am I to question God?

Is there anything I could have done to prevent Laura's suicide?

The answer to this often-asked question is "yes", but I would like to add a word into this question, which changed it for me to "no". The word I would like to add is "reasonably". See, when you change it to "reasonably done", then you take out all of the absurd things. I could have been with Laura 24/7/365 days a year which would have prevented the suicide. So when would I sleep? How would I have been able to provide financially for the family? How trapped would Laura have felt if I never left her side?

I have met several people who have lost a loved one to suicide. I have found this to be a guilt question in my life and theirs, and there is no place for it in my life or theirs. We are not responsible for the actions of others.

Where is God?

Sometimes I wonder what the answer to this question is and sometimes I am secure in the answer that is in God's Word. What I have found in God's Word is that He is with me. He was with me during Laura's illness. He was with me before I met Laura. He will be with me for all eternity. As it says in Hebrews 13:5, "Keep your life free from love of money, and be content with what you have, for He has said, "I will never leave You nor forsake You."

So as I continue my journey through the rest of my life here on earth, I must decide if I believe what the bible says or not. I find when I believe it I am better off. However, I struggle sometimes because my life did not turn out how I hoped it would when I was a teenager. I am not a dad. I am now a widower before the age of 60. I live a life alone in many ways. None of these things were part of my plan, but apparently, they were part of God's plan.

I thank God for His comfort. I thank Him for the comfort of my friends and family members that are still around me. I thank Him for the opportunity to minister to others

Why does God even care?

This is another question that is hard to understand the answer. Much like the question "why did this happen?", the answer must be accepted by faith in the Word of God. I know that I certainly do not deserve God's care and affection. But God chose in His infinite grace and mercy to have a relationship with me. He offers that same infinite grace and mercy to all. As one of the most known passages in scripture, John 3:16 tells us, "For God so loved the world, that He gave His only Son, that whoever believes in Him should not perish but have eternal life."

So, I do not care what the answer to this question really is. All I care is that He does. Honestly, if God did not care, I do not know where I would be today. I would not know where my hope would come from or my will to continue on with my life. Because God cares I know that I can face everything that will happen in my life.

That does not mean at times when I struggle believing God's Word that I question if God cares for me. It does mean that when I ground myself in His Word, I not only believe that God cares but I trust it. I can lean into His loving arms and be at peace.

Where is the Church?

What I found is that as a generalization the Church as a whole was absent. Most people would prefer not to talk about suicide. They also have a tendency to avoid a survivor. I believe that is because they do not know what to say. I believe this is very true because frankly, before Laura committed suicide, I would not have known what to say. So let me make some suggestions. Rather than telling someone only that you are sorry for their loss, you might want to ask him or her questions. Some good ones I found meaningful are:

- Is there anything specifically I can pray for you for this coming week?
- Is there anything I can do to help? If you ask them this, you must be willing to do what they ask. I know a couple who after the loss of their college age daughter responded to this question by asking, "Can you come over and feed our dogs and take them for a walk because we just do not have the energy to do that ourselves?"
- Is there any way that I can be an encouragement to you?

Bible verses and words of encouragement can be helpful, but make sure that your relationship with the person is such that your words will be well- received and not considered to be some sort of platitude. Because if someone who was not a close friend quoted me a Scripture verse, even though the verse may be true and applicable, I felt like they were being condescending and hurtful. I needed to find those verses myself and apply them to my situation.

There were several couples in my church that were friends that came around me and were present for me. An example is when I was in church the Sunday after Laura's suicide, I sat at the back of the church because I was not sure that I could make it through the service without starting to bawl. If that had occurred I wanted a fast way out. As I was sitting alone in the back and praying, I looked up and saw four couples coming back to me. They sat down next to me and one of them simply said, "We didn't want you to be alone." That was so amazingly helpful to me. So my encouragement to those in a church body and someone loses a loved one to suicide is to just be present. You really do not have to say much; your presence in a time of need speaks volumes.

To church leadership I would say one thing: Do not avoid a suicide survivor! Like me, they will probably see it as if you do not care. It played a role in my decision to change churches a little over a year after Laura's death. Again it is about presence and asking questions, not telling survivors something unless they ask. One question leadership might ask is if it would be helpful to come and talk about what is going on in the survivor's life.

When will my pain of loss go away?

I really would like an answer to this question because I am tired of having times in my life where I feel the loss of Laura. As I am writing this just a few days after my birthday and a few days before my eighth Christmas without Laura, I have been going through some times of pain. My pain is not as severe as it was the first year but it is still there.

I know that the ultimate answer is it will completely go away when I get to heaven, but I am not sure that it will ever completely go away as long as I am in my earthly body. Revelations 21:4 says "He will wipe away every tear from their eyes, and death shall be no more, neither shall there be mourning, nor crying, nor pain anymore, for the former things have passed away." I do know that God's grace is sufficient for me to deal with my pain. All I need to do is accept His grace. Sometimes that is easier said than done. 2 Corinthians 12:9 says, "My grace is sufficient for you, for my power is made perfect in weakness." So, I pray regularly that God helps me to accept His grace that He is offering to me.

What is God's plan for my life now?

I am not sure that this question is any different for me than it is for anyone else. I do not have a crystal ball. God has not revealed to me His complete plan for my life either. There is a big part of God's plan for me that is the same as it has always been.

I am to do all things for His Glory. 1 Corinthians 10:31 says, "So, whether you eat or drink, or whatever you do, do all to the glory of God." So, I strive to do what I believe God would have me do in my life with this in mind.

I am to make disciples of all nations. Matthew 28:19-20 says, "Go therefore and make disciples of all nations, baptizing them in the name of the Father and of the Son and of the Holy Spirit, [20] teaching them to observe all that I have commanded you. And behold, I am with you always, to the end of the age."

So right now, I believe God is calling me to do some things in my life. I believe that He has called me to help others who have lost loved ones to suicide. I am responding to His call in that area by writing this book and probably a second one, which will be a devotional. He has placed me in a church where we have started a group for suicide survivors. We meet twice a month for encouragement and prayer and the study of His Word.

I believe He has also called me to run a ministry called Engage – SDG. My ministry is creating Bible studies and videos to help Christians answer difficult questions. One of the questions I address is how to help a suicide survivor. This ministry is my way of making disciples.

Will I Ever get Used to Being Alone?

I do not know. It has been seven plus years since Laura committed suicide, and I am not used to it yet. I know that whether or not I ever get used to being alone, I am truly never alone because God is always with me. I need to truly work on being content with knowing that fact. I must take comfort in the fact that God is always there for me and always will be. I must learn to give my loneliness into His hands knowing and believing that He will take care of the situation.

How do I get over my Fears About New Relationships?

I must confess that this has been the most difficult part of my journey in many ways. I have what I would call an irrational fear. The fear I have is that I will meet someone, fall in love, remarry, and shortly after being remarried, I find that my new wife has a terminal illness that will cause me to be a caregiver again. I am not sure that I could do it again because the first time was hard enough.

I call this an irrational fear because I understand that God will provide me the grace I need to do what I need to do just as He did with Laura. I know this in my head, but I have not as of yet had it reach my heart. Maybe all I need for that to happen is for God to bring a woman in my life that will make the true difference. Maybe I will just finally be able to yield this fear over to God as I should and it will go away. I guess only time will tell.

Can I have a Relationship with a Woman that is not Romantic?

It seems to me that it is more difficult than it was when I was in high school and college. In part it is difficult and maybe even inappropriate to have a friendship relationship with someone who is married. There is always the appearance of the possibility of some sort of affair going on even if there is nothing happening.

In the case of single women, I have found it to be more difficult now than when I was young as well. First, there is difficulty in separating going out with a friend or a date. As I enjoy nice dinners, live theater, and things that seem like dates more than doing something with a friend, I do not want someone to get the wrong idea. Ultimately, however, if I were ever to have a romantic relationship with someone, I would want it to start out as a friendship and then evolve into a romantic relationship because of the closeness of our friendship.

What I have found so far is that there seems to be two types of women around my age: someone who is looking for a new husband because she has lost her past husband, and the other who has been single all her life and wants to remain single. Those who have been single all their life seem to be hesitant to have a platonic relationship with a man.

So at this point, the answer to the question is maybe. I am convinced that God will bring some women into my life where we can just be friends. It just has not yet happened, maybe because I am not ready and God knows it.

Can I Have Another Romantic Relationship?

Only time will tell. I am sure that it would be possible when the time is right and God has it in His plan for me. To this date I have not met anyone where I have a desire to have another romantic relationship. I will wait for the time patiently and be willing to have the answer be yes or no. I am convinced that God will provide me what I need no matter what the answer is to be.

What Happens to me as I get Older?

In some ways this is a fear that I have. I wonder since I have no spouse or children if I will end up dying alone; the prospect of that is not pleasant to me. However, I must remember that I am never alone because God said, "I will never leave you or forsake you." (Hebrews 13:5) So I do not truly know the answer but I must trust God as Proverbs 3:5-6 says,

> "Trust in the Lord with all your heart
> And do not lean on your own understanding.
> In all your ways acknowledge Him,
> And He will make your paths straight." (NASB)

As I continue my journey, I will endeavor to follow Proverbs 3:5-6. I will depend on God's grace to do this. I know at times I will fail, but I have a glorious God who will always forgive me.

Can I be at peace?

Much like joy, peace is a gift of the Holy Spirit so I can be at peace. As I struggle with being peaceful, I have found it helpful to meditate on John 14:27, "Peace I leave with you; my peace I give to you. Not as the world gives do I give to you. Let not your hearts be troubled, neither let them be afraid." I also find Philippians 4:7 to be helpful to meditate upon, "And the peace of God, which surpasses all understanding, will guard your hearts and your minds in Christ Jesus."

What a wonderful God I serve who chooses to grant me peace. I have decided to depend upon His grace and His promises so that I can live in peace no matter my circumstances. I am not always successful, but I am confident that I will have peace.

Can I ever have joy and rejoice and be thankful in Laura's death?

In 1 Thessalonians 5:16-18 it says, "Rejoice always, pray without ceasing, give thanks in all circumstances; for this is the will of God in Christ Jesus for you." More than seven years have passed since Laura's suicide, and I am certainly not in a place yet where I am rejoicing nor am I giving thanks in my circumstance.

Why would God want me to rejoice and be thankful that Laura is no longer with me? I ask myself. *What does it mean to rejoice and be thankful in all circumstances? It certainly cannot mean that I need to be happy about it, does it?*

Maybe the answer is because God says that I should rejoice and be thankful, therefore I must. I do not really like this answer because I am not a "have to" kind of believer; I prefer to be a "want to" kind of believer. Let me explain. In John 14:15 it says, "If you love me, you will keep my commandments." I used to believe it is a command to keep His commandments, but then I flipped my idea to think that maybe it is not a command but a promise. So, if it is a promise, then if I love Jesus more, I will be more obedient to His commands rather than the other way, which says if I obey His commands then I will love Jesus. Since Christianity is a faith-based religion, like no other, not a works religion like all others, it makes sense to me that by loving Jesus more, He will help me be more obedient.

So, it seems to make sense to me that if I look around at all the blessings in my life that God gave me, my attitude should be that of rejoicing and thanksgiving. In doing that, it will cause me to love God more and by doing that, I will become more obedient. Ultimately my hope is that by loving Jesus more, I will get to a point in my life where I can truly rejoice and be thankful in my circumstances without Laura.

My understanding of the concept of rejoicing and being thankful is that it is not necessarily being happy. It is more of an attitude of contentment. It is an understanding that "Every good gift and every perfect gift is from above, coming down from the Father of lights, with whom there is no variation or shadow due to change." (James 1:17) But we are talking about something that was evil happening to me, so does it fall into the same realm? Well, Job said to his wife, "You speak as one of the foolish women speaks. Shall we indeed accept good from God and not accept adversity?" In all this Job did not sin with his lips." (Job 2:10) (NASB) It seems that Job believed that he should rejoice and be thankful despite whether he received good or evil

There are some things that I can rejoice and be thankful in regarding Laura's suicide. I rejoice and am thankful that Laura is no longer suffering as she was on earth. I rejoice and am thankful that Laura is with Jesus her Savior and Lord. I rejoice and am thankful that Laura is waiting for me to join her with Jesus. I rejoice and am thankful that I have an enduring hope in spite of Laura's suicide. I rejoice and am thankful that God has never forsaken me during this long and difficult journey.

Almost seven and a half years after Laura's suicide, I believe I have figured out what it means to rejoice and be thankful in Laura's suicide. When I was on a prayer retreat with the men of my church, the Holy Spirit wanted me to figure this out. He directed me to James 1:2-4 which says, "Count it all joy, my brothers, when you meet trials of various kinds, for you know that the testing of your faith produces steadfastness. And let steadfastness have its full effect, that you may be perfect and complete, lacking in nothing." Now this is a passage that I have studied twice since Laura's death, but until then it had not sunk into my head nor my heart. Looking at this passage, I finally understood that Laura's death was a trial that was there to produces steadfastness in me. If I would let the Holy Spirit allow this steadfastness to have its full effect, then I would become more perfect and lack in nothing. So now understanding this and looking at Laura's death, I am more able to rejoice and be thankful. I am still not fully there, but I know that if I believe God's Word in this area, I will make it there completely.

I know that God will continue His work in me until I am complete and lacking in nothing. I am absolutely thankful for His grace and abundant love. Because of these truths, I am convinced that someday I will be able to completely rejoice and be thankful in my circumstances without Laura. When that will be, I do not know, but God does, and He will always lead me to that place.

Does knowing Jesus make all of the difference?

Absolutely! I truly do not know how I could have endured without my faith and trust in Jesus. If you do not know Jesus as I do, then please read the next chapter and find out why you need to know Him and how you can do it.

If you are on a similar journey as I am and was, then please do not do it alone. Do not do it without Jesus. Do not do it without the help of the Body of Christ, His Church.

CHAPTER 14

Hope is in God Alone

It is wonderful how God uses music to touch the soul and certain songs to minister to one's spirit at difficult times. As I wrote this book, I kept hearing this song by Plumb on the radio as I drove to different places. It really spoke to me and described my feelings about the trials Laura and I experienced.

Need You Now (How Many Times)
By Plumb

Well, everybody's got a story to tell
And everybody's got a wound to be healed
I want to believe there's beauty here
'Cause oh, I get so tired of holding on
I can't let go, I can't move on
I want to believe there's meaning here

How many times have You heard me cry out
"God please take this"?
How many times have You given me strength to
Just keep breathing?
Oh I need You
God, I need You now.

Jim Hansen

Standing on a road I didn't plan
Wondering how I got to where I am
I'm trying to hear that still small voice
I'm trying to hear above the noise

How many times have You heard me cry out
"God please take this"?
How many times have You given me strength to
Just keep breathing?
Oh I need You
God, I need You now.

Though I walk,
Though I walk through the shadows
And I, I am so afraid
Please stay, please stay right beside me
With every single step I take

How many times have You heard me cry out?
And how many times have You given me strength?

How many times have You heard me cry out
"God please take this"?
How many times have You given me strength to
Just keep breathing?
Oh I need You
God, I need You now.

I need You now
Oh I need You
God, I need You now.
I need You now
I need You now[9]

---

[9] Need you Now (How Many Times) Writers credits Tiffany Arbuckle Lee, Christa Wells, Luke Sheets, © 2012 Curb Congregation Songs, Shoecrazy Publishing, Kiss Me Not Publishing (all admin by Curb Congregation Songs / Platy Songs Used by permission.

Plumb's song is an expression of the deep desire of the heart to know God and be known by Him. I would be remiss if I did not tell you God's story for you and for me.

On September 27, 1967, during a Lutheran confirmation class, my teacher shared God's plan for each of us to have eternal life. That night I accepted Jesus as my personal Lord and Savior.

As you have been reading, my life has been far from perfect. I hope that at least you have seen how God remained faithful and shed His love on Laura and me all during our struggles and during the good times.

Perhaps you do not have the kind of relationship with God that I describe in this book, and you do not feel like you could cry out to God as we did.

God Created Humans to Be in a Relationship with Him

At the beginning of time, God make it plain that He desired a relationship with humans.

"Then God said, "Let us make man in our image, after our likeness. And let them have dominion over the fish of the sea and over the birds of the heavens and over the livestock and over all the earth and over every creeping thing that creeps on the earth."

So God created man in His own image, in the image of God He created him; male and female he created them." (Genesis 1:26-27)

God designed a loving relationship with humans for Himself. "Hear, O Israel! The Lord is our God, the Lord is one! You shall love the Lord your God with all your heart and with all your soul and with all your might." (Deuteronomy 6:4-5) (NASB)

God intended that humans would glorify Him. "So, whether you eat or drink, or whatever you do, do all to the glory of God." (1 Corinthians 10:31) God wants us to enjoy Him forever.

God promised us eternal life, but more than that, an abundant life. "I came that they may have life and have it abundantly." (John 10:10b)

So if God wants us to glorify Him and have eternal life, and He wants us to have an abundant life, what is it that keeps us from experiencing what God wants for us?

Our Personal Sin Has Separated Us from a Relationship with God.

Let me ask you a few questions, questions I have asked myself. Have you ever lied? Have you ever taken anything from work like a piece of paper, a paperclip, a pen or something small? Have you ever looked at another person and had lustful thoughts? Have you ever hated someone so much you wanted them to die? I know I have.

Jesus said that if you look at someone with a lustful eye, you have committed adultery with that person. He said that if you hated someone, you have committed murder.

> You have heard that the ancients were told, "You shall not commit murder" and "Whoever commits murder shall be liable to the court." But I say to you that everyone who is angry with his brother shall be guilty before the court; and whoever says to his brother, "You good-for-nothing," shall be guilty before the supreme court; and whoever says, "You fool," shall be guilty *enough to go* into the fiery hell.
>
> You have heard that it was said, "You shall not commit adultery"; but I say to you that everyone who looks at a woman with lust for her has already committed adultery with her in his heart. (Matthew 5:21-22, 27-28) (NASB)

Did you answer "yes" to any or all the questions I asked above? I had to answer yes. Then according to Jesus, like me, you are a liar, adulterer, and murdering thief.

Because God is Holy and cannot tolerate the presence of sin, He drove Adam and Eve, as sinners, from His presence. They had tried to hide from Him, but God saw them, just as He sees us. We are all sinners. All of us have sinned and are separated from God. "…for all have sinned and fall short of the glory of God" (Romans 3:23)

> "Behold, the Lord's hand is not shortened, that it cannot save,
> or His ear dull, that it cannot hear;
> but your iniquities have made a separation
> between you and your God,

and your sins have hidden His face from you
so that He does not hear." (Isaiah 59:1-2)

He is a God of justice and as such, has determined a penalty for our sins. That penalty is death. "For the wages of sin is death." (Romans 6:23a)

Sin Cannot be Removed by Our Good Works

Many people hope to earn a relationship with God through their own efforts and believe God will bless them for it. But **sin cannot be removed by our good works.** No matter how hard we try, or the number of good works we do, these cannot blot out our sins.

Since God is holy and man is sinful and separated from Him, the natural thing is to try to reach God through human efforts (good works, religion, philosophy, etc.).

What about you? How have you tried to reach God? God, through the prophet Isaiah, explained that our works fall short of God's holiness and perfection. "We have all become like one who is unclean, and all our righteous deeds are like a polluted garment." (Isaiah 64:6)

If we cannot settle our sin accounts with God by doing good works, then what hope do we have? "For by grace you have been saved through faith. And this is not your own doing; it is the gift of God, not a result of works, so that no one may boast." (Ephesians 2:8-9)

Paying the Price of Our Sins Jesus Died on the Cross and Rose Again

There is only one way to bridge the gap between God and man – the death and resurrection of Jesus Christ. **Jesus paid the price for our sins when He died and rose again to give us eternal life with God.**

God had a plan to reunite mankind with Him. He fulfilled His plan when He sent His Only Son, Jesus, to live a perfect life and then to take our sins upon Himself and die on a cross. Satan thought he had won – the Son of God had died. Then Jesus rose from the grave, defeating sin and death.

Who is Jesus? Jesus said He is God in human flesh. "I and the Father are one." (John 10:30)

Jesus died in our place. "…but God shows His love for us in that while we were still sinners, Christ died for us." (Romans 5:8)

Jesus rose from the dead. "For I delivered to you as of first importance what I also received: that Christ died for our sins in accordance with the Scriptures, that He was buried, that He was raised on the third day in accordance with the Scriptures…" (1 Corinthians 15:3-4)

Jesus proclaimed that He was the only way to God, the Father. "Jesus said to him, 'I am the way, and the truth, and the life. No one comes to the Father except through me.'" (John 14:6)

Everyone Who Trusts in Jesus Alone has Eternal Life

Yet it is not enough to know, to have head-knowledge, of the facts about Jesus. God's requirement is that **everyone who trusts in Jesus alone has eternal life.**

Through His death on the cross and resurrection, Jesus paid the price for the sins of everyone who had lived, was alive, and who would live in the future – this includes you and me. God, therefore, offered us eternal life as we trust the reality that Jesus paid the price for our sin.

How does one trust Jesus to receive this gift of eternal life? We receive Jesus by faith trusting in Him alone for salvation.

"…because, if you confess with your mouth that Jesus is Lord and believe in your heart that God raised Him from the dead, you will be saved. For with the heart one believes and is justified, and with the mouth one confesses and is saved." (Romans 10:9-10)

We each receive Jesus by personal invitation. "Behold, I stand at the door and knock. If anyone hears my voice and opens the door, I will come in to him and eat with him, and he with Me." (Revelation 3:20) "But to all who did receive Him, who believed in His name, He gave the right to become children of God…" (John 1:12)

Many years ago, God spoke to Laura and me about His free gift of salvation. Both of us trusted Jesus' gift and as a result, God has given us eternal life. You, too, can accept this free gift. "For all who call on the name of the Lord will be saved." (Romans 10:13)

So if you are ready to accept God's free gift of eternal life, then I invite you to pray from your heart this simple prayer – or one like it in your own words. "Lord Jesus, I need You. I realize that I am a sinner and cannot save myself. I need Your forgiveness. I believe You are the Son of God and that You died on the cross for my sins and rose from the dead. I repent from my sins and trust in You as my personal Savior and Lord. Take control of my life and help me to follow You in obedience. In Jesus' name I pray. Amen!"

Life with Jesus Begins Now and Lasts Forever

Once you have prayed a prayer like the one above, **your life with Jesus begins immediately and lasts forever.** Trust God to keep His promise – because He will.

Put your faith in His Word and not in your feelings. "Truly, truly, I say to you, whoever hears my word and believes Him who sent me has eternal life. He does not come into judgment, but has passed from death to life." (John 5:24)

"And the testimony is this, that God has given us eternal life, and this life is in His Son. He who has the Son has the life; he who does not have the Son of God does not have the life.

These things I have written to you who believe in the name of the Son of God, so that you may know that you have eternal life." (1 John 5:11-13) (NASB)

I know that my new life with God started the moment I accepted Jesus' gift of eternal life, and it will last forever. The reason that I can be confident of the claims I have made in this book rests on my faith in God and trust in Jesus Christ. This truth gives me hope that I can, in fact, live the abundant life that Jesus promised in John 10:10.

As I have grown older, I am learning that my relationship with God can be better tomorrow than it is today and was yesterday. The more I learn about Jesus Christ, the surer I am of His promises.

Each day of my journey with Laura, I knew that no matter what happened that day or the next, our salvation was certain in Jesus Christ. So, will yours be, if you have trusted Him as we did.

> "The Lord bless you, and keep you;
> The Lord make His face shine on you,
> And be gracious to you;
> The Lord lift up His countenance on you,
> And give you peace." (Numbers 6:24-26) (NASB)

SOLI DEO GLORIA

APPENDIX

Eternal Security Argument

Where is Laura Now

This is probably the most difficult question that anyone faces when they have a loved one who commits suicide. It is difficult because there are many Christians who believe that suicide is an unforgivable sin – I do not agree. I believe that the only unforgivable sin is the rejection of God's free gift of salvation through faith in Jesus Christ. In other words, the only unforgivable sin is the sin of unbelief.

In part I believe this to be true because otherwise no one would truly know whether they were saved when they faced death. I ask this question: If I committed a sin for which I had not asked for forgiveness before I die, would that mean that I would die in sin? If I died in unforgiven sin, would I then go to hell as opposed to heaven?

I strongly believe that Scripture teaches us that once we have accepted Jesus as our personal Lord and Savior, our sins are forgiven – past, present, and future. So therefore, our salvation does not depend upon whether we have asked for forgiveness for the last sin we commit before death but rather upon the promises of God. God gave us a promise that when we believe and accept Jesus as our personal Lord and Savior, our sins are forgiven. As it says in Romans 8:1, "There is therefore now no condemnation for those who are in Christ Jesus."

So, based upon this belief, I know that Laura is in the arms of her Savior Jesus Christ in heaven.

I do believe that Laura's act of suicide was a sin. I also do not know if Laura asked God for forgiveness after she took the pills that caused her to die.

I do know this. It is not because of Laura's faithfulness to God but because of God's faithfulness to her, along with the righteousness He imparts through Jesus Christ, and the truthfulness of His word – these are the reasons I can trust God that Laura is with Him.

Part of what leads me to this conclusion is my belief that once you accept Jesus as your Lord and Savior you are saved, period. You cannot lose your salvation. This is what many Christians call eternal security. If you have the same basic belief in eternal security that I do, you could probably move onto the next chapter, because the rest of this chapter I will spend discussing the concept of eternal security. This will not be a complete discussion that can be found in the Appendix; rather this is a synopsis of the discussion in order to reduce the length of this chapter. If you do not believe as I do, I would encourage you to read the argument which I set forth and defend by the Word of God.

I am Eternally Secure in My Salvation

These scriptural passages support the idea that we are eternally secure in our salvation because God keeps us secure. To me this makes perfect sense since scripture teaches that we can do nothing to earn our salvation – then how can we do anything to lose our salvation?

John 6:37 "All that the Father gives me will come to me, and whoever comes to me I will never cast out."

So according to John, if I come to Jesus in belief that includes trusting Him unto salvation, He will never drive me away. God is not going to cast me out once I believe.

John 6:37-39 "All that the Father gives me will come to me, and whoever comes to me I will never cast out. For I have come down from heaven, not to do my own will but the will of Him who sent me. And this is the will of Him who sent me, that I should lose nothing of all that He has given me, but raise it up on the last day."

In verse 37, Jesus promised that "whoever" comes to Him He will never drive away. In verse 38 He says He came to do the will of the father. According to verse 39 He says the Father's will is that He "shall lose none of all that He has given Me." This means us, as Christians. God has given us who believe to Christ, and He will not lose us.

John 10:27-29 "My sheep hear my voice, and I know them, and they follow me. I give them eternal life, and they will never perish, and no one will snatch them out of my hand. My Father, who has given them to me, is greater than all, and no one is able to snatch them out of the Father's hand."

Here Jesus says that as a Christian, God has given us to Jesus and that we are in the Father's hand. Therefore, no one can snatch us from the Father's hands, including us because we are someone.

Matthew 9:17 "Neither is new wine put into old wineskins. If it is, the skins burst, and the wine is spilled and the skins are destroyed. But new wine is put into fresh wineskins, and so both are preserved."

Jesus has made us new, a new creation – a new wine skin. God fills this new wine skin with the Holy Spirit, like new wine. Both are preserved!

Romans 4:20-21 "No unbelief made Him waver concerning the promise of God, but He grew strong in His faith as He gave glory to God, fully convinced that God was able to do what He had promised."

The eternal security debate hinges on this simple belief – is God faithful to do what He has promised? Over and over, God promises us our eternal inheritance (Eph. 1:13-14).

Romans 14:4 "Who are you to pass judgment on the servant of another? It is before his own master that he stands or falls. And he will be upheld, for the Lord is able to make him stand."

Our master is the Lord. We are His servants. Others cannot judge another's servant, only the Master! And our Master is "able to make him stand." Many will claim that Christians must stand firm until the end to prove they are saved (persevere), but God says it is HE who is able to make us stand! He is the one who keeps us to the end (1 Corinthians 1:8). That doesn't mean we won't stumble along the way. It does not mean that for periods of time in our lives we will not bear fruit, yet there will be periods of time in which we will bear much fruit.

1 Corinthians 1:8 "who (GOD) will sustain you to the end, guiltless in the day of our Lord Jesus Christ."

We will be blameless on the day of our Lord. He does this, not us. It is by His grace, not our works, so we cannot boast (Ephesians 2:9).

2 Corinthians 1:21-22 "And it is God who establishes us with you in Christ, and has anointed us, and who has also put His seal on us and given us His Spirit in our hearts as a guarantee."

How much more clearly can it be stated? It is God, not us, that empowers us to stand firm in Christ. It has nothing to do with what we do or don't do. It is God who has set His "seal of ownership" on us as believers.

We do not own God to be cast aside at our choosing (i.e. falling from salvation). It is God who owns us. And He has placed His Spirit in our hearts as a deposit, a sign of that ownership, "guaranteeing what is to come." If this were a "financial" transaction, if God would not fulfill His promise of "what is to come" (my eternal salvation), He would lose His deposit – the Holy Spirit and the blood of Jesus Christ! That cannot happen. If we have the Holy Spirit (by faith in Christ), God's deposit in us guarantees what is to come. We are secure in our salvation because God has promised it.

2 Corinthians 1:10 "He delivered us from such a deadly peril, and He will deliver us. On Him we have set our hope that He will deliver us again."

Paul had experienced "great pressure, beyond his ability to endure" (v8). But God delivered Him. The promise here, however, is even greater than continued deliverance from physical hardship. There is herein a sense of continued deliverance, beyond the physical to the eternal.

2 Corinthians 4:7-9 "But we have this treasure in jars of clay, to show that the surpassing power belongs to God and not to us. We are afflicted in every way, but not crushed; perplexed, but not driven to despair; persecuted, but not forsaken; struck down, but not destroyed;"

Trials will come upon us as Christians – that much is sure. But even though we are hard-pressed, perplexed, persecuted and struck down, we are NOT crushed, not in despair, abandoned, or destroyed. We are preserved (Matt 9:17) not from physical pain or death, but kept from the second death (Rev 20:6) – the destruction of the ungodly. (2 Pet 3:7)

Galatians 3:1-3 "O foolish Galatians! Who has bewitched you? It was before your eyes that Jesus Christ was publicly portrayed as crucified. Let me ask you only this: Did you receive the Spirit by works of the law or by hearing with faith? Are you so foolish? Having begun by the Spirit, are you now being perfected by the flesh?"

True Christians don't argue about how we are saved – we agree it is by grace through faith. Salvation is not of ourselves, lest no one should boast! We cannot work to gain our salvation. Yet many want to insist that we have to work to *keep* our salvation. Nonsense! We are saved by grace and we are kept saved by grace! Paul condemns the Galatians for trying human effort to keep saved after being saved by grace through faith.

Ephesians 1:13-14 "In Him you also, when you heard the word of truth, the gospel of your salvation, and believed in Him, were sealed with the promised Holy Spirit, who is the guarantee of our inheritance until we acquire possession of it, to the praise of His glory."

As a believer, we are "God's possessions." He will not let us go. He owns us because He bought us with the precious blood of Christ. (1 Peter 1:19) The Holy Spirit who guarantees our inheritance, which is eternal life with God, seals us.

Philippians 1:6 *"For I am* confident of this very thing, that He who began a good work in you will perfect it until the day of Christ Jesus." (NASB)

We can be confident in our security in Christ. He has begun "a good work" in us and will finish the job! It will be finished on the day of Christ Jesus, a reference to the rapture when we will be glorified.

Philippians 3:12 "Not that I have already obtained this or am already perfect, but I press on to make it my own, because Christ Jesus has made me His own."

John 10:28-29 says we are in Christ's and God's hand and no one can take us out. Here's why: Christ has taken hold of us! It is not we who are required to hold on to Him; it is He who holds on to us! So how can we take ourselves away from Jesus? We cannot because we are not stronger than Jesus.

2 Timothy 1:12 "I thank Him who has given me strength, Christ Jesus our Lord, because He judged me faithful, appointing me to His service,"

God guards what is entrusted to Him. What is that? Our very life, our eternal life and not just under certain circumstances, but "until that day"... probably the rapture or at the Judgment Seat of Christ.

2 Timothy 2:11-13 "The saying is trustworthy, for:

If we have died with Him, we will also live with Him;

^{12}if we endure, we will also reign with Him;

if we deny Him, He also will deny us;

^{13}if we are faithless, He remains faithful—"

Our old self is dead. We have been crucified with Christ (Gal 2:20). Christ died and yet lives forever. So too shall we if we have placed our trust in Him. Some may say, "but I have to endure" (verse12), then I shall reign with Him. But God is the One who makes me stand (Romans 14:4). He is able to guard what is entrusted to Him (2 Tim 1:12). And even with our faith, great or small, He remains faithful. He cannot deny Himself because He is in us!

Hebrews 7:24-25 "...but He holds His priesthood permanently, because He continues forever. Consequently, He is able to save to the uttermost those who draw near to God through Him, since He always lives to make intercession for them."

As long as He intercedes for us we are saved. And as long as Jesus lives, He intercedes for us. And Jesus lives forever! So, we are saved forever. In a sense, our security in salvation IS conditional - conditional on us trusting the high priest to continually intercede for us before God, yet His advocacy for us is not conditional on us – He will intercede for us. Thank God our High Priest is eternal!

1 Peter 1:3-5 "Blessed be the God and Father of our Lord Jesus Christ, who according to His great mercy has caused us to be born again to a living hope through the resurrection of Jesus Christ from the dead, to *obtain* an inheritance *which is* imperishable and undefiled and will not fade away, reserved in heaven for you, who are protected by the power of God through faith for a salvation ready to be revealed in the last time.'(NASB)

Our eternal inheritance is kept for us in heaven where it can never perish! What on earth can change our inheritance, our new birthright? Nothing. We are "shielded" by God's power, not our own. It is God who keeps our inheritance, not us. How can anyone lose his or her salvation if it is God who keeps it? The answer is they cannot.

1 Peter 1:18-19 "…knowing that you were not redeemed with perishable things like silver or gold from your futile way of life inherited from your forefathers, but with precious blood, as of a lamb unblemished and spotless, *the blood* of Christ." (NASB)

God has bought us with the price of His Son's life, His blood. Therefore, we are redeemed! Therefore, our redemption cannot perish as it is based on the full, imperishable payment of the blood of Christ.

Jude 1 "Jude, a servant of Jesus Christ and brother of James,

To those who are called, beloved in God the Father and kept for Jesus Christ:"

God keeps us "for Jesus Christ."

Jude 24-25 "Now to Him who is able to keep you from stumbling and to present you faultless before the presence of His glory with exceeding joy, to God our Savior, Who alone is wise, be glory and majesty, dominion and power, both now and forever. Amen."

Jesus Christ will present us who believe in Him as faultless. That means, without the kind of fault that would separate us from God. This is a sure belief, one from which nothing we can do will separate us from God. Jesus has done it all for us.

Based on His Grace

The Scriptures are also clear that our salvation comes ONLY because of the grace of God. It does not come from anything that we do. We did not become saved because we worked at it and succeeded.

Ephesians 2:8-9 "For by grace you have been saved through faith. And this is not your own doing; it is the gift of God, not a result of works, so that no one may boast. For we are His workmanship, created in Christ Jesus for good works, which God prepared beforehand, that we should walk in them."

We are saved through faith, not by works. It is not from ourselves. And if we are saved by the grace of God only, there is nothing we can do to undo it. Works didn't save us and works can't "un-save" us.

Grace is a free gift from God for those who believe on Jesus Christ for salvation. It is based on what Jesus has done for us, not on what we have done or haven't done. We have passed from spiritual death to spiritual life, a new life in Christ Jesus. All that we are now is through the grace of God.

We are kept secure, not by what we do, but by what Christ has already done for us. By God's power, we are thus secure in Christ forever.

If we were responsible for keeping our salvation, then we would have something to boast about. We are not and therefore, we do not!

1 Corinthians 1:4 "I give thanks to my God always for you because of the grace of God that was given you in Christ Jesus,"

Paul is being a little sarcastic here. Even though the Corinthians weren't acting much like Christians, God's grace is still with them through Christ Jesus. There is nothing we can do to lose it.

Romans 6:14-18

> "For sin shall not be master over you, for you are not under law but under grace.
>
> What then? Shall we sin because we are not under law but under grace? May it never be! Do you not know that when you present yourselves to someone *as* slaves for obedience, you are slaves of the one whom you obey, either of sin resulting in death, or of obedience resulting in righteousness? But thanks be to God that though you were slaves of sin, you became obedient from the heart to that form of teaching to which you were committed,

and having been freed from sin, you became slaves of righteousness. (NASB)

As believers, we are under grace, a grace that comes from God, not ourselves. Under the law, everyone is required to follow the law, but under grace, the only requirement is to accept Jesus Christ. After that, we have "been set free from sin."

Titus 3:47

But when the kindness of God our Savior and *His* love for mankind appeared, He saved us, not on the basis of deeds which we have done in righteousness, but according to His mercy, by the washing of regeneration and renewing by the Holy Spirit, whom He poured out upon us richly through Jesus Christ our Savior, so that being justified by His grace we would be made heirs according to *the* hope of eternal life. (NASB)

God saved us. We did not do it. This is because of His mercy and grace. We are now heirs having the "hope" of eternal life. But this is not an uncertain hope like we use the word today; it is a hope of full assurance that it is in God's hands, not ours. (see Hebrews 11:1)

Romans 5:1-2 "Therefore, since we have been justified by faith, we have peace with God through our Lord Jesus Christ. Through Him we have also obtained access by faith into this grace in which we stand, and we rejoice in hope of the glory of God."

According to Paul, we have been justified, we have peace with God and have "gained access" into this "grace in which we now stand" by faith. This grace in which we stand is through "our Lord Jesus Christ." It is not because of us.

We are His Possessions

Another reason to believe that our eternal life is secure is because we are God's possession. He owns all that we are. Just like any other possession, the owner makes the decision as to what will happen to it. In this case, God has promised us eternal life based on our belief in the atoning death and resurrection of the Lord Jesus Christ. Christ bought us with His blood. God owns us.

Romans 14:8 "For if we live, we live to the Lord, and if we die, we die to the Lord. So then, whether we live or whether we die, we are the Lord's."

To me, the whole eternal security debate is silly. I belong to the Lord. I am now His. I am His possession. I am His bondservant. Dead or alive, I belong to Him. He decides what happens to His possessions, not me! It's out of our hands—thank God!!!

Ephesians 1:13-14 "In Him you also, when you heard the word of truth, the gospel of your salvation, and believed in Him, were sealed with the promised Holy Spirit, who is the guarantee of our inheritance until we acquire possession of it, to the praise of His glory."

This passage was used above under "God Keeps Us," but is repeated here to emphasize that we no longer belong to ourselves, but we belong to Him. What happens to us is up to Him.

2 Corinthians 1:21-22 "And it is God who establishes us with you in Christ, and has anointed us, and who has also put His seal on us and given us His Spirit in our hearts as a guarantee."

This passage is also listed under "Our Future is Guaranteed," but here God's ownership of us is emphasized. Notice that the promise of our guaranteed future is linked to His ownership of us. We are His!

1 Corinthians 7:23 "You were bought with a price; do not become bondservants of men."

Both here and 1 Cor. 6:20, Paul says that we were "bought with a price." That price was the blood of Christ (1 Pet 1:19). We are His! Bought and paid for!

1 Corinthians 6:19-20 "Or do you not know that your body is temple of the Holy Spirit who is in you, whom you have from God, and that you are not your own? For you have been bought with a price: therefore glorify God in your body." (NASB)

Again, we have been bought and paid for by God. He now has the sole legal authority to decide what happens to His rightful possessions (us). And He has promised that we will inherit eternity! (Rev 21:7)

Our Name is Written in His Book

Throughout Scripture there are references to the Book of Life. The question one must ask is when is a name written in the Book of Life? Does God write it in pencil or in the shed blood of our Lord Jesus Christ? The ink is Jesus' shed blood and it cannot be erased.

Philippians 4:3 "Yes, I ask you also, true companion, help these women, who have labored side by side with me in the gospel together with Clement and the rest of my fellow workers, whose names are in the Book of Life."

Clearly God writes the Christian's name in the Book of Life, also called the "Lamb's Book of Life" (Rev 21:27). This is a very important book, kept in heaven (Luke 10:20), and is the record of who will be allowed to enter into a heavenly eternity–the New Jerusalem! If my name is in the book, I am in. If not, I am thrown into the lake of fire. (Rev 20:15)

Revelation 3:5 "The one who conquers will be clothed thus in white garments, and I will never blot his name out of the Book of Life. I will confess His name before my Father and before His angels."

When we are saved our name is written in the Lamb's Book of Life. But can a name ever be removed from the book? God clearly says no! Remember, he who conquers is anyone who has believed Jesus is the Son of God (1 John 5:5) through faith.

Revelation 21:27 "But nothing unclean will ever enter it, nor anyone who does what is detestable or false, but only those who are written in the Lamb's Book of Life."

So, if our name is written in the Lamb's Book of Life, we WILL enter the New Jerusalem for Christ's blood has made us pure!

Participants of a New Covenant

A God-given covenant is eternal. It never ends, and it is always sure. God never breaks a covenant. Covenants do not depend on our behavior or faithfulness, but they are dependent upon God's faithfulness.

Hebrews 7:22 "This makes Jesus the guarantor of a better covenant."

With His broken body and shed blood, Christ made a new covenant (Luke 22:20). Christ is the mediator of this new covenant (2 Cor. 3:6, Heb. 12:24). We participate in this new covenant through faith in Christ who guarantees it! Like God's original covenants, this new covenant can never be broken. It is dependent on who He is, not who we are or what we have done.

Hebrews 13:5 "Keep your life free from love of money, and be content with what you have, for He has said, 'I will never leave you nor forsake you.'"

This promise was first made to Israel, whom God will save when Christ returns, and they will possess the land forever. Here the promise is repeated for the sake of individual Christians who already participate in the new covenant (which Israel will participate in at the second coming; Jer. 31:31, Heb. 8:8). Since we are participants in the new covenant we are in, we cannot break it because the covenant is based on God's faithfulness, not ours.

2 Corinthians 3:5-8 "Not that we are adequate in ourselves to consider anything as *coming* from ourselves, but our adequacy is from God, who also made us adequate *as* servants of a new covenant, not of the letter but of the Spirit; for the letter kills, but the Spirit gives life.

But if the ministry of death, in letters engraved on stones, came with glory, so that the sons of Israel could not look intently at the face of Moses because of the glory of his face, fading *as* it was, how will the ministry of the Spirit fail to be even more with glory?"

We are as ministers of this new covenant and participate in it through the Spirit, which is given to those who believe. The new covenant replaces the old (Mosaic covenant), which no one could keep. By the Holy Spirit, however, we are competent ministers of the new covenant; He has made us competent! We do not do it. He does it.

In Full Assurance of Faith

Ephesians 2:18 "For by grace you have been saved through faith. And this is not your own doing; it is the gift of God."

We have access to the Father by the Spirit whom God has given us as a deposit guaranteeing what is to come (Eph. 1:13). We have been sealed by the Spirit for the day of redemption (Eph. 4:10), and we will be with Him forever (John 14:15). This means as believers, we shall always have "access" to the Father.

Ephesians 3:11-12 "This was according to the eternal purpose that He has realized in Christ Jesus our Lord, in whom we have boldness and access with confidence through our faith in Him."

Unlike unbelievers who only have a fearful expectation of judgment from God (Hebrews 10:27), Christians can approach God with confidence!

Hebrews 4:16 "Let us then with confidence draw near to the throne of grace, that we may receive mercy and find grace to help in time of need."

As a Christian, we have such assurance of our faith that we can, through prayer, approach His throne with confidence.

Hebrews 10:14 "For by a single offering He has perfected for all time those who are being sanctified."

We are perfect in God's eyes (made righteous through faith). And this is forever.

Hebrews 10:22 "…let us draw near with a true heart in full assurance of faith, with our hearts sprinkled clean from an evil conscience and our bodies washed with pure water."

We have full assurance of faith. No questions, no what ifs, no apprehension, but full confidence that God will complete what He has started (our salvation).

Hebrews 10:23 "Let us hold fast the confession of our hope without wavering, for He who promised is faithful."

What God has promised, He will fulfill. He is faithful.

Hebrews 10:39 "But we are not of those who shrink back and are destroyed, but of those who have faith and preserve their souls."

We have believed in the death and resurrection of Jesus Christ, and trusted Him alone to pay the penalty of our sin. So we have been saved. End of story.

Hebrews 12:28-29 "Therefore let us be grateful for receiving a kingdom that cannot be shaken, and thus let us offer to God acceptable worship, with reverence and awe, for our God is a consuming fire."

Nothing can touch His kingdom, and nothing can touch His possessions – which we are!

Sealed with the Holy Spirit

Ephesians 1:13-14 "In Him you also, when you heard the word of truth, the gospel of your salvation, and believed in Him, were sealed with the promised Holy Spirit, who is the guarantee of our inheritance until we acquire possession of it, to the praise of His glory."

As believers, we are marked with the Holy Spirit as God's possessions (2 Cor. 1:22). Our inheritance, as God's children, is guaranteed! Read that again – a "deposit guaranteeing our inheritance." As believers, we are "God's possession." He will not let us go. The Holy Spirit is the deposit! If God were to break this promise, He would lose the deposit of the Holy Spirit. And that cannot happen.

Ephesians 1:21-23 "...far above all rule and authority and power and dominion, and every name that is named, not only in this age but also in the one to come. ²² And He put all things in subjection under His feet, and gave Him as head over all things to the church, ²³ which is His body, the fullness of Him who fills all in all." (NASB)

How much clearer can it be? It is God, not us, who makes us stand firm in Christ. It has nothing to do with what we do or don't do. It is God who has set His "seal of ownership" on us as a believer. We do not own God, nor can we cast aside His promises anytime we choose (i.e. falling from salvation). It is God who owns us, and He has placed His Spirit in our heart as a deposit, a sign of ownership, "guaranteeing what is to come." If God says He has guaranteed it, there is nothing that can change the eternal security of the believer.

2 Corinthians 5:5 "He who has prepared us for this very thing is God, who has given us the Spirit as a guarantee."

Again, the Holy Spirit is the guarantor of what is to come! Our future is secured by God's deposit, the Holy Spirit.

Ephesians 4:30 "And do not grieve the Holy Spirit of God, by whom you were sealed for the day of redemption."

Our full redemption will come at the rapture when we receive a glorified body. We are sealed until that day.

John 14:15-17 "'If you love me, you will keep my commandments. And I will ask the Father, and He will give you another Helper, to be with you forever, even the Spirit of truth, whom the world cannot receive, because it neither sees Him nor knows Him. You know Him, for He dwells with you and will be in you.'"

The Holy Spirit will be "with you forever." There is no conditional statement to this promise. And "forever" is forever.

2 Timothy 2:13 "...if we are faithless, He remains faithful—for He cannot deny Himself"

Our bodies are now the temple of the Holy Spirit. God has given the Holy Spirit to us as a deposit. We are part of His family. We are His children. We are in Christ. We are His possession. If we as Christians were able to lose our salvation, God would need to "disown Himself." He would have to separate Himself from Himself (the Holy Spirit), something He cannot nor would not do.

Nothing Can Separate Us

Romans 8:38-39 "For I am sure that neither death nor life, nor angels nor rulers, nor things present nor things to come, nor powers, nor height nor depth, nor anything else in all creation, will be able to separate us from the love of God in Christ Jesus our Lord."

This is certainly one of the most powerful scriptures in terms of our security in Christ. There is nothing, absolutely nothing, in all of creation (which includes everything except God, Jesus, and the Holy Spirit...and He has promised He won't abandon us—Hebrews 13:5) that can separate us from God in Christ Jesus, who has reconciled us to God. So since we are in creation, we cannot separate ourselves from Him!

Revelation 3:7-8 "And to the angel of the church in Philadelphia write: 'The words of the holy one, the true one, who has the key of David, who opens and no one will shut, who shuts and no one opens.

"'I know your works. Behold, I have set before you an open door, which no one is able to shut. I know that you have but little power, and yet you have kept my word and have not denied my name.'"'

Jesus said, "I am the door; if anyone enters through me, he will be saved." (John 10:9) The door to the kingdom of heaven is Jesus...it is only through Him! Here is the promise that He will never shut that door.

Our Future is Guaranteed

Ephesians 1:13-14 "In Him you also, when you heard the word of truth, the gospel of your salvation, and believed in Him, were sealed with the promised Holy Spirit, who is the guarantee of our inheritance until we acquire possession of it, to the praise of His glory."

As believers, God has marked us with the Holy Spirit as His possessions (2 Cor. 1:22). Our inheritance, as God's children, is guaranteed! Read that again. A "deposit guaranteeing our inheritance." As a believer, I am "God's possession." He will not let us go. The Holy Spirit is the deposit! If God broke this promise, He would lose His deposit which is the Holy Spirit, and that cannot happen.

Romans 8:29 "For those whom He foreknew He also predestined to be conformed to the image of His Son, in order that He might be the firstborn among many brothers."

Predestined is *poorizo* in Greek and means that something has been determined or ordained. In this case, God Himself ordained our conformity to His Son. Since God has said that we will be conformed to the likeness of His Son, nothing can change that. It is done!

Philippians 1:4-6 "…always offering prayer with joy in my every prayer for you all, in view of your participation in the gospel from the first day until now. *For I am* confident of this very thing, that He who began a good work in you will perfect it until the day of Christ Jesus."

Be confident that "he who began a good work in you" (that is, God, starting at your salvation) will complete it! No conditions. No "ifs" or "buts". He WILL complete it.

1 Corinthians 13:12 "For now we see in a mirror dimly, but then face to face. Now I know in part; then I shall know fully, even as I have been fully known."

Now, we still live in this imperfect flesh. We see in part and we know only in part. But God has promised us a day when we shall see Him face-to-face and know Him fully! That day is at the resurrection when God glorifies us at the rapture. And our participation is guaranteed, for He has begun a good work, and WILL carry it on to completion (Phil 1:4-6).

2 Corinthians 1:21-22 "And it is God who establishes us with you in Christ, and has anointed us, and who has also put His seal on us and given us His Spirit in our hearts as a guarantee."

If God says He has guaranteed it, there is nothing that can change it. God is faithful and always keeps His word.

2 Corinthians 5:5 "He who has prepared us for this very thing is God, who has given us the Spirit as a guarantee."

God guarantees what is to come.

1 Thessalonians 4:17 "Then we who are alive and remain will be caught up together with them in the clouds to meet the Lord in the air, and so we shall always be with the Lord." (NASB)

This is a rapture verse. At the rapture, the dead in Christ receive their glorified bodies, then we (Christians) who are alive at that time will receive our glorified bodies (1 Cor. 15:51-52). Then, we will all meet the Lord in the air, and be "with the Lord forever." So whether you are alive or if you have died in Christ, at the time of the rapture you will be glorified (see "We Will be Resurrected" below) and be with the Lord forever.

1 Thessalonians 5:23-24 "Now may the God of peace Himself sanctify you completely, and may your whole spirit and soul and body be kept blameless at the coming of our Lord Jesus Christ. He who calls you is faithful; He will surely do it."

He will keep us blameless until the coming of our Lord Jesus at the rapture. He will do it! He will sanctify us through and through – completely – on that day.

2 John 2 "...for the sake of the truth which abides in us and will be with us forever:" (NASB)

Again, a promise made today for those in Christ, a promise which continues into eternity. The truth (Jesus is the truth) lives in us (now) and will be with us forever.

We Will be Resurrected

1 Corinthians 15:12-13 "Now if Christ is proclaimed as raised from the dead, how can some of you say that there is no resurrection of the dead? [13] But if there is no resurrection of the dead, then not even Christ has been raised."

Our future resurrection to glory is just as certain as Christ's resurrection to glory three days after His death. It will happen for every Christian. It is an unconditional promise stated multiple times in Scripture.

2 Corinthians 4:14 "...knowing that He who raised the Lord Jesus will raise us also with Jesus and bring us with you into His presence."

God has promised our future resurrection to glory.

1 Thessalonians 4:14-16 "For if we believe that Jesus died and rose again, even so God will bring with Him those who have fallen asleep in Jesus. For this we say to you by the word of the Lord, that we who are alive and remain until the coming of the Lord, will not precede those who have fallen asleep. For the Lord Himself will descend from heaven with a shout, with the voice of *the* archangel and with the trumpet of God, and the dead in Christ will rise first." (NASB)

These verses about the rapture of believers (both dead and alive) point to the fact that we will be resurrected. This event is certain for all those that are "in Him." Note that in verse 17, God says we will "be with the Lord forever." This promise is fully assured today!

Romans 6:5 "For if we have been united with Him in a death like his, we shall certainly be united with Him in a resurrection like his."

We will be resurrected just like Jesus and be united with Him. God says it will happen. It is God's unconditional promise! Through faith we have been united with Him in Christ's death (Gal. 2:20); so too we will be united with Christ in His resurrection!

Romans 8:23 "And not only the creation, but we ourselves, who have the firstfruits of the Spirit, groan inwardly as we wait eagerly for adoption as sons, the redemption of our bodies."

We can only "wait eagerly" for something that we KNOW is going to happen. We WILL be fully redeemed.

Romans 8:29 "For those whom He foreknew He also predestined to be conformed to the image of His Son, in order that He might be the firstborn among many brothers."

As believers, our predestination is that we WILL BE conformed to the likeness of His Son! In other words, our future has already been written – Biblical predestination! It WILL happen because God has promised it!

Philippians 3:21 "...who will transform our lowly body to be like His glorious body, by the power that enables Him even to subject all things to Himself."

God promises He will transform our lowly bodies so that they will be like His. There is only one condition – faith in Jesus Christ. Then there are no "ifs." He *will* transform us.

Kept from Wrath

1 Thessalonians 5:9-10 "For God has not destined us for wrath, but to obtain salvation through our Lord Jesus Christ, who died for us so that whether we are awake or asleep we might live with Him."

We are not destined for wrath.

1 Thessalonians 1:10 "...and to wait for His Son from heaven, whom He raised from the dead, Jesus who delivers us from the wrath to come."

He rescues us from the coming wrath. This is also a great pre-tribulation rapture verse. We wait for Him to rescue us (the rapture) from the coming wrath (the tribulation). We are rescued (taken off the earth) from what is about to happen on earth (the tribulation).

Romans 5:9 "Since, therefore, we have now been justified by His blood, much more shall we be saved by Him from the wrath of God."

God has no wrath for a believer.

Romans 8:1-2 "There is therefore now no condemnation for those who are in Christ Jesus. For the law of the Spirit of life has set you free in Christ Jesus from the law of sin and death."

There is no condemnation...ever...for the believer. We are free from the law and free from death!

Romans 9:33 "as it is written, 'Behold, I am laying in Zion a stone of stumbling, and a rock of offense and whoever believes in Him will not be put to shame.'"

The "stone" is Jesus. The one who trusts in Jesus will "never be put to shame." Never! (See also Rom. 10:11, 1 Pet. 2:6.)

Revelation 3:5 "The one who conquers will be clothed thus in white garments, and I will never blot his name out of the Book of Life. I will confess his name before my Father and before His angels."

Revelation 21:7 says only those whose names are written in the Lamb's Book of Life will enter the new Jerusalem. Revelation 20:15 says those not found in the Book of Life will be thrown into the lake of fire. Here Jesus promises that for "He who conquers" (believes in Him), He will "not erase his name from the Book of Life."

Revelation 3:10 "Because you have kept my word about patient endurance, I will keep you from the hour of trial that is coming on the whole world, to try those who dwell on the earth."

The hour of testing is the coming tribulation (Daniel's 70th Week). John is writing to the church in Philadelphia and says the body of believers there have "kept my word" and "not denied my name" (v8). They believe! Jesus promises they will be kept from the coming tribulation, which is for unbelievers (Rom. 1:18; 2:8; 2 Thess. 1:8; Eph. 5:6).

Revelation 2:11 "He who has an ear, let Him hear what the Spirit says to the churches. The one who conquers will not be hurt by the second death.'"

A conqueror is one who believes Jesus is the Son of God (1 John 5:5). Here the promise states that he who conquers will not be hurt by the second death, which is the lake of fire (Rev. 20:14). Once you believe, you can't be thrown into the lake of fire. God has promised!

Revelation 20:6 "Blessed and holy is the one who shares in the first resurrection! Over such the second death has no power, but they will be priests of God and of Christ, and they will reign with Him for a thousand years."

The first resurrection is unto life; as described in 1 Cor. 15. God will raise Christians imperishable, in glory, in honor, etc. Those who have been promised a new, glorified body cannot be hurt by the second death (i.e. thrown into the lake of fire). And God has promised our resurrection (first resurrection). See "We Will be Resurrected" below.

Have an Inheritance

Romans 8:17 "...and if children, then heirs—heirs of God and fellow heirs with Christ, provided we suffer with Him in order that we may also be glorified with Him."

We know that we are children of God (v16). As His children, God says that we are "heirs."

Ephesians 1:11 "In Him we have obtained an inheritance, having been predestined according to the purpose of Him who works all things according to the counsel of His will,"

God has made us heirs of His kingdom. Our inheritance in Christ is part of God's plan of salvation. We are predestined to reign with Christ. It is our destiny.

Colossians 1:12 "giving thanks to the Father, who has qualified you to share in the inheritance of the saints in light."

We have an inheritance that cannot be taken away for the Father has qualified us.

Colossians 3:23-24 "Whatever you do, work heartily, as for the Lord and not for men, knowing that from the Lord you will receive the inheritance as your reward. You are serving the Lord Christ."

Knowing that we have this inheritance as a reward should affect how we live. We don't work hard now to keep our inheritance because it is guaranteed, but we work to please Him who has given us this gift of life.

1 Peter 1:3-5 "Blessed be the God and Father of our Lord Jesus Christ, who according to His great mercy has caused us to be born again to a living hope through the resurrection of Jesus Christ from the dead, to *obtain* an inheritance *which is* imperishable and undefiled and will not fade away, reserved in heaven for you, who are protected by the power of God through faith for a salvation ready to be revealed in the last time." (NASB)

Wow, another passage that just seems to sum it all up. We have a "new birth" into a "living hope" based on what Christ has done (the resurrection). And now we have an inheritance that can never perish, spoil or fade. Why? Because God keeps it in heaven by His power!

John 8:35-36 "The slave does not remain in the house forever; the son does remain forever. [36] So if the Son makes you free, you will be free indeed." (NASB)

By faith, the Son (Jesus Christ) has set us free (from sin – verse 34). We are now heirs with Christ into an inheritance that can never perish (1 Pet 1:3-5). We are also now children of God (John 1:12). Here Jesus says that if we are a child of God, then we belong to the family of which God is the Father "forever." We are children of God by faith.

Revelation 21:7 "The one who conquers will have this heritage, and I will be His God and He will be my son."

John is explaining that after the Great White Throne judgment (of the lost), there will be a new heaven, a new earth and a New Jerusalem. He says, "He who conquers will inherit all this." It seems important to understand who a "conqueror" is. A conqueror is anyone who believes that Jesus is the Son of God (1 John 5:5). If you believe, you WILL inherit all this!

Have Eternal Life

John 5:24 "Truly, truly, I say to you, whoever hears my word and believes Him who sent me has eternal life. He does not come into judgment, but has passed from death to life."

At the moment of salvation, you are given a new life in Jesus Christ. You go from being spiritually dead to being spiritually alive. You now have eternal life…without condition. The only condition is to accept Jesus Christ in the first place.

John 3:16 "For God so loved the world, that He gave His only Son, that whoever believes in Him should not perish but have eternal life."

Over and over in the gospel of John, God promises eternal life for those who believe. It is a promise of God. God always keeps His promises.

Romans 6:22-23 "But now that you have been set free from sin and have become slaves of God, the fruit you get leads to sanctification and its end, eternal life. For the wages of sin is death, but the free gift of God is eternal life in Christ Jesus our Lord."

The result of faith in Jesus Christ is eternal life. God grants eternal life by His grace. That is the meaning of salvation. And if you HAVE eternal life, but then lose it, that means it was something short of eternal.

John 10:28 "I give them eternal life, and they will never perish, and no one will snatch them out of my hand."

"They will NEVER perish." Eternal life would be just a little short of eternal if it could be lost. And if it was lost, then one would certainly perish. But God tells us "they will NEVER perish".

1 John 5:13 "These things I have written to you who believe in the name of the Son of God, so that you may know that you have eternal life." (NASB)

We KNOW we HAVE eternal life. We KNOW now, not later, not when we die. And if we have eternal life right now, it can't be lost – otherwise it was something less than eternal.

Have Been Forgiven

Romans 4:7-8
"'Blessed are those whose lawless deeds are forgiven,
and whose sins are covered;
blessed is the man against whom the Lord will not count his sin.'"

God forgave us our sins through the sacrifice of His Son. This forgiveness is past tense. Our sins no longer count against us. God will not go against His word and start counting our sins against us again which is what He would have to do if we could lose our salvation. In other words, you cannot sin your way out of eternal life. You ARE forgiven! (But remember Rom. 6:1-2 – do not go on sinning.)

1 John 2:12 "I am writing to you, little children,
because your sins are forgiven for His name's sake."

Our sins have been forgiven, past tense. And that includes all your sins, past, present and future. You have been washed clean by the blood of the lamb and that's how God now sees you.

1 Corinthians 6:11 "And such were some of you. But you were washed, you were sanctified, you were justified in the name of the Lord Jesus Christ and by the Spirit of our God."

You WERE washed! Your washing is done. It is complete.

Acts 10:43 "To Him all the prophets bear witness that everyone who believes in Him receives forgiveness of sins through His name."

At the point that anyone "believes in Him", they receive "forgiveness of sins".

Acts 2:38 "Peter said to them, 'Repent and be baptized every one of you in the name of Jesus Christ for the forgiveness of your sins, and you will receive the gift of the Holy Spirit.'"

Forgiveness must be completed BEFORE you receive the Holy Spirit. So anyone who repents (believes in Christ) is forgiven, and receives (filled with, sealed by) the Holy Spirit, ALL of which happens at the point of belief!

Colossians 1:14 "in whom we have redemption, the forgiveness of sins."

As a Christian, you have been redeemed, bought and paid for (see "We are His Possessions" above). We have "forgiveness of sins" right now. Even our continued sinning has been washed white as snow and no longer counts against us (Rom 4:8).

Have Been Justified

Romans 5:1, 9 "Therefore, since we have been justified by faith, we have peace with God through our Lord Jesus Christ.

Since, therefore, we have now been justified by His blood, much more shall we be saved by Him from the wrath of God."

As believers in Christ, we HAVE been justified – made righteous in the eyes of God. If it were possible to lose your salvation, God would have to un-justify us.

Romans 8:30 "And those whom He predestined He also called, and those whom He called He also justified, and those whom He justified He also glorified."

The progression of promises here from God will be fulfilled.

Titus 3:7 "so that being justified by His grace we would be made heirs according to *the* hope of eternal life." (NASB)

Having BEEN justified, we will become heirs and have eternal life. Again, this is a progression of promises from God. To lose salvation would mean God has to go back on many of His promises to believers.

Romans 6:3-5 "Or do you not know that all of us who have been baptized into Christ Jesus have been baptized into His death? Therefore we have been buried with Him through baptism into death, so that as Christ was raised from the dead through the glory of the Father, so we too might walk in newness of life. For if we have become united with *Him* in the likeness of His death, certainly we shall also be *in the likeness* of His resurrection,"

Being "born again" is a spiritual birth, moving from spiritual death to spiritual life. At the same time, God tells us "our old self was crucified with Him." In other words, our old nature is dead. Therefore, to lose your salvation, God would literally need to kill you spiritually and bring you back to life in your old self. Sounds silly? It is.

Have Been Born Again

1 Peter 1:23 "since you have been born again, not of perishable seed but of imperishable, through the living and abiding word of God;"

Once born again, we are born imperishable. Our physical birth is of a perishable seed, but our spiritual birth an imperishable birth through God. Once born again, you cannot become perishable again. You cannot become un-born again.

Keeping the Faith (By Works)

Galatians 3:3 "Are you so foolish? Having begun by the Spirit, are you now being perfected by the flesh?"

"You foolish Galatians! Who has bewitched you?" declares Paul in verse 1. These are some pretty harsh words for those who think they have to work to keep their salvation! Our salvation is based on what Christ has done, not on anything we have done. In the same way, keeping our salvation is based on what Christ has done, not on anything we can do!

Matthew 7:22-24 "Many will say to Me on that day, 'Lord, Lord, did we not prophesy in Your name, and in Your name cast out demons, and in Your name perform many miracles?' And then I will declare to them, 'I never knew you; depart from Me, you who practice lawlessness.'

The Two Foundations

"Therefore everyone who hears these words of Mine and acts on them, may be compared to a wise man who built his house on the rock.'" (NASB)

This is a powerful scripture about eternal security. Those that Jesus "never knew" were never saved. For Jesus is the Shepherd who "knows His sheep" (John 10:14) and yet tells these many that "I never knew you".

He does not say, "I once knew you but do not any more", nor does He say, "you have lost the right to be known." No, He NEVER knew them. They were never saved!

Matthew 25:11-12 "Afterward the other virgins came also, saying, 'Lord, lord, open to us.' But He answered, 'Truly, I say to you, I do not know you.'

Like Matt 7:22-24 above, the virgins in this parable are told by the bridegroom (Jesus), "I don't know you." And therefore, the door will not be opened for them.

1 Corinthians 3:15 "If anyone's work is burned up, he will suffer loss, though he himself will be saved, but only as through fire."

Anything not done in faith is sin (Rom 14:23). So any works not done in faith will be burned up. But even though all of a man's work is burned up, he himself "shall be saved." Why? Because of faith. What we DO doesn't get us into heaven. What we believe does.

Promise to Conquerors

When a person believes in Jesus as their personal Lord and Savior they become a conqueror.

Revelation 21:7 "The one who conquers will have this heritage, and I will be His God and he will be my son."

Nine times in Revelation Jesus makes a specific promise to "he who conquers." Some say these promises are for only those Christians who keep the faith until the end and then they become conquerors. Nonsense! God tells us that those who believe in Jesus HAVE conquered the world (1 John 5:5)! Why have Christians conquered? Christians have conquered because we are IN Christ who has conquered the world (John 16:33). All the promises to conquerors are for anyone who believes in Jesus. They are conquerors. (See "Conqueror" under "Following Jesus")

Revelation 2:7 "He who has an ear, let him hear what the Spirit says to the churches. To the one who conquers I will grant to eat of the tree of life, which is in the paradise of God.'"

If you are one "who conquers", God promises that you will eat from the tree of life. The tree of life will be in in the New Jerusalem, which comes down to the New Earth (Rev 22:2). Only the righteous made so through faith in Jesus Christ will ever enter this city. If you believe, you are a conqueror, and you will eat from the tree of life.

Revelation 2:11 "He who has an ear, let him hear what the Spirit says to the churches. The one who conquers will not be hurt by the second death.'"

If you are one "who conquers", God promises that you will not be hurt by the second death, that is, being thrown into the lake of fire (Rev 20:14).

Revelation 2:17 "He who has an ear, let him hear what the Spirit says to the churches. To the one who conquers I will give some of the hidden manna, and I will give him a white stone, with a new name written on the stone that no one knows except the one who receives it.'"

If you are one "who conquers", you will eat some of the hidden manna.

Revelation 2:26 "The one who conquers and who keeps my works until the end, to him I will give authority over the nations,"

If you are one "who conquers", you will rule with Christ. This is one of the seven promises to conquerors has an additional condition: "and does my will to the end." Those who say we can lose our salvation point to this verse, that if we don't do God's will to the end we won't be saved (see below under "Some say we can lose our salvation"). But a nearly identical promise (Rev 3:21) is stated without any condition.

Revelation 3:5 "The one who conquers will be clothed thus in white garments, and I will never blot his name out of the Book of Life. I will confess his name before my Father and before His angels."

If you are one "who conquers", your name will NEVER be blotted out of the Lamb's Book of Life. All those in this book make it into eternity with Christ! (Rev. 20:15)

Revelation 3:12 "The one who conquers, I will make him a pillar in the temple of my God. Never shall he go out of it, and I will write on him the name of my God, and the name of the city of my God, the new Jerusalem, which comes down from my God out of heaven, and my own new name."

If you are one "who conquers", you will be a pillar in the temple of God – most likely the "temple" in the New Heaven and New Earth, which is not a physical temple, but God and Christ themselves! (Rev. 21:22)

Revelation 3:21 "The one who conquers, I will grant him to sit with me on my throne, as I also conquered and sat down with my Father on His throne."

One of the promises to "him who conquers" is that they will sit with

Christ on His throne! Who is a conqueror? Believers (1 John 5:5)! Because we are IN Christ who has conquered the world (John 16:33).

Some Say We Can Lose Our Salvation

You need to stand firm

Matthew 10:22 "and you will be hated by all for my name's sake. But the one who endures to the end will be saved."

The idea that Christians must endure to the end to prove that they are saved comes primarily from Matthew's gospel, here and in Matthew 24:13. Interestingly, both the Calvinist and the Arminian use these passages to argue against the true security of the believer. The Calvinist says the believer must persevere to the end to prove they are saved. The Arminian says the Christian must stand firm to the end or they will lose their salvation. Neither is true! The idea of reaching the "end" is spoken to the JEWS. The JEWS that make it to the end of the tribulation period will be saved. The entire context of Matthew 24 is the 7-year tribulation period.

Matthew 24:13 "But the one who endures to the end will be saved."

The entire context of Matthew 24 has to do with the Jews and the seven-year tribulation that they will face in the end times. JEWS who make it to the end (the remnant chosen by grace) will be saved when Christ returns to earth. This has nothing to do with Christians persevering or enduring to the end to ensure their own salvation (see Matthew 10:22 above).

Falling Away

Luke 15:24 "for this son of mine was dead and has come to life again; he was lost and has been found.' And they began to celebrate." (NASB)

The story of the prodigal son is often used to show that you can be saved, then lost, then saved again. Especially common is using the phrase "alive again" to show that someone can be alive, saved, then dead, lost and thus lose salvation, and then "alive again" – saved again. I don't think this is what the story says at all. In fact, I believe it shows exactly the opposite.

If the son was a believer before he left, the complete story shows that even though the son went off into the world, he was always the son of the father, eternally secure, who welcomed him back with open arms. The son was never not his father's son. So even though he went and did some terrible things and he felt he had a license to sin, the father never disowned him! Thus, this speaks to eternal security, not to losing of one's salvation.

Alternatively, the story of the prodigal son could be about all people. If the son was not a believer before he left, the story shows that the father wishes none to perish, even those who have done terrible things in the past. Like the shepherd who finds the 100th sheep and rejoices, so too this father rejoices when one wayward child returns to him in faith.

1 Corinthians 10:11-12 "Now these things happened to them as an example, but they were written down for our instruction, on whom the end of the ages has come. Therefore, let anyone who thinks that he stands take heed lest he fall."

"These things" are examples of Israel's disobedience and the resulting consequences. God calls believers to holy living, and when we fall short, there are consequences. This passage is about standing firm in the face of temptation (v13). It's not that we lose our salvation when we sin, but we may stumble and fall. As Paul says in verse 23, "Everything is permissible"— but not everything is beneficial.

Galatians 5:4 "You are severed from Christ, you who would be justified by the law; you have fallen away from grace."

Paul is writing about those who are continuing to try to be righteous by obeying the law. For example, verse 2 talks about those who still want to require circumcision. Paul asks them why they are trying to follow the law. If you try to follow some of the law, you have to follow all the law (verse 3; also see Gal 5:11). What Paul, inspired by the Holy Spirit, writes to us here is that we should forget the law! God's grace is sufficient! If we try "to be justified by law" we are missing out on God's grace. The phrase "fallen away from grace" does not mean we will lose our salvation; it means we have not yet fully accepted God's grace! There are earthly and eternal consequences, such as the loss of joy and peace on earth and rewards in heaven, but not the loss of eternal life.

Hebrews 6:4-6 "For it is impossible, in the case of those who have once been enlightened, who have tasted the heavenly gift, and have shared in the Holy Spirit, and have tasted the goodness of the word of God and the powers of the age to come, and then have fallen away, to restore them again to repentance, since they are crucifying once again the Son of God to their own harm and holding Him up to contempt."

"If they fall away" seems to suggest the saved can fall away from God. But it is actually saying that this is impossible! It is impossible because to "fall away" and then be brought back to repentance is like crucifying the Son of God all over again, and that can't happen. That "falling away" is hypothetical is clear because it is impossible!

God is telling us that if we could lose our salvation we could never get it back without Christ dying for us again! In other words, someone cannot be born-again again, so it is impossible to get un-born again in the first place. As one commentator put it, those who reject "once saved, always saved" can only replace it with "once lost, always lost."

Note that some argue that this is not talking about true believers. I disagree. They have "shared in the Holy Spirit." They are true believers. It's just that "falling away" is impossible for the believer!

2 Peter 1:10 "Therefore, brothers, be all the more diligent to confirm your calling and election, for if you practice these qualities you will never fall."

The claim is that the contra-positive of this verse is also true, that if you DO NOT do these things, then you WILL FALL, meaning lose your salvation. I agree that the contra-positive is true, so the key here is what does it mean to "fall"? The Greek here is *ptaio* meaning to stumble. Do Christians stumble? Of course, we do! That doesn't mean then that God un-saves them. Talk about walking in fear!

2 Peter 3:17 You therefore, beloved, knowing this beforehand, take care that you are not carried away with the error of lawless people and lose your own stability."

This is another passage which seems to indicate that believers can "fall from their secure position"–meaning to lose salvation. The Greek again here is of utmost help. To "fall" is the Greek *ekpipto* which means to fall or stumble. "Secure position" is the Greek *sterigmos* meaning steadfastness. This means that when you follow false teaching, you will fall or stumble from steadfastness. 1 Cor. 16:13 says "Be on your guard; stand firm in the faith." In other words, be steadfast in your faith (as a believer). When we are not, we stumble. It doesn't mean we lose our salvation! Remember, it is God that makes us stand until the end! (Rom. 14:4)

Cuts Off (Are there fruitless Christians?)

Mark 4:13-20

> And He said to them, "Do you not understand this parable?
> How will you understand all the parables? The sower sows
> the word. These are the ones who are beside the road where
> the word is sown; and when they hear, immediately Satan
> comes and takes away the word which has been sown
> in them. In a similar way these are the ones on whom
> seed was sown on the rocky *places*, who, when they hear
> the word, immediately receive it with joy; and they have
> no *firm* root in themselves, but are *only* temporary; then,
> when affliction or persecution arises because of the word,
> immediately they fall away. And others are the ones on
> whom seed was sown among the thorns; these are the ones
> who have heard the word, but the worries of the world, and
> the deceitfulness of riches, and the desires for other things
> enter in and choke the word, and it becomes unfruitful.
> And those are the ones on whom seed was sown on the
> good soil; and they hear the word and accept it and bear
> fruit, thirty, sixty, and a hundredfold." (NASB)

The parable of the sower is often cited by those who say we can lose
our salvation because of the phrase "falls away" (e.g. Matt 13:21 speaking of
the seed that grows up in the rocky soil that "falls away" when persecution
comes). But the Greek in Mark 4 and Matthew 13 is *skandalizo* meaning a
stumbling. In Luke 8 the word used for "fall away" is *aphistemi* meaning to
withdraw. This is NOT a loss of salvation. This is a picture of a Christian
shrinking back in the face of persecution, not letting their light shine before
men. It is a picture of a Christian being choked out by the cares of this
world (the seed that grows up among the thorns), not trusting the Lord with
all their hearts for all their needs. As a result, they are fruitless Christians.

I know many believe that there is no such thing as a "fruitless" Christian,
but there are. Peter tells us that there are "ineffective and unproductive"
(i.e. fruitless) Christians (2 Peter 1:8). Paul chides the Corinthians for being
carnal or worldly in their thinking (1 Cor. 3:1) – being "babies" in Christ.

Likewise, the plant in the rocky soil and the plant among the thorns are saved (there was germination) – the seeds were just unproductive. And even the branch that bears no fruit in John 15:2 is still connected to the true vine (see below; it is NOT "cut off" but "lifted up")!

Luke 3:9 "'Even now the axe is laid to the root of the trees. Every tree therefore that does not bear good fruit is cut down and thrown into the fire.'"

Along with Matthew 3:10, Matt. 7:19 and Luke 13:9 are about being "cut off" and thrown into the fire. This is all about "good" trees and "bad" trees producing good fruit and bad fruit (Matt. 7). In fact, most of Matt. 7 is a contrast of two ways: two gates, two types of trees, two fruits, two groups at judgment, two kinds of builders and two kinds of foundations. One of the two ways leads to the kingdom of God; the other way to destruction. The emphasis here is on choosing the right way, being a good tree that bears good fruit, building your house on the rock, which is Christ. It is not about a "good" tree (someone who is saved) being cut down.

John 15:1-2 "I am the true vine, and my Father is the vinedresser. Every branch in me that does not bear fruit He takes away, and every branch that does bear fruit He prunes, that it may bear more fruit."

Like Luke 3:9 above, many see John's writing as proof that God will "take away" every branch that bears no fruit, meaning a believer can be "taken away" and "thrown into the fire" if he is fruitless. They combine this with the Parable of the Sower above to show if a Christian is fruitless, then they are not saved.

First, it is improper to make doctrine from an allegory or parable. The overwhelming picture from Scripture is that believers are secure in their position. More importantly, the Greek word here for "cuts off" is *airo* meaning to lift up! The passage should read in English "He LIFTS UP every branch in me that bears no fruit." God lifts up the branches connected to the vine (believers) that bear no fruit SO THAT they will become fruitful. Picture a gardener lifting up a grape vine out of the dirt or mud and tying it off to a trellis. Believers that are bearing fruit He prunes.

Finally, UNBELIEVERS are not connected to the vine (Jesus) but are gathered and cast into the fire. This is a picture of the coming judgment for unbelievers when Hades is cast into the lake of fire (Rev 20:14).

Romans 11:20-23 "Quite right, they were broken off for their unbelief, but you stand by your faith. Do not be conceited, but fear; [21] for if God did not spare the natural branches, He will not spare you, either. Behold then the kindness and severity of God; to those who fell, severity, but to you, God's kindness, if you continue in His kindness; otherwise you also will be cut off. And they also, if they do not continue in their unbelief, will be grafted in, for God is able to graft them in again." (NASB)

Some say this means that if a believer doesn't "continue in His kindness", he or she will be "cut off." If cut off, they suggest he or she can be "grafted in again" when they stop their unbelief. This verse, however, and the whole chapter (and Romans 9 and 10) is really about the nation of Israel. They are the natural branches (v 21), the chosen people of God who have been "cut off" because they reject Jesus Christ. Some will be saved (v14) during the Church Age and be grafted in again. Even as He turns to the "you" in verses 21-22, meaning the Church (believers), it cannot be saying that salvation comes or is maintained by kindness. Kindness is not the gate to salvation, faith in Christ is.

James 2:17 "So also faith by itself, if it does not have works, is dead."

This is the "big one" that people use to show that if you are not a "fruitful Christian" then your faith is "dead" – meaning you are unsaved. Either you've never been saved or you are cut off (see John 15:2). Again, this is an unfortunate English translation. The Greek word translated as "dead" is *nekros*, which can mean 1) without life; lifeless (in other words physically dead); 2) spiritually dead (unsaved); or 3) inactive as respect to doing right; destitute of power; inactive. Obviously, the individuals referenced in this verse are not number one, without life. And number two goes against the clear teachings of Paul that we are saved by faith ALONE and NOT by works (Eph. 2:8-9). Number three is what James means here! Faith by itself is inactive, destitute of power and inactive. This is exactly what Peter says in 2 Peter 1:8, that there are Christians who are "ineffective and unproductive" in their faith.

2 Peter 1:8 "For if these qualities are yours and are increasing, they keep you from being ineffective or unfruitful in the knowledge of our Lord Jesus Christ."

Generally, those who teach that you can lose your salvation do not use this verse. I put it here to show that there are Christians who are "ineffective and unproductive." In other words, fruitless. But as you possess these qualities in greater abundance (goodness, knowledge, self-control, godliness, etc., basically the fruit of the Spirit) you will start becoming a fruitful Christian.

Abandoning the faith (sinning your way out of heaven)

Galatians 6:1 "Brothers, if anyone is caught in any transgression, you who are spiritual should restore him in a spirit of gentleness. Keep watch on yourself, lest you too be tempted."

Some claim that a believer being "caught in sin" needs to be "restored." In other words, they suggest they can be brought back to a saving relationship with Christ. I believe this verse is about helping someone back to a spiritual walk with Christ, turning away from the world and turning back to God. They are still saved. "Restoring" someone is NOT salvation. It is talking about the restoration of fellowship with other believers. This idea is confirmed with the understanding of Church discipline found in Paul's writing in 1 Corinthians 5 and what Jesus says in Matthew 18. This is clear in that we can't save anyone! Only God saves. Yet the verse says, "you who are spiritual should restore." A believer can restore another believer through loving fellowship and mentorship, but only Christ can save.

1 Timothy 4:1 "Now the Spirit expressly says that in later times some will depart from the faith by devoting themselves to deceitful spirits and teachings of demons,"

This verse has nothing to do with losing salvation. It is a warning that some believers will be deceived. They will be deceived about things they must do to be more holy and righteous. Verse 3 talks about teachers who forbid marriage and order abstinence from certain foods. They are teaching the law all over again and God calls them deceiving spirits. Some will "abandon the faith" and follow these false teachings. It does not mean they are suddenly unsaved. Instead, it means that they will stop living by faith and try to live by the Law. Some translations say some will "fall away" from the faith. Again, this is in the Greek means to withdraw – not lose salvation!

Hebrews 10:26-27 "For if we go on sinning deliberately after receiving the knowledge of the truth, there no longer remains a sacrifice for sins, but a fearful expectation of judgment, and a fury of fire that will consume the adversaries."

This is the same "knowledge" as in 2 Peter 2:21. It is a "precise and correct knowledge" according to *Strong's Greek and Hebrew Dictionary*. It does not mean a saving faith. Compare the saving "belief" talked about in John 3:16 according to Strong's – to think to be true, to be persuaded of, to credit, place confidence in. Knowledge of something is different from acceptance and belief of something. This verse is saying if you receive and understand the truth (that Christ died on the cross, rose again in Glory, and salvation is only through accepting Him) but do not accept it (believe it to be true, place confidence in, accept it, accept Him as savior), there is no sacrifice for sins left, because that is the ONLY sacrifice for salvation!

Other relevant verses are in Hebrews 2:1-4, 3:12-14, 10:16-31.

2 Peter 2:20-22 "For if, after they have escaped the defilements of the world by the knowledge of the Lord and Savior Jesus Christ, they are again entangled in them and are overcome, the last state has become worse for them than the first. For it would be better for them not to have known the way of righteousness, than having known it, to turn away from the holy commandment handed on to them. It has happened to them according to the true proverb, "A dog returns to its own vomit," and, 'A sow, after washing, *returns* to wallowing in the mire.'"

First read the rest of this chapter (verses 1-19). The context of this entire chapter is false prophets and false teachers. They are the "they" of verse 20 and are clearly not saved in the context of the rest of the chapter – for their "condemnation" is mentioned several times. The key here is what kind of "knowledge" do they have? The Greek here for knowledge is *epigenesist* meaning correct knowledge. But this is not the same as saving knowledge (which is the Greek *pisteuo* – meaning believe to be true AND entrust for salvation). It is simple intellectual knowledge of what salvation is all about and not a saving knowledge, or belief, of Jesus Christ as one's personal Lord and Savior.

James 5:19-20 "My brothers, if anyone among you wanders from the truth and someone brings him back, let him know that whoever brings back a sinner from his wandering will save his soul from death and will cover a multitude of sins."

Like Galatians 6:1, some believe this is about a believer helping someone back to faith and away from death. The focus here, however, is on "someone" bringing him back and turning him from sin. Someone can point out someone else's sin in love and help them back to following Christ. Only Christ can save.

Revelation 2:5 "Remember therefore from where you have fallen; repent, and do the works you did at first. If not, I will come to you and remove your lampstand from its place, unless you repent."

This verse is part of a letter to the church at Ephesus, and too, is often quoted as proof you can lose your salvation. The church had been doing good in the eyes of the Lord (v2-3) but then they began to drift from the love they had at first. God's call to them is to remember the love they had earlier, living in love and not growing weary. If they do not recall this love, then Jesus would remove their lampstand from its place. This is NOT about a loss of salvation. It is about the loss of the church at Ephesus! In fact, the church in Ephesus did eventually cease to exist. Today, Ephesus (which is in Turkey) is virtually 100 percent Islamic.

Revelation 2:26 "The one who conquers and who keeps my works until the end, to him I will give authority over the nations,"

There are seven promises to "him who conquers" in Revelation (see above under *Promises to Conquerors*). This promise to conquerors has an additional condition: "and does my will to the end." Those who say we can lose our salvation point to this verse, that if we don't do God's will to the end we won't be saved. A nearly identical promise, however, (Rev 3:21 - To him who conquers, I will give the right to sit with me on my throne) – is stated without condition. Also, Rev 21:7 states that conquerors will "inherit all this" without condition.

Revelation 3:5 "But if our unrighteousness serves to show the righteousness of God, what shall we say? That God is unrighteous to inflict wrath on us? (I speak in a human way.)"

Those that say you can lose your salvation point to the fact that you can be blotted out of the Book of Life. But this verse is saying the exact opposite! If you are a conqueror (someone who is born again; see 1 John 5:4-5), it says you will NEVER be blotted out of the Book of Life. Never!

Old Testament

1 Samuel 28:16 "And Samuel said, 'Why then do you ask me, since the Lord has turned from you and become your enemy?'"

Some say that Saul lost his salvation because he did not obey the Lord (v18). The Lord did "depart" from him (took His Holy Spirit from him, something He promises not to do for those in Christ as part of the new covenant) and God did judge him by taking his kingdom from him as well as taking his life and his son's lives (1 Sam 31:2-6). Samuel, who is dead and in Abraham's bosom and was brought up out of the earth (Hades) by the medium (1Sam 28:13), says to Saul that when he dies tomorrow "you and your sons will be with me" (1 Sam 28:19). Saul was saved (he did NOT lose his salvation), but God did take His Holy Spirit from him and there were consequences for his actions.

1 Samuel 28:19 "Moreover, the Lord will give Israel also with you into the hand of the Philistines, and tomorrow you and your sons shall be with me. The Lord will give the army of Israel also into the hand of the Philistines."

Saul did not obey the Lord (v18) and the Lord departed from him (v16). In fact, Saul's last act is to seek a medium for wisdom and advice instead of seeking the Lord. The medium calls Samuel up from Hades (v13) and gives Saul a final prophecy: Saul and his sons are to die the next day, and so as predicted, it happens the next day (1 Sam 31:2-6). Yet, Samuel also tells Saul that he and his sons "will be with me" that next day. Despite Saul's disobedience and the Lord departing him, He still is with Samuel when he dies. He is in Abraham's Bosom in Hades.

The Big "ifs"

Colossians 1:22-23 "...he has now reconciled in his body of flesh by his death, in order to present you holy and blameless and above reproach before Him, if indeed you continue in the faith, stable and steadfast, not shifting from the hope of the gospel that you heard, which has been proclaimed in all creation under heaven, and of which I, Paul, became a minister."

Salvation IS conditional. IF you believe that Jesus paid the price for your sins, THEN you will be saved. The condition is faith; the result is salvation from God. Once you are saved, the overwhelming picture from Scripture (see all the passages listed above) is that your salvation is unconditional. God has promised you an inheritance that He keeps. What you do cannot save you; it is not by works so no one can boast (Eph. 2:8-9). If you were now responsible for KEEPING your salvation, you would have something about which to boast.

Galatians 6:9 "And let us not grow weary of doing good, for in due season we will reap, if we do not give up."

Our eternal rewards are based on what we do. All God's judgment is based on our deeds. But the judgment to which we go is based on faith. Believers will appear before the Judgment Seat of Christ and will be rewarded for what they do while in the body (2 Cor. 5:10). Unbelievers appear before the Great White Throne Judgment and will be thrown into the lake of fire (Rev 20). The Galatians passage is an exhortation to continue to "do good," NOT to keep your salvation. This is not about our salvation but about our heavenly reward.

1 Thessalonians 3:8 "For now we live, if you are standing fast in the Lord."

In this chapter Paul is encouraging the Thessalonians to "strengthen and encourage their faith" in the face of "trials" (v2-3). He reminds them that we are destined for persecution as believers (v3-4). In verse 7-8, Paul is commending them for standing firm in the Lord despite their trails. They are continuing in good works, not shrinking back or falling away (withdrawing) in the face of persecution (See the Parable of the Sower explanation above). In the NIV, verse 8 says, "For now we really live, since you are standing firm in the Lord." The Thessalonians' faith was an encouragement to Paul. [Notice that the NIV does not contain the word "if."]

1 Timothy 2:15 "Yet she will be saved through childbearing—if they continue in faith and love and holiness, with self-control."

No one teaches that women are saved through childbearing. All of us are saved by faith! So what does this passage mean? Good question. I don't really know what Paul is saying about women and childbearing. If, however, this is conditional security, then we must all ALSO continue in "love" and "holiness with propriety" too! Again, I think this is an exhortation to continue practicing "good deeds" (v10).

Hebrews 3:6 "but Christ is faithful over God's house as a son. And we are his house if indeed we hold fast our confidence and our boasting in our hope."

Hebrews here has a message of warning to those who think they are believers but are not. Verse 12 says, "see to it, brothers (Hebrews, not other Christians), that none of you has a sinful, unbelieving heart." Verse 18 says, "...so we see that they were not able to enter, because of their unbelief." Heb. 4:2 says, "...but the message they heard was no value to them because [they did not] combine it with faith."

Hebrews 3:14 "For we have come to share in Christ, if indeed we hold our original confidence firm to the end."

In other words, we share in Christ when we combine hearing the message with belief and have faith. This statement is exactly the same message as Rom. 10:14, "How, then, can they call on the one they have not believed in? And how can they believe in the one of whom they have not heard?" The true warning here in Hebrews 3 and 4 is a warning against unbelief. Furthermore, Paul writes in 2 Cor. 13:5, "Examine yourselves to see whether you are in the faith; test yourselves." Why? Because some have heard and NOT combined it with faith.

1 Corinthians 15:1-2 "Now I would remind you, brothers, of the gospel I preached to you, which you received, in which you stand, and by which you are being saved, if you hold fast to the word I preached to you—unless you believed in vain."

"In vain," the context of the rest of the chapter is to "believe" WITHOUT experiencing in person the resurrection of Christ. Verse 14: "And if Christ has not been raised, our preaching is useless and so is your faith." Without the resurrection, your belief is in vain and your faith is useless. And if Christ has ...not been raised, your faith is futile; you are still in your sins." (v17)

But Doesn't Our Security Give Us a ™"License to Sin"? Yes and No.

Galatians 5:13 "For you were called to freedom, brothers. Only do not use your freedom as an opportunity for the flesh, but through love serve one another."

As a believer, we still have free will. We are free to focus on Christ and live by the Spirit or to focus on this world and indulge in sin. It is a daily choice for the believer.

Galatians 5:16 "But I say, walk by the Spirit, and you will not gratify the desires of the flesh."

When we are focused on Him, when we set our eyes on Him, when we live by the Spirit, God promises that we will not gratify the desires of our sinful nature.

1 Corinthians 6:12 "'All things are lawful for me,' but not all things are helpful. 'All things are lawful for me,' but I will not be dominated by anything."

Everything is permissible; that sounds like a license to sin. So should we use this license as an excuse to sin? No! (See Rom 6:1-2) Not everything is beneficial.

Later in verse 15 about sexual sin, Paul writes, "Never." Why would you use your freedom to become "one flesh" and "united" with a prostitute (sin) when you are "united with Lord" and "one with Him in spirit?" Good question. Why do we continue to sin when we are united in spirit with the creator of the universe?

Titus 2:11-14 "For the grace of God has appeared, bringing salvation to all men, instructing us to deny ungodliness and worldly desires and to live sensibly, righteously and godly in the present age, looking for the blessed hope and the appearing of the glory of our great God and Savior, Christ Jesus, who gave Himself for us to redeem us from every lawless deed, and to purify for Himself a people for His own possession, zealous for good deeds."

The grace of God, working through the Holy Spirit, will teach us to say "No" to the world. We don't need to do anything on our own. We simply need to set our eyes on Him and live by faith.

Romans 6:1-2 "What shall we say then? Are we to continue in sin that grace may abound? By no means! How can we who died to sin still live in it?"

We do have a "license to sin." It is the "freedom" written of in Gal. 5:13 and about that which is permissible in 1 Cor. 6:12. Actually, a "license to sin" is maybe more accurately a "freedom from sin," since we have been forgiven of all of our sins: past, present and future. Does this mean we should use this license? "By no means!" Paul writes. In the NASB it says, "May it never be!" The NKJV says, "Certainly not! How shall we who died to sin live any longer in it?"